1982

MORALITY AS
A BIOLOGICAL
PHENOMENON

MORALITY AS A BIOLOGICAL PHENOMENON

THE PRESUPPOSITIONS OF SOCIOBIOLOGICAL RESEARCH

Edited by GUNTHER S. STENT

University of California Press
Berkeley, Los Angeles, London

University of California Press
Berkeley and Los Angeles, California
University of California Press, Ltd.
London, England

Copyright © 1978, revised edition © 1980,
Dr. Silke Bernhard, Dahlem Konferenzen, Berlin.

Printed in the United States of America

Library of Congress Cataloging in Publication Data
Main entry under title:

Morality as a biological phenomenon.

　　Edition for 1978 by Dahlem Workshop on Biology and Morals
held in Berlin, 1977.
　　Includes index.
　　1. Ethics, Evolutionary—Congresses.　2. Sociobiology—Philosophy—Congresses.　I. Stent, Gunther Siegmund,
1924–　II. Dahlem Workshop on Biology and Morals, Berlin, 1977.
Morality as a biological phenomenon.
BJ1311.M67　1980　　170　　80-15948

CONTENTS

INTRODUCTION

G. S. Stent

Ever since the Greeks first formulated the moral nature of man as a central problem of Western philosophy, there have existed two rival views: that of idealistic ethics advocated by Plato and that of naturalistic ethics advocated by Aristotle. The idealistic view considers moral behavior as being in accord with an ideal moral law. By contrast, the naturalistic view considers moral behavior as a strategy for optimizing human welfare. That both of these views have managed to coexist in the West for more than two thousand years suggests that, despite their prima facie contradictory stance, both views must contain elements of deep truth.

The naturalistic view of morality, which sees man as a phenomenon of nature, is naturally more congenial to scientists. It brings morality within the purview of biology and thus offers the hope of grounding moral law in sound scientific principles, rather than, as had been the case in prescientific times, in a morass of hand-me-down superstitions. But however reasonable the naturalistic view may have seemed through the millennia, the grounding of moral law in biology had to remain a utopian vision as long as biological knowledge itself remained very primitive during Antiquity, Middle Ages, and Renaissance. However, with the rise of Darwinism in the last century and its firm demonstration of the biological nature of man, the naturalistic view received tremendous impetus. As Charles Darwin himself knew, natural selection operates not only on the physical features of animals but on their behavior as well. And so it became quite plausible to envisage that also human behavior in general, and moral behavior in particular, is the product of selective, evolutionary forces. Thus not only the existence of a moral code but also of its actual content would be justifiable by discovering what adaptive value, or fitness, it brought to the human species in the evolutionary struggle for survival.

How are the evolutionary origins of human morality to be approached? The most obvious approach is via the study of the social behavior of animals. For just as we can ask how there arose the intricate and superbly adapted facet eye of the honeybee, so can we ask how it was possible for natural selection to give rise to the intricate and superbly adapted society of the beehive. But despite Darwin's awareness of the importance of social behavior for his theory, it was only in the 1930s that the evolutionarily oriented study of animal behavior really got under way, with Konrad Lorenz as one of its Founding Fathers. By the 1950s, the subject had become an established academic discipline under the name *ethology*. And in the 1960s, the rather qualitative evolutionary reasoning that Lorenz had brought to ethology was given a more quantitative and sharper formation by William Hamilton's theory of "kin selection." According to the kin selection theory, the evolutionary fitness of a particular behavior is not given solely by the extent to which that behavior serves the reproductive success of a particular animal. Fitness must take into account also the extent to which the reproductive potential of that animal's close relatives is served. Kin selection can thus account for the—on the first sight anti-Darwinian—evolution of such behaviors as the alarm call of birds. For though by drawing attention to itself the alarmist bird reduces its own chances of leaving offspring, its self-sacrificial behavior does raise the reproductive success of its close relatives in the flock, and hence augments what is now called its "inclusive fitness" as a social animal. This conceptual advance presented by "inclusive fitness" led to the development of an ethological subdiscipline styled "sociobiology" specifically concerned with the evolution of the social behavior of animals. Of this subdiscipline Edward O. Wilson's treatise entitled *Sociobiology* published in 1975 provided the first comprehensive account. Admittedly, there exist differences of opinion among biologists regarding the achievements of sociobiology to date. These opinions range from the sanguine view of one of the leading sociobiologists, Richard Alexander, who thinks that he and his colleagues have produced the most important advance in the understanding of evolution since Darwin, to the dim view of one of the leading contemporary students of evolution, Richard Lewontin, who thinks that current sociobiology is little more than a caricature of Darwinism. But regardless of whether sociobiology has or has not any substantial achievements to its credit, it would be downright cranky for any biologist to deny that the professed general scientific goal of sociobiology is not intrinsically worthwhile.

Why then did the publication of Wilson's scholarly *Sociobiology* cause such a controversy? Why was Wilson made the object of both laudatory feature stories in the news media on the one hand, and the target of invective, and even personal assault, from political activists on the other hand? Because in the final chapter of his treatise, otherwise devoted mainly to insects and other lower orders, Wilson claimed that the methodology and findings of sociobiology are applicable also to the social behavior of our own species, *Homo sapiens.* Thus Wilson proposed that his New Synthesis can provide for human sciences such as anthropology and sociology a firm, and presumably objective, scientific basis. It should be noted, however, that much of the virulent criticism directed against Wilson was not based on the grounds that the naturalistic view of morality embodied in his New Synthesis is philosophically mistaken. That is to say, most of Wilson's critics do not deny that moral behavior is to be viewed as a strategy for optimizing human welfare. That naturalistic viewpoint most of Wilson's ideological opponents actually share with him and believe in as fervently as does he. No, their criticism is based mainly on an outright rejection of the scientific premise fundamental to sociobiology that human behavior is genetically determined. They believe that human behavior is determined by the environment, and not by human genes. So it seems that this argument is susceptible to an objective resolution, since the validity of the proposition that human behavior is genetically determined ought to be subject to empirical tests. But there is a fundamental difficulty in the way of testing the validity of that proposition, namely that the very concept of "genetic determination" of *any* complex feature of an animal, not just of human behavior, is still rather elusive. For although, thanks to the triumphs of molecular biology, "genetic determination" is now a highly meaningful concept when applied to the microscopic structure of protein molecules, and possibly also when applied to their physiological function, it is much less meaningful when applied to a macroscopic trait such as "blue eyes." Here what the genes can be usefully said to "determine" is not the blue eyes, nor even their blueness, but only the *difference* between the brown and the blue eye trait. But again, most of Wilson's critics did *not* attack him on these esoteric logical grounds, because almost all of them believe, as does Wilson, that the general notion of genetic determination of complex traits is, on the whole, sound. They reject only its special application to human behavior.

More recently Wilson published another book entitled *On Human Nature*. That book is ostensibly an expansion of the controversial final chapter of *Sociobiology* into a full prospectus for the sociobiological project of grounding the human sciences in biological principles. Although from *On Human Nature* Wilson's New Synthesis emerges as still basically the same as that which he had adumbrated in 1975, his original strident claims on its behalf are now partially neutralized by many caveats, disclaimers, and reservations. Surprisingly, however, in *On Human Nature* Wilson mentions neither of the two authors, the social anthropologist Marshall Sahlins nor the ethologist Richard Dawkins, whose popular and readily accessible books on the sociobiology controversy published in 1976 were read just as widely as Wilson's own earlier treatise. Sahlins evidently wrote his *The Use and Abuse of Biology* in order to show that one who has some professional acquaintance with the study of human social behavior can find grave faults with Wilson's New Synthesis. Sahlins first discusses what he calls "vulgar" sociobiology, as exemplified by the popular writings of Konrad Lorenz and of Robert Ardrey, Desmond Morris, Lionel Tiger, and Robin Fox. Vulgar sociobiology, according to Sahlins, aims to account for human social behavior as an expression of needs and drives of the human organism, needs and drives that became part of human nature in the course of biological evolution. Such an account of human behavior, says Sahlins, demands a one-to-one correspondence, or isomorphism, between the character of these human biological needs and drives and the features of human social systems. But—and this is Sahlins's first important claim—no such isomorphism exists between human biological needs and drives and the features of social systems, because the presence of *culture* interrupts any straightforward causal chain between human biology and human social structures. Culture has evidently freed human behavior patterns from being inexorably determined by biological needs and drives. This follows from the anthropological findings that, on the one hand, the *same* human motives appear in different cultural forms, and that, on the other hand, different motives appear in the same cultural forms. Hence there can be no biological determinism of human social behavior, and insofar as *Homo sapiens* is concerned, vulgar sociobiologists are whistling in the dark.

Sahlins's point of the futility of any sociobiological project that neglects the central role of culture in the shaping of human social behavior seems well taken. Moreover, Sahlins may be correct in claiming that the vulgar authors whose writings he consigns to the ashcan of sociological literature have not taken the role of culture sufficiently into account. But Sahlins's argument does *not* show that there is no conceivable, more sophisticated version of sociobiology which *could* take the role of culture into account and which might thus provide a biological account of human social behavior after all. First, it certainly simplifies the analysis of any phenomenon if its structural features *are* isomorphic with a set of underlying causes. But it is not true, as Sahlins appears to think, that a one-to-one correspondence between antecedents and consequents is an absolute requirement for their causal relation. If Sahlins's general demand for such a cause-effect isomorphism were valid, it would also be futile to search for a biological account of embryonic development. Except for the isomorphism between nucleotide sequence in the genes and amino acid sequence in the proteins, there is no ensemble of properties in the egg for which there exists a one-to-one correspondence with the properties of the mature animal. Second, and more important, Sahlins seems to take it for granted that the symbolic character of cultural tradition puts it squarely outside the biological realm. But unless Sahlins regards "culture" as some kind of transcendental phenomenon, with laws and dynamics beyond the reach of scientific analysis, independent of the biological structures of the human (and humanoid) organisms that originated and perpetuated it, it is far from self-evident why there cannot be in principle a sociobiological account of culture.

Sahlins eventually returns to this problem and declares that the nature of the relation between culture and biology is, as he says, "hierarchical," just as is the relation between biology itself and physics and chemistry. According to Sahlins, "culture is biology plus the symbolic faculty," just as "biology is physics and chemistry plus natural selection." So Sahlins does admit that biology has something to do with culture after all. Namely, as he says, biology "puts at the disposition of culture a set of means for the construction of a symbolic order." Consequently, all it would take for a culture-inclusive supersociobiology of the future to connect that symbolic order with biology is a theory of meaning, just as it took a theory of biological information for molecular biology to connect heredity with physics and chemistry. And since the present lack of a theory of meaning (presumably to be supplied one of these days by cognitive psychology) is just as debilitating for Sahlins's own field of social anthropology in its attempt to account for culture as it is for sociobiology, it seems quite unreasonable for Sahlins to single out only sociobiology for special criticism in its inability to deal with culture.

Next, Sahlins trains his guns on "scientific" sociobiology, which according to him is vulgar sociobiology plus the theory of kin selection. Sahlins clearly holds scientific sociobiologists, such as Wilson and Alexander, in somewhat higher regard than their vulgar colleagues, Lorenz and company. To their credit, the scientific sociobiologists have understood that kinship is the primary feature to be explained by any social science. Hence for Sahlins, Wilson and Alexander at least qualify as discussion partners. Sahlins finds that "the issue between sociobiology and social anthropology is decisively joined on the field of kinship." It would follow, therefore, that if, in view of the admitted central importance of kinship for human behavior, actual kinship relations, as ascertained by social anthropologists, do not turn out to be ordered in accord with the predictions of the kin selection theory, then the project of scientific sociobiology collapses. And—this is Sahlins's second important claim—the ethnological record shows "that there is not a single system of marriage, postmarital residence, family organization, interpersonal kinship, or common descent in human societies that does not set up a different calculus of relationship and social action than [sic] is indicated by the principles of kin selection." In support of this claim, Sahlins cites data from New Guinea, from the Sudan, and from all the Nesias—Micro, Mela, and Poly. These data show that, contrary to the demands of kin selection, under the kinship conventions of these societies not all of the closest biological relatives render each other mutual aid, that is, are actually considered as kin.

Suppose we accept Sahlins's ethnological data; does it really follow that scientific sociobiology collapses? No, because the mere fact that extant kinship relations do not match exactly those predicted from kin selection theory may mean simply that additional, complicating factors are at work (i.e., that sociobiological theory is merely approximate), a conclusion which, I am sure, most scientific sociobiologists would readily accept. Moreover, in all the examples (except one) adduced by Sahlins, a person is biologically related much more closely to culturally defined kinsmen than to what passes for non-kin within his social horizon. Hence the role of kin selection in kinship convention seems more confirmed than refuted by his data. To make the sociobiological project really collapse, Sahlins would have to produce a countertheory of kinship whose predictions give a much better quantitative account of the data than do the predictions of the kin selection theory. In the absence of offering any better countertheory, Sahlins's rejection of scientific sociobiology on the basis of his kinship data is not very convincing.

After having supposedly demolished the sociobiological approach to human behavior, Sahlins moves on to a general consideration of the current conceptual status of evolutionary theory. According to him, "the Darwinian concept of natural selection has suffered a serious ideological derailment in recent years," a disaster to which sociobiology made a primary contribution. How has evolutionary theory actually been "derailed"? Here Sahlins makes his third important claim: evolutionary theory has been corrupted by the identification of natural selection with the operation of the free market economy. To document this allegation, Sahlins cites examples from the sociobiological literature in which the authors resort to economic terminology, such as "cost benefit analysis," "investment," and "profit," and regard animals as entrepreneurs seeking to maximize their genetic capital. Once more, Sahlins weakens his valid criticisms of sociobiology by exaggerating his case. First, sociobiologists (contrary to their own pretensions, apparently accepted by Sahlins) are only on the fringe of present-day evolutionary biology. Hence the sociobiological "derailment" of natural selection theory by obstructing its tracks with economic baggage is a rather local phenomenon, of little significance for the general status of current evolutionary thought. Second, the mere borrowing of the notion of the free market does not by itself invalidate the sociobiological approach to natural selection, no more than the borrowing of the concepts of mechanical and hydraulic engineering by Descartes and his contemporaries invalidates human physiology. That Sahlins is able to present some cases from the sociobiological literature where shoddy reasoning based on the economic metaphor has led to ludicrous propositions does not mean that Wilson's New Synthesis is to be rejected.

Finally Sahlins raises an issue that, though he considers it only in the context of the debate surrounding sociobiology, reaches down to the very foundations of science: Can there be such a thing as a science that is an objective exercise of pure reason, not subject to influence by human affects or culture? David Hume, who held that "reason is, and ought to be the slave of the passions" had already replied in the negative. More recently, such contemporary historians and philosophers of science as Thomas Kuhn, Paul Feyerabend, and Stephen Toulmin have maintained that the notion of culture-free, eternal scientific truths is merely an illusion. Without giving any sign that he is aware of stirring up this epistemological hornet's nest, Sahlins makes his fourth and final important claim: since the seventeenth century natural history, and its eventual successor biology, have been shaped by an ideological dialectic with social thought, from Thomas Hobbes to Adam Smith, from Smith to Darwin, from Darwin to William Graham Sumner, and finally from Sumner to E. O. Wilson. In this dialectic across time the model of capitalist society is applied to the animal kingdom, and this bourgeoisified animal kingdom is then reapplied to the interpretation of human society.

Here, as is the case for his other three important claims, Sahlins makes what appears to be a valid point. But since the reciprocal contamination of scientific thought and culture is not an exclusive debility of sociobiology, in that it applies even to the hard physical sciences (not to speak of his own social anthropology), Sahlins's indictment of sociobiology and his stigmatization of it as "Scientific Totemism" loses most of its force. To point out that sociobiology, just as other scientific disciplines, lacks true objectivity is not enough for a convincing indictment. Sahlins has to show that there is a better approach than sociobiology to the understanding of the social behavior of animals. And this Sahlins does not, and I imagine cannot, do.

Thus far from having struck a decisive blow against Wilson's claim of providing a biological account of human social behavior, Sahlins's book has only further strengthened Wilson's case. For if not even the scholarly critique of a well-known social anthropologist like Sahlins makes a sound and convincing argument against Wilson, then one might suspect that maybe the sociobiological position is impregnable. In my opinion, most of the critics of sociobiology, Sahlins included, have erred in attacking sociobiology on either political or scientific grounds. For on those grounds sociobiology is not dramatically weaker than most other so-called human sciences. Insofar as the application of biology to the understanding of human social behavior is concerned, it is not so much the case that the sociobiological project is intrinsically impossible. Rather, it is the case that many sociobiologists, by virtue of philosophical and political naiveté, lack of sociological insights, and overbearing exuberance, have greatly overblown the significance and scope of their findings. On their part, many humanists, social anthropologists, and Marxist-oriented biologists have overreacted to these exaggerated claims. In their, not wholly unjustified, fear of the political consequences of the work of sociobiological would-be social engineers, these critics of sociobiology have gone too far and dismissed as completely worthless also what there is of value in the sociobiological approach to animal societies.

I think that if there is to be effective criticism of the claims of sociobiology with regard to human social affairs, then this criticism has to be made on philosophical grounds, and in particular on moral philosophical grounds. For it is not difficult to show that Wilson and his fellow sociobiologists are clearly misusing the concepts of moral discourse. To illuminate this deficiency of sociobiological thought, we may examine the moral concepts of "altruism" and "selfishness" with which much of sociobiological theory is presently preoccupied. And this examination is greatly aided by Richard Dawkins's highly successful, prosociobiological popular book entitled *The Selfish Gene*. Dawkins epitomizes the sociobiological viewpoint of man, by saying that we are machines created by our genes. These genes have managed to survive in a highly competitive world only by virtue of their ruthless selfishness. And since our genes are selfish, it is only to be expected that our social behavior is similarly selfish. This is quite a startling argument. Under the ordinary, everyday morally relevant parlance, *selfishness* means disregard by one person for the interests of other persons, whereas *altruism* means regard for the interests of others. But how can genes, not being persons, have regard or disregard for the interests of other persons? In order to avoid having to impute personhood and intentionality to genes, Dawkins puts forward wholly unconventional, value-free definitions of the concepts of selfishness and altruism. According to Dawkins, an entity is altruistic if it behaves in such a way as to increase another entity's welfare at the expense of its own, with welfare being defined as "chances of survival." Selfish behavior has exactly the opposite effect. Thus Dawkins's special, sociobiological meanings of altruism and selfishness are beyond good and evil, since they concern consequences for survival rather than regard for interest, and they pertain to "entities" rather than to persons.

By contrast, the conventional, morally relevant meanings of altruism and selfishness make sense only within the context of interpersonal relations, and for these meanings intent, rather than consequence, is the necessary and sufficient criterion. For instance, if child A takes away chocolate from child B because it wants to eat the chocolate itself, child A is morally selfish. However, since child A has thereby reduced the chances of tooth decay in child B, child A's morally selfish act is at the same time sociobiologically altruistic. Dawkins then shows that apparently altruistic behavior, such as the alarm call of birds, is really selfish after all. For according to the principle of kin selection, the selfish genes of the alarmist bird have actually increased the welfare of their own informational replicas in the other birds of the flock. It is easy to see that such sociobiological playing with the words *altruism* and *selfishness* is unlikely to contribute very much to our understanding of moral behavior.

It should be noted moreover that sociobiologists not only denature the concepts of moral discourse but they also sow confusion about the central concept of genetics, namely the "gene." One of the main triumphs of molecular biology was the identification of the Mendelian gene as that element of genetic material, or of DNA, in which the amino acid sequence of a particular protein is encoded. It is in this molecular biological sense that nearly all working geneticists now employ the term "gene." But how the ensemble of genes, or genome, of the animal is related to the ensemble of its overt features, or its phenome, is an extremely complex and as yet quite unsolved conceptual problem. In particular, it is not sensible to consider that the genome embodies a "program" for the embryonic development of the animal. The conceptual obstacle to formulating a genetic theory of development lies mainly in the crucial role played by the enormously complex context in which the genes find themselves in the course of embryonic and postembryonic development.

It is this presently utterly obscure relation between phenome and genome, rather than the free market economy simile that troubles Sahlins, which is one of the hidden skeletons in the closet of neo-Darwinian evolutionary theory. Since it is clear that natural selection selects the overt features of the animal, but since it is also clear that what is passed on to future generations are the covert genes, we must know the ontogenetic relation between genome and phemome before we can understand how evolution really works. To cover up this conceptual deficit, sociobiologists arbitrarily define the gene as that hereditary unit that natural selection happens to select. But since that unit is certainly not what geneticists mean by "gene," the sociobiological "Selfish Gene" is neither selfish, in the context of morality, nor is it a gene, in the context of genetics.

One important reason for insisting on a hygienic use of the gene concept, by the way, is to remove all grounds for the claim that *Homo sapiens* is a unique animal that can transcend its genes. There may be good reasons for criticizing sociobiological extrapolations from animals to humans, but the human transcendence of genes is not one of them. The notion of transcendence of our evolutionary genetic heritage has, in fact, been a characteristic, essentially apologist, stance taken by many ethologists that have made claims for the moral relevance of animal studies. Such ethologists usually first show why evolution has endowed us with a selfish, aggressive, and on the whole, rather nasty set of genes. They then reject the seemingly justified accusation that they are providing a naturalistic justification for an immoral society. To make this rejection, they claim that, on the contrary, they are paving the way for the City of God by pinpointing those beastly aspects of our human genetic heritage that we must struggle to "transcend." But the idea of any organism, including man, transcending its genes is a biological absurdity. Within the context of biology as a branch of natural science, and upon proper consideration of any conceivably scientifically valid relation between the genome and phenome, transcendence of genes is no more possible than natural selection of the unfit.

Dawkins, like Sahlins, raises the troublesome question of whether there can be such a thing as a value-free study of the social behavior of animals (let alone of humans). And like Sahlins, Dawkins seems unaware that he is touching here on one of the most hotly debated issues in the contemporary philosophy of science. In his book, Dawkins feels he is in danger of being accused of committing the "Naturalistic Fallacy," that is of being misunderstood by those people, all too numerous, who cannot distinguish a statement of what is the case from advocacy of what ought to be the case. But Dawkins's text shows why these people are so numerous: in studying the social behavior of animals, it is evidently extremely difficult, if not impossible, to state what is the case without implying also what ought to be the case. The reason for this is that the words in terms of which the sociobiologist states what is the case—such as *pain, hunger, aggression, parent, queen, worker, courtship, slave, rival,* or *soldier,* not to mention *selfishness* and *altruism*—all connote functions, roles, and values. Such use of functional, value-laden terminology is well-nigh unavoidable, since these words are properly descriptive of the typology that the sociobiologist recognizes in the animal behavior he observes. But for these words it is not true, as Dawkins claims it is, that the sociobiologist can define them "how he likes for his own purposes, provided he does so clearly and unambiguously." On the contrary, in doing his work the sociobiologist brings to the objects of his study his intuitive understanding of these words, which he shares with all other persons speaking his language without need of explicit definition. The student of animal behavior thus arrives, willy-nilly, at propositions from which an ought *can* be inferred from an is. Consequently, anyone who would bring sociobiological propositions to the domain of human social behavior must be aware, as Dawkins is not, that in this context the "Naturalistic Fallacy" is itself false: here the description of what *is* the case *can* imply what ought to be the case. Therefore, when in the last chapter of his treatise E. O. Wilson extends his sociobiological considerations to man, he can rightly be considered to have entered the ethical domain, and hence to have opened himself up to critique on moral grounds. Nevertheless, regardless of these conceptual deficits of sociobiology as it has developed thus far, we can ask: is it not possible that there will be some day a better, conceptually more adequate biological account of human social behavior?

Before attempting to answer that question we must turn to Immanuel Kant. Just as biology had been given a new departure by Darwin, so had moral philosophy been given a new departure by Kant some eighty years prior to the appearance of the *Origin of the Species*. Kant's fundamental epistemological claim was that we live in two metaphysically distinct worlds. One of these worlds is that of science, whose natural objects are seen as being governed by laws of causal determination. The other world is that of morals, whose rational human subjects are seen to be governed by laws of freedom which each individual imposes on his own actions. Thus from the Kantian viewpoint the main task in understanding the nature of morality would be to discover and explicate the metaphysical principles presupposed by moral judgments, rather than the discovery of biological generalizations about human welfare or evolutionary mechanisms. These metaphysical principles can be discovered only by examining the facts of moral experience and by analyzing the logic of moral judgments. This Kantian view is, of course, not very congenial to modern biologists. How can they accept the Darwinian view of the biological nature of man while granting Kant's insistence that belief in an autonomous free will, independent of natural law, is a necessary presupposition of morality? In any case, it is obvious that from the Kantian viewpoint the sociobiologist project of grounding morals in Darwinism is *radically* mistaken. The biology of morals would fail because it brings a categorical confusion to the problem of ethics. Biologists are thus faced by a dilemma. On the one hand it must seem self-evident to them that the sociobiological approach to moral behavior has *some* merit. After all, since man's familial roots do lie in the animal kingdom, it would seem perverse to deny that observations on the social behavior of animals cannot in some way illuminate the nature of human morals. On the other hand, it seems equally apparent that the antinaturalistic notion of an autonomous free will and of a categorical obligation to obey universal moral law cannot be dismissed as so much nonsense in any attempt to fathom the nature of morals.

In my view, this dilemma is only one of many such dilemmas that arise from the paradoxical character of the set of basic concepts about the world intuited by human reason, concepts thanks to which reason constructs reality from experience. The internal inconsistencies of rational concepts are not so grave that they prevent us from building a superficially coherent picture of reality for a rational conduct of everyday life. In fact, these inconsistencies become apparent only when scientists and philosophers pursue the analysis of that picture to the bottom of the night. Then, once the analysis has proceeded far beyond a certain depth, basic incompatibilities or ambiguities come into view that cannot be resolved unless some fundamental intuitive concepts about the world are altered. These alterations may reintroduce logical coherence, but making them has grave cognitive and affective consequences: it alienates man from the reality that he constructs in the service of everyday sane human life.

Kant, of course, recognized that the relation of science to ethics is inherently paradoxical. As he pointed out, our intuitive attribution of freedom of the will to the person contradicts our intuitive attribution of causal necessity to nature. And as rational beings we cannot abandon the idea of moral freedom any more than we can abandon the idea of scientific causal necessity. Thus our view of the relation of the person to his actions must be fundamentally different, when we view the person either as a moral agent or as a natural object. As scientists we must regard the person as a material object forming part of the causally determined events of the natural world; but as moralists we must regard the person as an intelligent subject forming part of the world of thought that is independent of the laws of nature.

How can this paradox arising from the incoherence of the set of rational concepts be resolved? If it is to be resolved at all, then remedy must be given to what I think continues to be a defect of traditional philosophical arguments. Namely, moral philosophers have generally considered only the moral reasoning of the adult, mature human mind. They give little thought to the processes by which moral competence, indeed reason itself, arises in childhood development, except that they usually reject the idea that the felt obligation to obey moral law is a product of social learning. This rather general neglect of childhood by moral philosophers seems surprising, since the development of moral competence is a phenomenon that, from the technical point of view, has always been empirically accessible. It was certainly accessible in Kant's time, since the types of study of children pioneered by Jean Piaget fifty years ago did not require atomic fission or the electron microscope. This ready empirical access to *ontogenetic* moral development can be contrasted with the inaccessibility to direct study of the *phylogenetic* development of morals, on which sociobiological interest is mainly focused. Accordingly, it would appear that it is the study of childhood development by cognitive psychologists that can presently offer one of the potentially most fruitful meeting grounds for biology and moral philosophy.

In view of the controversy generated by the publication of Wilson's *Sociobiology*, Silke Bernhard, the founder-director of the Berlin Dahlem Konferenzen, felt it would be propitious to hold a workshop on the theme "Morality as a Biological Phenomenon." She thought that an interdisciplinary discussion between persons of goodwill could show that it is possible to move a little farther toward resolving the ancient paradox of naturalistic versus idealistic ethics than had been the case for the recent debates between the proponents and opponents of sociobiology. Accordingly, she requested an organizing committee, consisting of N. Bischof, F. J. G. Ebling, C. Fried, F. A. Jenner, G. W. Kowalski, E. Turiel, B. A. O. Williams, and myself to plan such a workshop. Our committee chose as the stated goal of the workshop "to examine the limits of the naturalistic approach to morality" reflecting our shared belief that whereas the naturalistic approach is not without validity, it nevertheless *has* limits that must fall short of providing a full account of morality. The meeting was held in Berlin from November 28 to December 2, 1977, with twenty-five participants coming from France, Germany, Great Britain, Switzerland, and the United States.

In my opening remarks to the workshop participants I pleaded for terminological rectitude, insofar as this is possible in talking about the difficult subject which we came to discuss. I expressed my hope that we would avoid using terms, or referring to concepts, with meanings other than those under which they are commonly understood in ordinary parlance. In my view, it is due to recent failures to adhere to this single principle of terminological hygiene, or to avoid what W. Stegmüller recently called "semantic pollution of the intellectual environment," that the present scene of morality as seen from the biological perspective is so turbid. Fortunately, there seemed to be a general consensus among the participants that, whatever else morals may be, or whatever is their biological basis, the concept of morality pertains to an *intentional state* of an agent. Accordingly, the benign or malign consequences of action are relevant for the consideration of the moral component of behavior mainly insofar as the consequences can reveal the intentional state of the agent. There are people, of course, for instance behaviorists, who hold that biology can have nothing to say about intentional, or "mentalistic" states. In the light of the evident intentional aspect of morality, such people would be fully justified in holding that morality as a biological phenomenon is a nonsubject. But such people would *not* be justified in redefining the concept of morality by simply replacing covert intentionality by its overt consequences as the criterion of the moral component of behavior, just so that biology can be brought to bear on something called "morals" but which is not, in fact, the morals of ordinary discourse.

It would be difficult to conceive of any conference more "interdisciplinary" than this workshop, whose participants included not only biologists, philosophers, psychologists, and social anthropologists but also a theologian, a jurist, and a sinologist. As is evident from the papers presented in this volume, the workshop brought together scholars with widely divergent perspectives on the nature of morality and on the approaches likely to be fruitful for its study. Thomas Nagel, for instance, held that ethics, as developed by moral philosophers, is an autonomous subject with its own internal standards of analysis and discourse, to which biology cannot, in principle, make any interesting contributions. Donald Campbell, by contrast, held that it is high time that ethics is rescued from the sterile grasp of moral philosophers and put where it belongs, namely into the hands of evolutionary biologists and psychologists. Or, Charles Fried expressed his conviction that the element of choice is central to any conception of morality, whereas Ming Wei Tu maintained that for more than two millennia Chinese society has operated with a concept of morality under which individual choice plays no significant role. And whereas Norbert Bischof took the stand that biologically relevant universal aspects of human morality, such as the incest taboo, clearly provide an empirical nexus of biology and morals, Clifford Geertz and Jack Goody found that such alleged universals, the incest taboo not excepted, have no real existence, being merely unsophisticated farragoes of fundamentally disparate anthropological phenomena. But I think it is fair to say that, despite these initially divergent perspectives, our discussions made some progress toward at least clarifying the true issues that are at stake in the debates which the sociobiological approach to morality has recently provoked and that most of us left Berlin with an enlarged intellectual horizon. I am sure I speak for all the Workshop participants when I thank Silke Bernhard and the Dahlem Konferenzen for making possible this unique opportunity to examine a most critical interface between philosophy and modern biology.

PART
1

EVOLUTION
AND MORALS

THE CONCEPTS OF SOCIOBIOLOGY

J. Maynard Smith

During the past ten years, several new ideas have been applied to the evolution of social behavior in animals. In this essay, I first describe these new ideas, and then discuss their possible relevance to human societies.

"FUNCTIONAL" AND "CAUSAL" EXPLANATIONS IN BIOLOGY

Most questions in biology require answers at two levels. If one asks "Why does the heart beat?" the "causal" answer would refer to the fact that the heart muscle has a spontaneously contractile rhythm, that the heart is innervated by motor neurons, and so on. The causal explanation, then, is a here-and-now answer in physiological terms. But one could answer "to pump the blood round the body." This "functional answer," corresponding to Aristotle's final cause, might seem illegitimate in the context of science because of its teleological form. It is in fact legitimate only if it can be translated into an explanation in terms of natural selection—that is, "those mammals which in the past had hearts which were more efficient pumps left more descendants."

Thus the "function" of an organ is taken to mean those of its effects which have been responsible for its evolution by natural selection. The terms "functional" and "causal" are perhaps unfortunate, because they are liable to confuse. Thus a functional explanation is itself a causal one, in terms of causes acting over evolutionary time. It seems, however, that the terms are now so entrenched in the biological literature that we must vision ourselves to living with them.

Behavioral patterns, just as do anatomical structures, require both a causal and a functional explanation. A robin in spring attacks other robins entering a particular area because it has an "innate releasing mechanism" causing it to do so (causal explanation); by doing so, it holds a territory in which it can mate and rear offspring (functional explanation).

The new ideas in sociobiology have arisen from a more rigorous insistence that teleological explanations in biology be reducible to explanations in terms of natural selection and population genetics.

INDIVIDUAL, GROUP AND KIN SELECTION

No satisfactory axiomatization of Darwin's theory of evolution is available. I think, however, that any such axiomatization will have to be in terms of hypothetical entities having the properties of multiplication, variation, and heredity. The only entities with these properties are genes. The body is not replicated—it dies. This has led Dawkins (1) to propose that evolution theory be reformulated in terms of genes rather than organisms. In a sense, this is what is done in population genetics, but in population genetics "fitnesses" (probabilities of survival and reproduction) are ascribed to genotypes (sets of genes) without any explanation of *why* a particular genotype has a particular fitness. Consequently population genetics by itself can say nothing about the evolution of phenotypes (that is, of structure and behavior). If we are interested in the evolution of phenotypes, we must usually start with individual organisms.

A model of evolution by "individual selection" is, briefly, as follows. Suppose a population contains individuals of two kinds, $\bar{A}$ and $\bar{a}$ (for example, robins which do and do not attack intruders). Suppose also that there is a gene $\bar{A}$ which (averaged over the contemporary environments, and for the genes present at other loci) makes it more likely that a robin with gene Ā will belong to class Ā. Then if Ā robins are fitter than ā—leave on the average more offspring—the gene Ā will increase in frequency in the population. We can assert this because an individual passes exactly half its genes to each of its offspring. (There are important exceptions to this rule, but they need not concern us here.)

For many purposes, explanations in terms of individual selection are entirely adequate. We find the function of an organ by asking how it contributes to the survival of an individual possessing it. Some structures and behaviors, however, seem to reduce the fitness of the individual but they increase the chance of survival of the group to which the individual belongs. A classic example is the act of a worker bee in stinging an animal attacking the hive; if the attacker is a mammal, the sting stays in the wound and the bee dies. Sociobiologists refer to such acts, perhaps unfortunately, as "altruistic." How is their evolutionary origin to be explained?

One proposed explanation is "group selection" (10), in which the unit of selection is the population, not the individual. Populations of altruistic individuals are more likely to survive and reproduce than those containing selfish individuals. There is a continuing debate about this process (for a recent review see [4]). Group selection can work only if there are reproductively isolated populations of which most die out or split into two, and between which migration is rare. My own view is that the conditions needed for the operation of group selection rarely exist in nature, and that therefore it can be invoked as an explanation for the origin of altruistic behavior only in very special circumstances.

An alternative proposal is "kin selection" (2). Suppose a gene A̲ causes an individual that carries it to perform an act Ā, with the effect of reducing the fitness of the individual but increasing the fitness of some of its relatives. The result of performing the act Ā may be to increase the frequency of the gene A̲ in the future, because relatives of the individual may also carry copies of gene A̲.

Hamilton showed how one can calculate an "inclusive fitness" that predicts whether gene A̲ will increase in frequency, in terms of the reproductive cost to the individual, the reproductive benefit to each relative, and the degree of

genetic relationship between the individual and its beneficiaries. He also showed, particularly for social insects,
how the structure of animal societies can be explained in
the terms of inclusive fitness. In recent years, Hamilton's
ideas have been applied more widely (9).

A simple if somewhat trivial example may help to clarify
the inclusive fitness principle. *Tribonyx mortieri* is a flight-
less rail from Tasmania of which, for unknown reasons,
there are substantially more males than females. Adults
form stable pairs (1 o and 1 o) or trios (2 oo and 1 o). In a trio
both males mate with the female, which raises a problem.
Since one of the males could drive out the other, why does
he not do so? If he did, he would father all the female's children, instead of only half of them. If a trio were able to raise
more than twice as many young as a pair, it would pay the
stronger male to tolerate his partner; but the fact is, trios
raise only about 1.4 times as many offspring. It turns out that
the two males in a trio are almost always brothers. Now if
the stronger male were to drive out his brother and thereby
deprive him of any chance of producing offspring, it can be
shown that although the stronger male would increase the
number of his own direct descendants, he would decrease
the frequency of his genes in future generations. In Hamilton's terminology, he would decrease his "inclusive fitness."

Kin-selection can operate whenever relatives live close to
one another and unlike group selection, it does not require
that the species be divided into reproductively isolated
groups.

THE THEORY OF GAMES AND "EVOLUTIONARY STABLE STRATEGIES"

Contests between animals for a territory, a mate, or a
position in a hierarchy are often settled conventionally,
without escalation of physical violence (3). Although I do not
doubt this conclusion, I have long been puzzled by how
such conventional behavior could have evolved. Clearly it
is an advantage for the group, since it reduces the frequency of injury, but group selection explanations are suspect. An explanation in terms of individual selection is possible by borrowing some ideas from the theory of games (5,
6).

Suppose that a population of individuals compete in pairs. Individuals adopt different strategies and, after a number of contests, reproduce their kind in proportion to the "payoffs" which they have accumulated. Evolution by natural selection will drive the population to an "evolutionary stable strategy," or ESS. An ESS has the property that if almost all the members of a population adopt it, their (individual) fitness is greater than that of any "mutant" individual adopting a different strategy. Application of this idea leads to the following conclusions:

1. If escalation is dangerous, and if there is no readily discernible asymmetry associated with the contest, the population will evolve toward a mixture of aggressive and timid individuals (these could differ genetically, or an individual could vary its tactics).

2. "Retaliation," in which an individual behaves conventionally unless its opponent escalates, whereupon the individual escalates in return, is likely to be a feature of ESS's in contest situations.

3. If there is a discernible asymmetry between contestants (for example, in size, or between "owner" and "intruder"), this is likely to be taken as a cue for the conventional settlement of contests. Surprisingly, a contest between an owner and an intruder will be conventionally settled even though there is no difference in payoff or in size and strength.

These ideas are of recent origin and have hardly been exposed to observational test, yet they do appear to account for much conventional behavior without recourse to explanations in terms of group selection. The concept of an ESS can be applied also to parental nurturing behavior, to competition between plants, and in fact to any context in which the best strategy for an individual depends on how other individuals are behaving.

ANIMALS AND MAN

Wilson (9) has written a major, albeit controversial, treatise on social organization in animals, in which he attempts to interpret the facts in Darwinian terms, and in particular in terms of inclusive fitness. It is perhaps too early to judge the success of Wilson's enterprise. In any case the main source of controversy has been his claim that an evolutionary approach can illuminate not only animal but also human societies.

Wilson does not allege that the *differences* between various human societies are caused by genetic differences between their members. Such differences Wilson accepts as being culturally transmitted, basically because historically documented changes in social organization have occurred too rapidly to be explained by genetic change. What he does claim is that there are universal characteristics of human societies which exist because of universal features of human nature that evolved by natural selection.

At one level this claim is obviously true. All human societies (unlike ant societies) depend on acoustic communication, and this certainly depends on a human aptitude which has evolved by natural selection. But can anything more interesting be said? Wilson believes something more can. He interprets the almost universal occurrence of some form of incest taboo, of an economic role differentiation between the sexes, of religious ritual associated in some way with an ethical imperative, of barter and exchange, and of the nuclear family as the building block of almost all societies as all being consequences of our genetic makeup.

Two main criticisms have been made of his position: that it is Social Darwinist, and that there is no evidence that behavioral characteristics in man are genetically determined. I will consider them in turn.

SOCIAL DARWINISM

It can be argued that any attempt to show that human characteristics are innate rather than acquired will be used to justify the status quo, because social reform can hope to alter acquired characters but not innate ones. Radicals, from the authors of the Declaration of Independence to Karl Marx, have tended to take up an environmentalist stance, and conservatives from Plato onward, a hereditarian stance. (There are exceptions—for instance, the conservative Skinner espouses environmentalism whereas the radical Chomsky has a hereditarian viewpoint.) Wilson's arguments do appear to lend themselves to the defense of the status quo. For instance, in America there is at present circulating a film, *Sociobiology, or Doing What Comes Naturally*, which makes a crude use of sociobiological images (one could hardly call them arguments) to justify such views as woman's place is in the nursery and in bed, and man's in the boardroom and on the football field.

I do not think one ought to reject Wilson's arguments merely because they can be used to justify social policies one dislikes. It is better to examine the evidence relating to man on its own merits and also to point out that a thing may be "natural" without being right. As far as sex role differentiation in human society is concerned, we have no idea how ancient it might be, and the evidence for innate cognitive or temperamental differences between the sexes is tenuous. Suppose, however, that future research does show that role differentiation is indeed ancient, and that there are statistically significant innate differences between the sexes. This still would not make it right to force men and women into different social roles. Equality of opportunity would still seem to me the right social policy, although it might not result in equal numbers of men and women performing particular roles.

Wilson's own position on the "naturalistic fallacy" is not clear to me. He says in his book that "Scientists and humanists should consider together the possibility that the time has come for ethics to be removed temporarily from the hands of the philosophers and biologicized." He has since made it clear, however, that he does not hold the view that if a thing is natural it is therefore right. It may be that all he intended by the above remark is that it is up to biologists to explain how man evolved the capacity to hold ethical beliefs. I agree with this view, but it is not particularly new. It was held by Darwin, and it is hard to see what other opinion an evolutionary biologist could hold. What is new, perhaps, is that concepts such as kin selection, reciprocal altruism (8), and ESS's may help us answer the question.

BIOLOGICAL DETERMINISM

Two different but related criticisms have been made of Wilson's genetic assumptions concerning man.

1. There is no evidence for a gene in man determining how aggressive he will be, or whether he will commit incest, or any other morally relevant trait. This statement is both true and irrelevant. It is certainly true that we do not know of a pair of alleles, A and a, which determine that all

men carrying A are aggressive and all men carrying a are not. But the existence of such alleles is not necessary for Wilson's argument. All he needs suppose is that there are genetic differences between people influencing how likely they are to be aggressive in particular circumstances. As it happens, we have only rather indirect evidence even for this much weaker assumption; unequivocal evidence is hard to come by in man, because controlled human breeding experiments are morally impossible. But, it would be very odd indeed if this assumption were not true. In other animal species, genetic variance for behavioral traits can be readily found, and I shall assume that the same is true for man until a good reason is provided for supposing otherwise.

If we do suppose that such genetic variance exists, is Wilson justified in assuming that traits such as incest avoidance have an innate basis? This is a much more difficult question: it brings me to the second criticism of Wilson's genetic assumption:

2. Genetics is concerned with differences, not with universals. Given two persons of different heights, we can reasonably ask whether the difference was caused by a difference between their genes or between their environments. Given appropriate evidence, we might be able to conclude that the height difference was genetically determined. But it would not be correct to assert that a person's height is genetically determined, because we know that it would have been different if he had been raised differently.

There are characteristics that are "genetically determined" in the sense that individuals of a given genotype will develop the characteristic in almost all environments compatible with life. The presence of a backbone is genetically determined in humans in this sense. Similarly the amino acid sequences of our proteins are genetically determined in this sense. But the characteristics treated by Wilson as human universals are not of this kind. There are environments in which some human genotypes do commit incest, or are reluctant to participate in ritual acts, or adopt roles atypical for their sex and society. So what can it mean to say that there are such human universals which are innate?

Clearly it cannot mean that these behaviors are present

in all human beings at all times. At best, it could mean that most human beings behave in these ways in most environments. In any case, the postulation of innate, socially relevant characteristics of human behaviors has been taken to imply that almost all human societies will acquire these characteristics, regardless of initial conditions or conscious intentions. I do not know how this implication can be justified, but it certainly cannot be justified by evolution theory. Human universals, if they exist, will be discovered by studying human beings. For example, it may or may not be true that the nuclear family is sufficiently common to be considered as a universal institution, but the question whether it is true is one for anthropologists to answer and not for biologists. The comparative data about family structure in animals do not provide any answer; there are monogamous primates (gibbons), promiscuous ones (chimpanzees), and polygynous ones (gorillas).

To make matters worse, even if a particular behavior has been shown to have existed in almost all human societies in the past, this tells us nothing certain about the future. For example, very few societies in the past have had easy access to a safe and effective contraceptive under female control. Generalizations about human sexual behavior based on societies of the past may not hold in the future.

It does not follow from these criticisms that biologists have nothing to say about human behavior, but I think we must be modest. The main generalization to have emerged from ethology is that animals, including higher animals, cannot be understood as blank sheets on which the environment writes what it will. Instead, animals must be seen as having a complex internal structure which ensures that they will learn to do some things very readily and others hardly at all. The same is likely to be true in man—as is becoming increasingly obvious from work in linguistics and psychology. What the evolutionary biologist can add is that if there is an internal structure of this kind, there must be a selective reason for its presence.

I conclude with one example where biology does seem to have something to contribute to the understanding of human behavior. Until recently, I held the view that incest taboos in man, however universal, are entirely cultural in origin. Three things have made me change my mind. The first was the realization that if the deleterious effects of inbreeding are sufficiently serious to have been responsible for the evolution of self-incompatibility in plants, they would also provide a strong selection pressure for reducing inbreeding in animals. The second was the discovery by a number of workers that, in the wild and the laboratory, many animals, including primates, have behavior patterns which reduce the frequency of incestuous matings. The third was the work of Shepher (7) on Israeli kibbutzim, suggesting very strongly that if given a choice human beings avoid incestuous matings. Of course, the details of the incest taboo in different societies may have a cultural basis. But it seems very likely that our ancestors avoided incest long before they could talk.

REFERENCES

(1) Dawkins, R. 1976. The Selfish Gene. Oxford: Oxford University Press.

(2) Hamilton, W. D. 1964. The genetical theory of social behaviour. J. Theor. Biol. 6: 1.

(3) Lorenz, K. Z. 1966. On Aggression. London: Methuen.

(4) Maynard Smith, J. 1976a. Group selection. Q. Rev. Biol. 51: 277.

(5) ———. 1976b. Evolution and the theory of games. American Scientist 64: 41.

(6) Maynard Smith, J., and Price, G. R. 1973. The logic of animal conflict. Nature 246: 15.

(7) Shepher, J. 1971. Mate selection among second generation kibbutz adolescents and adults. Archives of Sexual Behaviour 1: 293.

(8) Trivers, R. L. 1971. The evolution of reciprocal altruism. Q. Rev. Biol. 46: 35.

(9) Wilson, E. O. 1975. Sociobiology. Cambridge, Mass.: Harvard University Press.

(10) Wynne-Edwards, V. C. 1962. Animal Dispersion in Relation to Social Behaviour. Edinburgh: Oliver and Boyd.

ANALOGS OF MORALITY AMONG NONHUMAN PRIMATES

H. Kummer

INTRODUCTION

In biology, two characters are analogous if they serve the same kind of function although their specific construction and phylogenetic origin are different. A classical example is the wings of birds and insects. Function in the biological sense is ultimately seen as the contribution of a character to the fitness of its organism, that is, the organism's design for survival and reproduction (17).

The contribution to the individual's reproductive survival is clearly not a defining attribute of moral behavior (see Markl et al., this volume), that is, the goals of the moral person do not necessarily coincide with those of the biologically fit individual. Nevertheless, human moral norms cannot have been entirely at cross-purposes with biological fitness, since some populations of our species did survive. To a considerable degree, "culture is a reinterpretation of biological

Original work by the author and his collaborators was supported by the Swiss National Science Foundation, grant No. 5271.3. I thank Jane Goodall, Walter Bodmer, and Walter Goldschmidt for their ideas and criticism of the first draft of this paper.

imperatives" (Goldschmidt, personal communication). It is therefore legitimate for biology to search for aspects of moral behavior that enhance reproductive survival, in full acknowledgment of the fact that at least the conscious goals of moral norms can be independent of biological ends.

The title proposed to me for this paper by the Workshop organizing committee makes two implicit assumptions: (1) nonhuman primates have no morality, (2) instead they have some behavioral arrangements that functionally replace morality.

The first assumption is a tenet rather than a scientifically established fact, and it therefore should be questioned. I propose to do this by searching for evidence of two behavioral characteristics that we could expect if morality were present among nonhuman primates: the absence of selfish opportunism in certain actions even if the animals' mental and behavioral capacities would allow it, and the occurrence of sanction.

Selfish opportunism is understood here as the use of flexible strategies that maximize the replication of the subject's genes, his inclusive fitness. This includes "reciprocal altruism" (16) and the care for close relatives who share some of the subject's genes. Why should the absence of such selfish opportunism be an indicator of moral behavior? Obviously, a behavior can optimally serve reproductive survival and still be moral, such as denying oneself a momentary gratification in the service of one's long-term health or of one's children. But since we have as yet no access to the moral reasoning of a nonhuman primate, we cannot discriminate between moral and biologically selfish behavior if their effects coincide. Only if the effects of an ape's behavior consistently deviated from the fitness goal could we conclude that another factor besides selection were at work. If, in addition, biological analysis could not explain the deviation by the animal's mental or behavioral inability to do what is best for its genes, the additional factor might (but not must) be some kind of a moral norm. Obviously, deviation from selfish opportunism is neither a strictly necessary nor a sufficient criterion of morality. Nevertheless, it seems to apply to a wide range of potentially moral behavior in humans (such as celibacy or aid given to a stranger one is certain not to meet again). To summarize, my first criterion must, for rea-

sons of methodological constraints, exclude from consideration those moral behaviors that functionally coincide with
biologically fit behavior.

The second implication of the title is that nonhuman primates, while lacking morality, have behavioral arrangements that functionally replace it. Investigating this assumption requires that we know what the functions of morality
are in a human society. Since these functions are not immediately evident to me, I must try to formulate a respective
hypothesis. We then can examine whether nonhuman primates have indeed any functional analogs of morality or
whether, perhaps, the problems that morality solves are not
posed to them.

Before setting out on this search we should be aware of
our limitations. Morality and sanction have not been the declared topics of any primatological studies, and to use data
for purposes other than those for which they were collected
is always hazardous. We are somewhat better off with regard to the question of selfish opportunism. This is essentially the concern of sociobiology and has been the declared
topic of several recent studies on primates (e.g., Kurland (8)).

It is obvious from this introduction that the functional approach, while biologically interesting, nevertheless misses
the principal attributes of morality for which a phylogenetic
study of *component capacities* for morality is the most relevant. (This approach is included in Bischof's paper, this
volume).

SELFISH OPPORTUNISM VERSUS RULE-
CONFORMITY

In the first sections, we shall search for deviations from
selfish opportunism that might be clues for the presence of
moral rules.

An organism's physical equipment and its behavioral versatility determine what damage it can inflict on and what
help it can extend to other organisms. One common function both of moral and moral-analog behavior seems to consist in favoring certain other organisms, either by harming
them less or by helping them more than others. The question is: which are the ones to be favored?

In 1954, Konrad Lorenz (10) described examples of social
behavior which he interpreted as analogs to moral behav-

ior: for example, a dominant jackdaw interfering with a quarrel among two subordinates regularly takes the side of the lower-ranking contestant. A jackdaw that intrudes in a nest is, upon a call from the resident, immediately attacked by the other members of the colony. A stag does not attack his rival unless the latter is ready for it. In social species with dangerous beaks or teeth, a reliable inhibition prevents full-scale attacks against females or young, or against a rival that displays a particular submissive gesture. Lorenz seemed impressed by his observation that in several of his examples, a subject favored all members of its species, or at least all its weaker members indiscriminately, regardless of their individuality or of the subject's relationship with them. Lorenz therefore concluded that such behavior had evolved for the benefit of the species. Although the behavior seemed neither reflected nor moral, the fact that it appeared with such regularity and without reference to the subject's individual benefit made it comparable to equally absolute and unconditional rules of moral conduct.

The difficulty with this view is the assumption that natural selection can produce behavioral characters that benefit the species as a whole. As evolutionary biologists point out, the species "is not an adapted unit and there are no mechanisms that function for the survival of the species. The only adaptations that clearly exist express themselves in genetically defined individuals . . ." (17). The least onerous explanation of any evolved behavior and therefore the first hypothesis to be tested is that, on the average, it benefits the subject itself. If the hypothesis were correct, social behavior should be more selfishly opportunistic than in Lorenz's examples. Moral-analog behavior should not favor all members of the species indiscriminately; rather, it should give preferential treatment to the subject's relatives, who carry some of its own genes. It should also favor particularly useful cooperators and it should treat high-ranking group members with caution and preferences because they are more dangerous opponents as well as more effective protectors than low-rankers.

The stags and jackdaws in Lorenz's examples do not behave in this manner, and their behavior seems to contradict the opportunism hypothesis. We can, however, argue that these species simply lack the differentiated behavioral programming, the cognitive ties, or the capacity for discriminant learning required for such subtly conditional behavior. Lorenz makes it clear that the defense response of a jackdaw is released by a general key stimulus, not by the recognized individuality of the threatened companion. Even a black rag held by a human triggers the defense, and it will do so even if the "predator" is the otherwise preferred caretaker of the animals. These species might favor all members of their species or of their group equally because they are incapable of doing anything more selfishly opportunistic. This explanation might save the theory of individual selection, but only if we can show that species with clearly greater abilities (such as monkeys and apes) are more opportunistic in their moral-analog behavior. We shall now examine relevant examples from primates as to whether they indeed reveal more opportunism, that is, more precise scaling of moral-analog behavior to the benefit of the subject's genes.

KILLING OF CONSPECIFICS

In recent years, the Lorenzian picture that dangerous social species are reliably inhibited to kill members of their own species has been corrected. Lions kill other lions over prey, and several nonhuman primates have been reported to occasionally kill conspecifics in natural populations. More often than not, the victims are infants. The best documented case is that of the Indian langur (4). Infanticide was observed in seven troops. In each case, the single adult male of a troop was attacked, chased off and replaced by an adult male from outside the troop. Immediately after the takeover, the new male in each case killed the infants that were still nursing, the total toll in the seven groups being thirty. A few days after losing their infants, the mothers came into estrus; they were now ready to bear the new male's offspring rather than to continue nursing the children of the previous male. By immediately killing the offspring of his predecessor, a male extends his breeding period within the group. Since no male was seen to kill his own infants, and since some males even rescued their own infants at great risk, the behavior of male langurs toward their offspring is selfishly opportunistic. It benefits not the species, but the reproductive success of the subject at the expense of that of the former males, of the mothers, and of their killed infants. If key stimuli and inhibitions exist, they do not protect every infant langur against every male of his species. A primate baby may be very attractive to adults not only for cuddling and protecting, but also for maltreatment.

Jane Goodall (personal communication) recently observed warlike events among the two communities of chimpanzees at Gombe. Males of the northern community on ten occasions severely attacked female strangers, and in two cases killed and ate the females' infants. On three occasions, they attacked males of the southern community, which were familiar to them, when the victims were single or accompanied by a female. All three males were severely injured, were never sighted again, and presumably died. These events have not been explained to date.

PROTECTION AND ALLIANCE

Protection of one group member by another is frequent in primate groups. In cases for which detailed reports are available, such aid was mainly extended to members of the subject's own subgroup or kin. A study by Massey (12) demonstrates that the members of a pigtail macaque group not only helped a relative under attack more often than a nonrelative but even aided a close relative more often than a distant one. Attacks were directed at relatives and nonrelatives with equal probability. On the whole, the aid/attack ratio was in favor of a subject's relatives. These data do not force the conclusion that a monkey is aware of his pedigree, rather they indicate that the socialization process allows that close kin grow up together. The monkey therefore becomes more familiar and intimate with kin than with nonkin, providing for a degree of familiarity sufficient to permit preferential treatment.

Thus the data on killing and protection do not allow us to reject the selfish-opportunism hypothesis.

RESPECTING A POSSESSIVE RELATIONSHIP

Individuals of many species establish exclusive one-to-one relationships with a place, a nest, a mate, or, for a much shorter time span, with a piece of food. When such a relationship is "respected" by others, we are tempted to speak of "possession" and to suspect that the respecting individual behaves in analogy to a moral rule at the expense of his own interests.

Our experiments on hamadryas baboons demonstrated that a male does not take a female of another male by force once he has seen them interact as a pair (7). His inhibition to take the female holds also against males of an alien troop even if he is, within limits, dominant over that male. These results seemed to contradict the selfish-opportunism hypothesis; the inhibition apparently benefits the species by maintaining order and stability in the troops, at the expense of the inhibited rivals. More recent results, however, revealed some selfishness in the behavior of rivals. First, when hamadryas males see a male of their troop trapped, they immediately lose their inhibitions and appropriate his females. Second, a rival is more likely to overcome his inhibition if the possessor ranks low in the female's preference (Bachmann, in preparation). There is evidence that the inclinations of the female affect the outcome of a fight over her. Thus, rivals act as if they had considered the "vote" of the female before deciding whether a fight over her would be profitable. Third, possessors of harems in a wild troop were attacked and deprived of their females by those young males to whom the possessors were most familiar and probably most closely related (1). My interpretation of this behavior is that a hamadryas rival attacks the most familiar possessor because he knows the latter's fighting power and defense motivation and would therefore be able to predict his own chances more reliably than if he tackled a stranger. This advantage may outweigh the damage he does to the replicates of his own genes by attacking and depriving a relative.

Male chimpanzees at Gombe do not forcibly take prized food, especially meat, from the hands of even a subordinate male; rather, they use begging gestures to obtain a piece. Jane Goodall (9) was at first tempted to see "the crude beginnings of a sense of moral values" in this behavior, but eventually preferred the hypothesis that "a male in possession of such a prize may become more willing to fight for it." His more dominant rivals may feel hesitant in asserting their normal prerogatives when they fail to detect the normal apprehension in the subordinate possessor of the meat. This is a selfish-opportunism explanation that probably applies to most cases of respect for possession in animals. However, all that can be said for this explanation is that it cannot presently be rejected and that it seems more parsimonious than a hypothesis involving moral norms.

SEXUAL FIDELITY

Many nonhuman primates do not form permanent pair bonds. When a female chimpanzee is receptive, males may take turns in mating with her in full sight of each other and without signs of jealousy. Or, as is the case with anubis baboons, a male may appropriate a female for a few hours or days and then be harassed by his rivals. In this species, subordinate males may snatch a copulation while the momentary consort of the female is engaged in warding off more serious rivals (3). In the polygynous society of hamadryas baboons, no adult male has been observed to mate with a female of a harem other than his own in more than one thousand observation hours. Explanations based on selfishness could be constructed, but evidence to support them would not be available. Hamadryas females, however, occasionally mate with juvenile males. In doing so, they carefully hide from their leader's sight, check on his whereabouts at intervals, and visit him with submissive gestures in between matings (5).

A captivity experiment on the equally polygynous gelada baboons established that an adult female, when left alone with a male other than her own, will avoid or accept him, depending on her own rank in her regular harem: the lower her rank, the less she resists the advances of the alien male (6). Other evidence of this study shows that low ranking females have reduced access to their own male.

On the whole, the data on sexual fidelity agree with the selfish-opportunism hypothesis.

FALSE INFORMATION

Giving false information to a conspecific has been too rarely studied and observed in nonhuman primates to judge whether it is given more often to nonrelatives or to members of other groups. In an experiment by Menzel (14) on a group of young chimpanzees, a group member was informed by the experimenter on the location of hidden food. Normally, this chimp led the group to the food which was then shared: but on occasions, a leader who often failed to obtain any food led the group in a wrong direction, then suddenly ran across to the food and thus managed to secure his share.

Familiar companions may be able to extract more complete information from each other's behavior than from strangers. Mason and Hollis (11) found that two monkeys previously acquainted with each other communicated more rapidly about which of four handles produced a food reward. Since relatives are in general also more familiar, such a difference should favor relatives.

The examples cited in the previous sections suggest that injuring and helping among nonhuman primates occurs variably, either in ways that are not understood, in ways that benefit the subject's relatives, or in ways that seem to weigh his individual gains against the risks. Even when we are aware that alternative hypotheses have not been formulated and therefore were not rejected, the data clearly do not reject the selfish-opportunism hypothesis. The present impression is:

1. Insofar as animals adhere to a strict rule of conduct, such as not to kill conspecifics, they do so under the effect of key stimuli and inflexible releasing mechanisms.

2. When a species has the necessary cognitive abilities for selfishly variable social behavior, its members make use of it. For example, if the members of a species favor all group members alike against all nongroup members, they may simply have no means to discriminate among close and distant relatives within the group. Since group members are on the average more closely related than members of different groups, this two-type classification is the best possible approximation to the biologically ideal pattern of favoring.

There is at present no evidence among nonhuman primates of conduct which is clearly below the degree of opportunism that their cognitive abilities permit.

SANCTION

The presence of sanction is a second criterion which we would expect to find among primates if they had moral rules. The simple and most obvious sanction is the expulsion of the wrongdoing member from the group, which can be lethal both in a tribal human and in a monkey society.

Monkeys and apes frequently leave their native group. The reasons are not very clear, but often seem to consist in the search for better reproductive chances in a neighboring group. I know of no case where an individual was expelled in a concerted group action after it had harmed group members. A spectacular failure to expel destructive members was recently observed by Jane Goodall (personal communication) and her coworkers in the Gombe chimpanzees. An adult female, named Passion, and her daughter Pom, were seen to steal, kill, and eat three infants of other females of their own community and were suspected of having killed at least six others. The mothers of the victims fought back, learned to avoid the two dangerous females, and were on occasion defended by adult males; but the killers simply tried again, and in the end they were usually successful. In consequence only two infants have survived in the last three years. Nevertheless, the community has taken no decisive action against its destructive members.

A monkey or ape defends himself, allies with a familiar companion against a less familiar one within the group, and joins his group in threatening or fighting another group. But these are actions taken on the spur of the moment. He seems unable to identify a group member as *generally* destructive and to take sides with one of two quarreling parties if he is on equally friendly terms with both. It seems as though he lacks the following cognitive prerequisites of sanction:

1. He is unable to separate the affective value of an intimate versus a less intimate companion from an objective assessment of the companion's usefulness as an ally or enemy. A primate can harbor a grudge against another for a short time, but if the latter is an accepted close companion, the relationship will not be severed. The generalization "He did it to me several times and will probably do it again" seems obscured by the emotional tie; the companion's true value of the subject cannot be properly integrated across time.

2. The motivation for sanction may also rest on the inference: "He did this to her; one day he will do it to me." Such inference not only requires self-consciousness, for which we have some evidence in chimpanzees (2), but the

insight that "I am one like she (or he). What now happens to her can happen to me."

I know of no evidence of such consciousness of equality. A baboon often enters a trap even after having just seen another one being caught in it.

My preliminary assumption, admittedly without solid evidence, is that sanction does not occur among nonhuman primates because their time- and self-consciousness is not sufficiently developed to integrate the objective value of a companion (let alone of themselves) across time and context to a degree such that the evaluation can outweigh the emotional ties.

REWARDS

If nonhuman primates do not use sanction, do they perhaps use rewards? The cultural anthropologist, Walter Goldschmidt (personal communication), holds that moral behavior in humans is positively reinforced by what he calls the subject's "acceptance" by his society. Such approval is inexpensive, and its effectiveness is not limited by physiological satisfaction as would be the case with a food reward. Looking for a similar reward of social life among nonhuman primates, one readily thinks of social grooming. Primatologists agree that its function is not the removal of ectoparasites alone. It is an interaction typical of an intimate relationship; grooming and especially being groomed are desirable activities on which much time is spent. But if grooming is a reward or an incentive, what does it reinforce? Seyfarth (15) presents evidence for the hypothesis that a subject prefers to groom with partners who rank above him in dominance, and he assumes that grooming increases the protective tendency of these most powerful and therefore valuable allies toward the groomer. This opportunistic view of grooming is partly confirmed by Stammbach (in preparation). Grooming among his female hamadryas baboons was positively correlated with two independent factors; one of them again was the partner's dominance rank; the other equally powerful correlate was a personal preference (established by choice experiments) unrelated to rank. On what this preference is based is unknown; we cannot presently exclude the possibility that it is a quality such as nonaggressiveness or predictability. So far, nothing suggests that grooming or any other social behavior among primates is specifically timed as a post hoc reward for a specific action that was useful to the groomer.

SELF-ESTEEM

In a moral society, the individual respects the norms not only in order to avoid sanction and to seek the reward of acceptance but also to weigh his value of himself by the degree to which his conduct throughout life matches the ideal which his culture has set up for an individual of his class. Approaching the ideal is at the same time a third kind of incentive for moral behavior and a new, nonbiological "function" of morality: the meaning of the subject's life to himself. No method of animal psychology or ethology has yet been designed to demonstrate a symbolic representation of personal values. Therefore, even speculations about its existence in nonhuman primates are futile.

AMORAL PRIMATES: A REDUCTIONISTIC FALLACY?

Neither of our two criteria has given us any indication of morality among nonhuman primates. This may have at least three reasons: (1) The methods used so far were basically inadequate or at least too crude; (2) The biological tradition of seeking the least onerous of several explanations caused us to overlook available evidence because moral behavior may always be explained more simply than by morality—unless the subject protests. A keen observer among my friends recalls a mother dog that consistently prevented her pups from entering a flower bed that she was not allowed to touch herself (Bodmer, personal communication). The dog may well have internalized the commands of her master, but the least onerous explanation will simply have her remove the pups from a place she has experienced as causing trouble. The possibility that primatologists explain away whatever they see in the line of moral behavior is a question mark for the above conclusions that should not be taken lightly. Nor is it certain that social carnivores might not be more suitable subjects than primates for the study of protomoral behavior. (3) Even so, primatologists would probably have acknowledged *striking* evidence for morality in their animals. Since they have not, the possibility remains that monkeys and apes are indeed amoral. One of the greatest hopes of learning otherwise is the well-known work on communication with chimpanzees by Premack, Gardner, Rumbaugh, Fouts, and others.

PREDICTABILITY AS A POSSIBLE FUNCTION OF MORALITY

If monkeys and apes have no morality, they might nevertheless have evolved analogs. The question presupposes that we know the specific functions of moral norms in human societies. This section attempts to sketch such a possible function.

Many moral rules appear as a cultural attempt to revert to nonopportunism. As regards killing, respect of possession, or false information, they tend to prescribe the same course of conduct in (nearly) all situations and toward (almost) all conspecifics. Advanced codes include nongroup members, alien races, and even all animate beings among the class of the favored. To a biologist, this seems at first rather striking. Why should biological evolution produce a species endowed with superb behavioral flexibility and then "allow" a superimposed cultural development to undo just that achievement and, as it were, regress to rigid behavioral rules?

Behavioral versatility, one may argue, is an advantage, but only in certain contexts. Man as a hunter, forager, or toolmaker can hardly be too clever and versatile; he will always benefit from more foresight and a greater arsenal of selfish schemes. But man as a social companion can be too astute even in his own interest. Every being can become more dangerous simply by becoming less predictable, regardless of whether it appears in the role of an enemy, a competitor, or a cooperator. The essential benefit of social life is cooperation; its essential disadvantage competition. Cooperation requires that each participant be able to predict the other's actions. Effective defense against competition and attack also rests on the ability to foresee what the opponent will do. Thus, behaving in a predictable way increases the benefits and alleviates the risks of social life. A protohominid benefited from being as unpredictable as possible to his prey, but he had to remain predictable within narrow limits to his companion on the hunt and to his group at the home site. If we assume that man's preadaptations offered no way to evolve a brain that was shrewd with tools, predators, and prey, but simple and predictable in dealing with his companions, the evolution of moral capacities might have been the adaptive answer: a selective suppression of shrewd flexibility in the social context. The biological function of morality would be twofold: first, to increase the help and to reduce the damage done to the social companions; and second, to increase predictability both in the helper and in the competitor. The two functions are independent of each other: members of one group might never help and also frequently do damage to another group. But whether or not they fight according to a predictable code still makes a great difference to the enemy. In the first case, the enemy is favored (e.g., as a conspecific) even though he is harmed.

In narrowing the versatility of the primate brain in the social context, humans may seem to revert to almost preprimate levels of rigidity. But this is not so. Even if moral norms were entirely successful in enforcing "good" behavior, the advantage of the versatile brain would not be lost. Moral norms are passed on by tradition, and a tradition can be changed in adaptation to new ecological and social conditions far more rapidly than a genetically evolved character. The narrow range of a particular set of moral norms can shift within the larger band width of evolved flexibility.

HOW COULD MORALITY EVOLVE?

Even if the foregoing speculation that morality is on the whole biologically useful could be verified, it would not explain how it could evolve by individual selection. It is conceivable that mutually preferential treatment even of two group members would, on the average and in the long run, benefit both. On rational grounds, the other group members should then seek admission to this bond or contract. However, the temptation to break its rules for short-term benefits would be constantly present, and since an average benefit does not guarantee a gain in every single situation, the shrewd member will find occasions to break out that are even to his long-term advantage. The Dove-and-Hawk paradigm analyzed by Maynard Smith (13) suggests that the Evolutionarily Stable Strategy (ESS) could be improved by a contract which insured that every member of the social unit behaved as a Dove. However, the immediate benefit for any one member who singly reverts to the Hawk strategy is so great that the contract cannot exist without reinforcements, particularly cooperative sanction. This process and the ensuing possibility of group selection is developed further in the Markl et al. report in this volume (see also Campbell, this volume).

WHAT ARE THE ANALOGS OF HUMAN MORALITY?

If morality evolved as a protection against a degree of shrewd versatility that threatened the benefits of social life, then I cannot see that monkeys and apes have any analogous arrangements. Their social behavior, with all its versatility, seems sufficiently predictable at least among familiar companions; the problem may simply not arise.

Human morality can increase the benefits of social life beyond the level which noncultural mechanisms of behavior can produce. One example is cooperative sanction. The case of the infant-killing females at Gombe reveals no analogous control mechanism, even though the problem is very real in this example. Another example is seen where moral norms further loyalty among relatives (especially if this is done in more precise agreement with genetic relatedness than nonhuman cognitive abilities would permit), or among mates, or members of small groups. If morality thus *adds* to human fitness a portion which nonhumans cannot in any way realize, there are, again, no analogs. Only if it *substitutes* some fitness-increasing aspects of nonhuman primate behavior can we seek for analogs. In this sense, and forcing the issue, the analog of predictability induced by moral norms among humans would be the predictability induced by cognitive, that is, ultimately genetic, constraints among nonhumans.

With this possible exception, it seems at present that morality has no specific functional equivalents among our animal relatives. Their societies benefit their members even though their individuals are essentially guided by selfish opportunism. Human morality is intimately related to the evolution of cognitive abilities, which made it both necessary and possible.

REFERENCES

(1) Abegglen, J. J. 1976. On Socialization in Hamadryas Baboons. Doctoral dissertation, University of Zurich.

(2) Gallup, G. G. 1970. Chimpanzees: Self-recognition. Science 167: 86–87.

(3) Hausfater, G. 1975. Dominance and reproduction in baboons (Papio cynocephalus). Contributions to Primatology 7. Basel: Karger Basel.

(4) Hrdy, B. S. 1974. Male-male competition and infanticide among the langurs (Presbytis entellus) of Abu, Rajasthan. Folia primatol. 22: 19–58.

(5) Kummer, H. 1968. Social Organization of Hamadryas Baboons, A field study. Biblio. primatol. 6. Basel: Karger and Chicago: University of Chicago Press.

(6) ———. 1975. Rules of dyad and group formation among captive gelada baboons (Theropithecus gelada). Proc. Symp. 5th Int. Congr. Primatol. Soc., Nagoya, 1974, pp. 129–159. Tokyo: Japan Science Press.

(7) Kummer, H.; Götz, W.; and Angst, W. 1974. Triadic differentiations: An inhibitory process protecting pair bonds in baboons. Behav. 49: 62–87.

(8) Kurland, J. A. 1977. Kin Selection in the Japanese Monkey. Contributions to Primatology 12. Basel: Karger Basel.

(9) Lawick-Goodall, J. van. 1974. In The Shadow of Man. Glasgow: Fontana Books, Collins & Co.

(10) Lorenz, K. 1954. Moral-analoges Verhalten geselliger Tiere. Forschung und Wirtschaft 4: 1–23.

(11) Mason, W. A., and Hollis, J. H. 1962. Communication between young rhesus monkeys. Anim. Behav. 10: 211–221.

(12) Massey, A. 1977. Agonistic aids and kinship in a group of pigtail macaques. Behav. Ecol. Sociobiol. 2: 31–40.

(13) Maynard Smith, J., and Parker, G. A. 1976. The logic of asymmetric contests. Anim. Behav. *24*: 159–175.

(14) Menzel, E. W. 1974. A group of young chimpanzees in a one-acre field. *In* Behavior of Nonhuman Primates. Eds. A. M. Schrier and F. Stollnitz, 5: 83–153. New York, London: Academic Press.

(15) Seyfarth, R. 1976. Social relationships among adult female baboons. Anim. Behav. *24*: 917–938.

(16) Trivers, R. L. 1971. The evolution of reciprocal altruism. Q. Rev. Biol. 46(4): 35–57.

(17) Williams, G. C. 1966. Adaptation and Natural Selection. A Critique of Some Current Evolutionary Thought. Princeton, N.J.: Princeton University Press (paperback 1974).

ON THE PHYLOGENY
OF HUMAN MORALITY

N. Bischof

INTRODUCTION

"Morality" is understood here as a human behavioral complex that is (a) essentially cross-cultural, or *universally* human, and (b) apparently absent in animals, or *specifically* human.

The first point suggests that morality is at least partly based on genetic adaptation, the second that this adaptation is a recent occurrence in phylogeny.

In the following paragraphs I shall examine:

1. What phenomena are meant when we speak of "human morality";

2. what kind of analogs to human morality can be found on the animal level;

3. how the emergence of these analogs can be explained phylogenetically; and

4. how human morality may have developed in the framework of these analogs.

At present, theories in this area cannot meet the usual standards of scientific verifiability. The following statements are presented as heuristic hypotheses and intended to stimulate discussion.

CHARACTERISTICS OF HUMAN MORALITY
Form Characteristics

Norms: In every human society we find certain generally accepted value judgments, or norms, that define a profile of differential approval for the total range of possible human behaviors. In the simplest case, these norms are reflected in the predominant behavioral patterns of the society: some behaviors meriting disapproval simply never, or hardly ever, appear. Moreover, these norms may be expressed in gossip or rumor (e.g., about neighboring enemy groups), or in the form of legends or myths. Only in high cultures are norms expressed explicitly as an oral or written code of law.

Sanctions: If an individual's behavior deviates from the norms, he must expect a hostile reaction, either from the injured person or his representative, or from the entire group or its delegated representatives. Such a reaction might consist in: (a) mild or severe *excommunication* (ranging from derision to casting out), (b) special *punishment*. Punishment is based on the idea that one action can counterbalance another: breaking norms disturbs an equilibrium which must be restored through expiation. In expiation the emphasis is not on the guilty person but on the offense, which explains phenomena like vicarious atonement.

Internalization: Norm-conforming behavior also occurs under conditions which preclude sanctions, for example, in the temporary absence of a punishing authority. The inhibition felt under such conditions is called "conscience," and acting against this inhibition results in negative affects (feelings of *guilt* or *shame*). Feelings of guilt seem to be related to disobedience to authorities. Feelings of shame connote the loss of social esteem. They reflect a regression to the stage of an irresponsible infant who is not yet to be taken seriously. Feelings of guilt and shame appear not only after norm-violating action but can also accompany the intention, and thus can prevent or foil the action. These feelings can also follow unintended norm violations. There is a certain tendency to develop milder social sanctions in this latter case except when an offense occurs unintentionally while *another* norm-offending intention is being carried out.

Content Characteristics

One set of moral norms can be understood as attempts to protect group members from the unbounded *self-interest* of others (the banning of murder, theft, witchcraft, slander, adultery).

A second set of norms, which some anthropologists see as the prototype of morality, is composed of *marriage rules* proscribing a too "near" and too "far" choice of partner (the incest and racial taboos, respectively).

A third set of norms regulate the relations with the *spiritual* world: prescriptions dealing with honoring gods, ancestors, or totems. The first three Mosaic commandments belong to this set. In pictorial allegories, they appear together on a special tablet.

A fourth set of norms apparently serves to establish and corroborate the individual's *personal maturity* (rules of moderation, asceticism, abstinence, rules against excessive or infantile drive gratification).

Finally, without claiming completeness for this list, we may mention a fifth set of norms that serves to spare the society of having to take notice of certain forms of behavior (norms of discretion in sexual intercourse, defecation, menstruation, birth, and death).

There appears to be no "general moral principle" from which all the concrete norms may be deduced, just as there exists no "general drive" or "general animal." Phenomena of life cannot be systematized as being special applications of a general formula. They are special branches of a common tree, a substantially different proposition.

MORAL-ANALOGOUS BEHAVIOR IN ANIMALS
Content Analogies

The specifically human character of morality might imply that intentions suppressed by morality are "bestial." This idea is illustrated in the figure of St. George as the dragon-slayer. However, "amoral" behavior does not appear in the animal world as frequently as such a suggestion would lead one to expect.

Lorenz (8) has introduced the notion of "moral-analogous" animal behavior. It denotes a group of instinctive inhibitions that constrains selfishness and guarantees a relatively uniform distribution of advantages and disadvantages in the group. According to Lorenz, rank orders in the animal world serve to help the weaker members, since the alpha-animal usually attacks the beta, as if in support of the gamma. Furthermore, animals possessing dangerous weapons do not frequently use them in intraspecies conflicts, but rather perform ritualized combat. The superior in such a contest contents himself, even though he could kill his opponent, with inflicting a comparatively minor "disadvantage." Lorenz also mentions the warning against, or even the attacking of, predators threatening a group member, even though this involves a risk for the warner himself.

Inbreeding, hybridization, and homosexuality are efficiently avoided in most animal species through behavior patterns based on a complicated interplay of instinctual forces. (For instinctive inbreeding barriers, see refs. (1), (2), and following section on Possible Explanations of Moral-Analogous Behavior.)

Animal behavior exhibits many analogs of lying and cheating, even toward members of the same group. Nevertheless these practices are kept within limits. Counteractive mechanisms are therefore postulated to exist (14), but have not yet been analyzed. In some species, if an individual has found access to certain resources, even higher-ranking group members do not compete for them. This has been established for food-resources in chimpanzees (5) and for claims to females in Hamadryas baboons (7). Frequently, the respecting of alien territory is also assigned to this group of behaviors.

Formal Analogies

Habit formation and "superstition": Animal behavior is never entirely predictable. Particularly animals that are able to learn from experience must be capable of making alternative choices when confronted with new situations. After the learning phase, behavioral variability is reduced by way of habit formation; the experienced animal behaves more predictably.

The pattern of habit formation seems to have the following motivational background. Unfamiliarity is dangerous and leads to emotional "arousal." This may be a fascinating experience if arousal tolerance is sufficiently high, as is typical in the juvenile stage. Otherwise, arousal produces anxiety. A situation is unfamiliar as long as no appropriate response to it is known. The appropriate response is learned either (a) from other group members, without substantial increase in arousal, or (b) through unaided exploration. The latter method presupposes a high arousal tolerance.

Signs of arousal reappear when an animal happens to deviate from a learned response. This may be expected since, in a way, the breaking of a habit renders the situation unfamiliar again (9). The animal may be prepared to cope with this increased arousal. Otherwise, considerable anxiety may result from the deviation. In this way, habits often appear to have a "superstitious" or "compulsive" flavor.

Mobbing and "shame": The rule that anything unfamiliar produces fear and anything familiar lends security applies also to encounters with conspecifics and leads to socioethologically fundamental distinction between group members and strangers. Conspecifics become familiar (a) through imprinting, (b) through certain forms of intimate social contact (feeding, copulation, grooming, duetting, also, notably, aggressive conflicts), or (c) through long association.

Generally, familiar conspecifics release attachment behavior, while strangers are apprehensively avoided or attacked. High degrees of familiarity are normally limited to members of the core family. If animals live in larger groups, they are forced to stay in close contact with conspecifics that are only slightly familiar and, therefore, represent a potential source of arousal. In such cases low familiarity has to be compensated by high uniformity of behavior.

If group members become conspicuous, whether through a physical deformity (5), or through unusual behavior (in wild geese: first copulation of a pair in spring), arousal is activated and the group will react, mildly or violently, by "mobbing" them.

Is there any indication that animals "mobbed" by their own group do experience something like "shame"? Unfortunately, the response to "mobbing" has not yet been studied explicitly. In wild geese a "cringing posture" appears in this situation, a posture also displayed by low ranking animals. Interestingly, the signal through which young males indicate courtship motivation is formally related to this posture.

Rank order and "conscience"

In hierarchically organized groups it may be observed that a behavior which could lead to intervention by high ranking animals is shunned even in the absence of such animals.

Frequently, alpha-animals will not tolerate sexual activities on the part of low ranking group members. In this situation, the affected group members may even undergo physical atrophy of their sexual organs (1). Chimpanzees (6) and dogs (16), when kept under human control, may permanently "internalize" prohibitions. They show signs of fear when tempted—even if encouraged by their master—to deviate from the "good" behavior pattern and they display a "bad conscience" if caught in or briefly after a transgression.

POSSIBLE EXPLANATIONS OF MORAL-ANALOGOUS BEHAVIOR

Biological systems establish a particular interplay of situations and behaviors. A scientific "explanation" of this interplay may attempt either (a) an analysis of the internal (physiological, psychological) causality that determines the course of this interplay, or (b) an analysis of the external (phylogenetic, selective) causality that explains why the system can survive only with exactly this form of interplay. In keeping with common scientific usage, I refer to the first kind of analysis as "causal" (in a narrower sense), and to the second as "functional."

The earlier assertion, favored by anti-Darwinian diehards, that moral-analogous behavior contradicts the principle of natural selection because selection can produce only unconstrained selfishness has been refuted by the recent work of sociobiology.

Ritualized Fights and ESS

Functional explanation: J. Maynard Smith has clarified the selective advantage of ritualized combat by applying his concept of "Evolutionarily Stable Strategy" ((10, 11, 12), see also his paper, this volume). An ESS is a strategy of behavior that, if used by all members of the group, could not be bettered by any individual group member adopting an alternative strategy.

Maynard Smith has shown that reckless, uninhibited aggressivity ("hawk"-strategy) is not necessarily more advantageous than ritualized combat ("dove"-strategy). Admittedly, a "dove" fighting a "hawk" might not be able to retreat uninjured, as the model supposes. A rattlesnake only willing to box and wrestle with his rival could not retreat quickly enough if the latter suddenly began to use his venomous teeth. But he would still have time, in a quick reflex movement, to bite back! This is not "dove"-behavior, though; it is what Price has called "retaliator" strategy. It turns out that retaliation is the ESS in the given case, with a sizeable minority of true "doves" tolerated. Generally, in animals with dangerous weapons a preference for ritual combat can be expected to evolve, but this should not go so far as to render a majority of individuals unable or unmotivated to retaliate if the partner violates the ritual.

Causal explanation

The causal analysis of these behavioral strategies is still in its infancy. Lorenz (9) reasonably argues that refraining from injurious fighting is not due to an overall reduction of aggressivity, but rather to the development of additional inhibiting factors.

Kinship and Altruism

Functional explanation: Altruistic behaviors (care of the young, social grooming, group defense, etc.) which are to the advantage of the recipient at a cost to the donor can be evolutionarily stable, as long as these behaviors are directed at relatives or the marriage partner, that is, at individuals whose descendants share part of the donor's genotype (15).

Causal explanation: To ensure that preferential treatment can be correlated positively with degree of kinship, it must be the case that the probability of meeting a relative is greater than that of meeting a nonrelative, or that the individual is able to process cues that are correlated with the degree of kinship.

The most important cue for kinship is *familiarity*, especially when established in early childhood, for example through imprinting. Familiarity established through sexual partnership is another example, since mates, albeit nonrelative, have common progeny.

The necessity of cues for kinship has been stressed by Dawkins ((3), p. 110). He mentions as an example the ability of some birds to distinguish their "own eggs" from those of strangers. But it must be noted that the category "strange" has two possible opposites—namely, what is my own and what is familiar to me. "Ownness" is cognitively far more complex than mere familiarity (= low level of stimulus novelty) is a sufficient signal for kinship.

The following mechanisms are important in this regard:

1. Mothers or parents quickly become familiar to their newborn or hatched offspring, perhaps even become imprinted on them.

2. Parents generally limit caretaking behavior to familiar children; unfamiliar ones are rejected, attacked, or even eaten.

3. Offspring accordingly seek out familiar conspecifics ("attachment motivation") and avoid unfamiliar conspecifics ("fear of the stranger").

4. As long as the attachment motivation persists in the life of an individual, it is more probable that an encountered conspecific is a relative.

5. The coupling of altruistic behavior with the familiarity requirement exerts the intragroup conformity pressure mentioned in the discussion of "mobbing."

Genetic Variability and Incest Barriers

Functional explanation: Homogeneity of the group is counteracted by outbreeding. If the infantile attachment motivation persisted until and throughout sexual maturity, inbreeding would be the obligatory result. Homozygosis, thus affected, would limit genetic variability, and hence evolutionary adaptability, to such an extent that the line could no longer compete with an outbreeding variant (1).

Causal explanation: The mechanism effective in inbreeding-avoidance is basically the following (2): in early childhood familiar conspecifics are markedly responded to with attachment, unfamiliar ones with fear. In adolescence, this pattern diminishes or even reverses: the family is avoided ("surfeit reaction"), unfamiliar conspecifics become objects of fascinated approach. This reversal is owing to an increased appetence for arousal and a reduced dependency in this phase. The same factors lead to dissatisfaction with a possibly low position in the intra-family rank order. All these changes entail the departure from the family and the formation of new relationships. In the adult stage some need for security reappears, but the new partner has meanwhile become sufficiently familiar through exploration and sexual interaction to be an appropriate attachment object.

POSSIBLE PHYLOGENETIC ROOTS OF HUMAN MORAL CATEGORIES

Are the moral-analogous motives that keep animal behavior balanced still present in man? Anthropologists often point to Frazer's argument (4), according to which culture would not need to proscribe what nature already prevents. If this were correct, only the excitatory forces in animal motivation would be preserved in man, whereas the inhibitory ones would have atrophied. But there is evidence in favor of moral-analogous inhibitions having survived anthropogenesis. Persons familiar since early childhood are conspicuously avoided as sex partners (1). An inhibition against infanticide, postulated by ethologists (9), has been reasonably substantiated in the case of infants who have been nursed at least once (13).

In the following, the thesis will be presented that the phylogenetic transition from moral-analogous behavior to human morality is characterized by three processes:

1. The instincts regulating animal behavior, both excitatory and inhibitory, are damped in man. They do not disappear, but they do lose their compelling character and turn into emotional appeals.

2. Their spectrum is broadened through additional differentiation.

3. Cultural superstructures shape this basic material into new and specifically human forms.

These changes are seen as corollaries of a development that took place not primarily in the realm of motivation but rather in the realm of *cognition*.

Time-Representation

The basic hypothesis is this: the evolutionary step decisive for man, achieved halfway only by chimpanzees, consists in "time-representation."

Every organism normally responds with *behaviors* to *situations* in such a way that the probability of survival of his genome is kept near a local maximum. A "situation" is defined through momentary features of the *environment* and through the current *needs* of the organism. The maximum achievable reproductive benefit of a behavior depends on the current environment-need constellation. If the situation is such that the two do not match (e.g., rich supply of solid food in the state of thirst), then even an optimal behavioral strategy can achieve only insufficient benefit.

Animal intelligence partly overcomes this limitation. When solving problems, higher primates appear to shift things around in their "imagination." In other words, they are able to *represent* not only the perceived environment but also other environments which are possible, but at the moment not yet extant. These environments are tested for their potential benefits, as compared with the current state of need. The best of these alternatives is then realized.

This basic strategy is limited to anticipating potential environments while the momentary state of need remains unchanged. Man has adopted a higher strategy. Here future states of need also play a role in the decision process. Such a strategy involves two features: (1) possible environments are tested relative to present *and* future needs for maximal benefit; and (2) the environment belonging to the maximally beneficial outcome is realized whenever this can be done, independently of, or even in contradiction to, the current need.

Emotional Consequences of Time-Representation

This behavior strategy goes far beyond the reaches of animal intelligence. Anticipatory imaging based on the current state of need remains fixed in the present. With the representation of future needs, the temporal fixation becomes movable. The set of situations with which the organism can cope, and now also *must* cope, is thus extended by one dimension—from the present space to the represented space-time continuum. This leads to an increase in strategic efficiency, but it also has drastic emotional consequences that basically affect and shape human morality.

Existential anxiety

The newly represented time-space is mostly filled with *uncertainty*. Its intellectually manageable parts remain tiny compared to the rest. Uncertainty is related to *unfamiliarity* and, like the latter, evokes *anxious*, rather than merely neutral, feelings. These feelings combine with whatever general threat is characteristic of the time (atomic bomb, war, pollution, plague, cancer) and culminate in the foreboding of our own inevitable death. This "existential anxiety" is specifically human; it is the first price we pay for time-representation.

Motivational instability

Even at the animal level there are always several needs competing in the determination of current behavior. As a rule, only one need can be met at a time; the others must be suppressed, at least temporarily. This feature alone gives rise to conflicts, which increase manifold when time-representation is introduced and future needs are also taken into account.

If future needs are to have a chance to compete with actual needs, it is necessary that the "energy" of the latter be somehow attenuated. The actual needs—excitatory and inhibitory—must be reduced from the status of massive determiners of behavior to that of motivating appeals.

Thus the individual force of conflicting motives is reduced, while at the same time their number is increased. The result is a poor stability of motivation. This is the second price to be paid for time-representation.

Simultaneous identification

Identity, or "sameness," is a phylogenetically old cognitive category. It achieves object constancy over time (the rabbit disappearing behind the bush and the one appearing on the other side are identical). Identity does not require equality—things can change, but remain themselves. In contrast, two *simultaneously* appearing objects may be equal, and they may be mistaken for each other, but on the infra-chimpanzee animal level, there is no behavior indicating that they are kept apart and nevertheless regarded to be the "same." The situation changes when future processes can be incorporated into the present. An object, or one's own body, must then be imaginable in a place different from the one actually occupied. Time-representation would not work without the identity relation being capable of simultaneously bridging spatial distance.

The most amazing of the now possible achievements is the awareness of the identity of oneself with one's own reflection in the mirror. This reflection shows a conspecific. Once the identity with *this* "conspecific" has been established, man cannot but see himself, to a degree, mirrored in *any* conspecific. The gap between "ego" and "others" is partly bridged by the new identity category.

As a consequence, man is capable of directing *social* motives (love, aggression, responsibility, etc.) toward *himself* (which has little to do with a neglected chick compulsively plucking its own feathers). Conversely, an individual's *self-ish* feelings may begin to protect *others*—since he cannot help identifying with them. (Greedy people cannot bear it when *others* waste their money; a young man emotionally exploited by his mother may participate in a demonstration against exploitation of the working class; we laugh when a clown stumbles.)

Again the space of motivational possibilities is substantially expanded, with numerous new sources of conflict opening up (an example is the conflict between expulsion and care of sick group members). This is the third problem incurred in time-representation.

Human Morality

An immense diversity of motives, ambiguous in directing action, but taking vengeance if neglected and overshadowed by omnipresent existential anxiety—this is the problem to be solved by human morality.

Mythological ideas

Human imagination, capable of dreaming up possible future environments and ego-states, is not bound to a strict down-to-earth level. It can produce mythological ideas that reduce the inherent emotional tensions. Here we find the consoling eschatologies of religions, and also the socialist utopia of a paradise of general solidarity, or the capitalist ideology of the unlimited possibilities of personal development.

Psychological realization

For such mythological motifs to become effective shields against anxiety and a solid foundation for emotional stability, their "psychological reality" must be raised to the highest possible level. The "psychological reality" of an idea depends on its being grounded in everyday experience. Unlike scientific or technical ideas, myths are not well confirmed by experience. Dogmatic repression of contradicting experience is of some help here. But by far the most effective procedure in translating myths into reality is to let them gain influence on *behavior*: to act them out, and to provide that others do the same. This is why myths breed morals.

Ritualization

An anxiety-reducing strategy practiced already on the animal level—the strategy of adhering rigidly to behavioral patterns that have once proved successful, or at least not harmful—is maintained by man. The previous success of such patterns may have been purely accidental, as in some magic superstitions, or it may have reflected causal connections actually encountered, albeit poorly understood. Such causal connections may involve *physical* factors, as in the experiences leading to dietary proscriptions, or *psychological* factors, as in experiences involving the emotional consequences of time-representation. Particularly the latter factors, being universally human, should lead to a certain uniformity and universality in basic moral norms.

Clan formation

A natural counterbalance to anxiety is attachment to familiar conspecifics. In man, the capability of imagination to move along the time axis allows genealogical conceptions to develop; the family can thus be extended to the clan. Because of its size, the clan provides more security than the relatively defenseless single family. But an individual cannot know each of his fellow clan members. *Familiarity* must therefore be supplemented by meticulously maintained *uniformity*, through common vernacular, common cultural knowledge, common totem, and especially through a common moral code. Since the readiness for altruistic behavior increases with familiarity, and since, therefore, the practice of such behavior is a means to raise the "psychological reality" of familiarity, there exists especially emphatic moral norms of altruism toward clan members. In fact, in primitive cultures altruistic norms apply only to clan members, and are often reversed for foreigners. This dichotomy is mitigated only slightly by the all-human identification process mentioned earlier.

Shame

Group members who violate norms are "mobbed." An animal that does not conform to the group usually behaves as if it does not understand why it is mobbed. It may react with conflict behavior, anxiety, or depression. The human, capable of self-reflection, can compare himself to the others and perceive himself to be deviant. Through identification with the group, he participates in their emotional reaction to his deviance. This intrinsic conflict may be the new element in human shame.

A person who is ashamed feels as if he has "lost face." Face, in this context, is something like a mask, concealing his identity from unauthorized eyes. So is the garment he wears. To recognize oneself in the mirror is to understand that one has two sides—an internal self and an external face. The internal self is centered on a core, but has no distinct *boundaries*. Only the mirror reveals that I am a Gestalt, with definite boundaries, constant over time.

These boundaries define how *others* perceive me. What I am to others may be different from what I am to myself. Tolerating such a discrepancy may be a comfortable way to conform to group expectations and at the same time gratify individual needs. *This* kind of insincerity has no counterpart in lower animals. Such a discrepancy, however, causes tensions in my feeling of identity: core and face do not match. Tensions of this kind seem to be typically involved in human shame.

Obedience and awe

Among the familiar conspecifics providing security, the parents are of paramount importance because they are most strongly motivated to offer protection and assistance. But to get the benefit of their protection one has to accept their superior rank position. Thus a connection between security and obedience is preestablished. Moreover, in a human group the parental figures are the ones who are in possession of the traditional knowledge accumulated by the culture; it is from them that one hopes to receive all the remedies for emotional disorder and anxiety. From this point of view we understand the particularly strong moral demand for awe of the parents, and also, the apotheosis of parental figures to deities acting as warrantors of the moral norms. Amorality can thus become a form of metaphysical disobedience.

Revenge and guilt

Retaliation can occur, even as an evolutionarily stable strategy, in animals. But in animals it remains bound to the current situation: reports of delayed revenge among animals are anthropomorphisms. With time-representation, revenge in the true sense is possible. Unlike animals, man must live with the expectation that anyone injured by him may *at some time* retaliate.

This retaliation expected at some uncertain time is an extremely grave cause of anxiety, particularly if it is believed to come from mythological powers retaliating for disobedience of moral norms. The expectation of inevitable but delayed punishment is manifested in the feeling of guilt. In order to reduce the tension of this expectation, actions are often performed that *anticipate* what is feared ("self-punishment"). Moreover, negative experiences (illness, loss, war, natural catastrophes) tend to be interpreted as retaliation for unnoticed personal offenses and hence arouse guilt feelings. Conversely, the interpretation of positive experiences as a reward for personal virtue, such as the (Calvinistic) view of prosperity as a visible sign of personal uprightness, originates in the same source.

Exogamy and original sin

In view of the special role of the theocratic kinship group as a factor compensating for existential anxiety, it is all the more difficult to act in conformance to the emotional aversion against incest. Therefore, particularly strict exogamy rules are necessary to prevent group members from trying to escape existential anxiety by allowing themselves to be devoured by the ogre-mother-goddess Kali. Emancipation from the familiar, however, must not result in the breaking up of cultural tradition. This is no simple task, as the corresponding mechanisms of family dissolution in the animal kingdom entail the serious challenge of parental authority and the discontinuance of all relations.

The tension created by this problem area is probably inescapable. In myth, the unavoidable step of gaining personal maturity is therefore frequently seen as original sin (Adam and Eve, Lucifer, Prometheus).

CONCLUSION: MORALITY AS A SELF-REPLICATING MEME COMPLEX

Dawkins (3) outlines the idea that cultural contents, such as moral norms and their mythological context, which he calls "memes," are propagated in a way that makes them comparable to genes.

Replication

Memes are structures that can, through imitation, spread from their material carrier (a human brain) to other carriers. Imitation can take place voluntarily, or by suggestion, or simply in response to threat: a meme can be successful just because it is appealing to particularly violent brains which then begin to spread it on crusades.

Similar to genes, which construct organisms to insure their own replication, some mythologies have created a kind of superorganism: the *institutions* of the churches, states, societies, and the like. And just as the archaeologist finds skeletons of organisms which no longer have any genes to pass on, we too may encounter cultural fossils—petrified institutions, or rigid dogmatic skeletons from which the myth has long escaped, but which may persist for hundreds of years until they crumble to dust under the powerful arrival of new, vital ideas.

Variation

Memes can emerge spontaneously, and they can undergo change at each replication. Variation is an important precondition to evolution: selection needs a rich supply of variants to be able to ensure adjustment and improvement.

To produce variation, memes take advantage of a genetically preformed feature: the autonomy claim of adolescence. Having actually come into being as an incest barrier, the youthful fever of independence, with its disgust at familiar surroundings and its setting out into the world of the unknown, is the appropriate nutrient soil for new ideas. It is therefore, in all cultures, the youth who ensure that old forms are reinfused with new vitality, or destroyed when their time has come.

Selection

The chance that a meme will be passed on or be forgotten depends upon, among other things, its content. It is aptly stressed by Dawkins that the selection of memes is independent of the selection of genes. There are interactions: memes can have a genetic effect; a society that hangs young thieves breeds honesty. However, it is not a necessary condition for the "success" of a moral norm that it somehow enhances the reproductive chances of the moral individual, let alone of his group. Faulty assumptions of this kind encumbered the older "biological" explanation of the incest taboo, according to which cultures allowing incest died out due to inbreeding depression.

But what is it that makes a moral idea successful? In genes success depends on "adaptation." What are memes adapted to? Each behavior is based on a complicated interplay of excitatory and inhibitory motives which are accompanied by corresponding affects and feelings. Such affects can be pleasant or unpleasant and the organism behaves in such a way as to seek and secure pleasant affects and avoid unpleasant ones. To this extent his behavior is purposive. The pleasantness of affects is in some way correlated with the reproductive payoff of the behaviors concerned. But the individual knows nothing of this connection, and even if he knew of it he would continue to do the things he likes because he likes them, and not because they perpetuate his genome.

The connection between affective reward and reproductive benefit is only a *statistical* one: behaviors carry the premium of being "pleasant" when the carrying of this premium has frequently enough paid its way in the past. And the premium is then rigidly adjoined to them even when, because of particular conditions, their biological purpose is missed.

Happiness, defined as the quintessence of all toward which we strive, is thus an archaic *signal* of reproductive success, but basically one that may be misleading, particularly in man. The acquisition of time-representation has led to dislocations in the realm of emotions: There are behaviors that appear as both duty and trespass, that harbor both happiness and horror; there are impulses with goals to be reached only if one acts against them, and so on. This does not impair the reproductive efficiency of man; but he is expelled from Paradise.

Mythological or moral ideas, then, do not evolve because they promote the physical survival of mankind. They are accepted or rejected according to the degree to which they assist in finding and holding on to points of equilibrium in the paradoxical field of human emotion. When they find their niche in *this* ecology, they then have the chance to endure, the chance that temples and palaces be built for them, virgins consecrated, and human hearts sacrificed in their honor, the chance that they be immortalized in hymns and carved into the face of rocks, the chance that martyrs bear witness to them, and that missionary conquistadores lay the world in ruin so as to make them triumph in millions of subjugated brains.

Acknowledgment

The author wishes to thank Helen Bommer for translating and Max Delbrück for revising the original manuscript.

REFERENCES

(1) Bischof, N. 1975. Comparative ethology of incest avoidance. *In* Biosocial Anthropology, ed. Robin Fox, pp. 37–67. London: Malaby Press.

(2) ———. 1975. A systems approach toward the functional connections of attachment and fear. Child Development *46*: 801–817.

(3) Dawkins, R. 1976. The Selfish Gene. Oxford: Oxford University Press.

(4) Frazer, J. J. 1910. Totemism and Exogamy. London: Macmillan.

(5) Goodall, J. 1974. In the Shadow of Man. Glasgow: Fontana Books.

(6) Köhler, W. 1921. Zur Psychologie der Schimpansen. Psychol. Forsch. *1*: 4.

(7) Kummer, H.; Götz, W.; and Angst, W. 1974. Triadic differentiation: An inhibitory process protecting pair bonds in baboons. Behav. *49*: 62–87.

(8) Lorenz, K. 1964. Moral-analoges Verhalten der Tiere-Erkenntnisse heutiger Verhaltensforschung. Universitas *19*: 43–54.

(9) ———. 1967. On Aggression. New York: Bantam Books.

(10) Maynard Smith, J. 1974. The theory of games and the evolution of animal conflicts. J. theor. Biol. *47*: 209–221.

(11) Maynard Smith, J., and Parker, G. A. 1976. The logic of asymmetric contests. Anim. Behav. *24*: 159–175.

(12) Maynard Smith, J., Price, G. R. 1973. The logic of animal conflict. Nature *246*: 15–18.

(13) Westermarck, E. 1907 and 1909. Ursprung und Entwicklung der Moralbegriffe, Vol. I and II. Leipzig: Klinkhardt.

(14) Wickler, W. 1971. Die Biologie der 10 Gebote. München: Piper.

(15) Wilson, E. O. 1975. Sociobiology. The New Synthesis. Cambridge, Mass.: Belknap/Harvard.

(16) Zweig, A. 1959. Tierpsychologische Beiträge zur Phylogenese der Ich-Ueber-Ich-Instanzen. Schweiz. Z. F. Psychol., Suppl. 37.

SOCIAL MORALITY NORMS AS EVIDENCE OF CONFLICT BETWEEN BIOLOGICAL HUMAN NATURE AND SOCIAL SYSTEM REQUIREMENTS

D. T. Campbell

A SCIENTIFIC MEDIATIONAL NORMATIVE ETHICS

We need to make clear our relation to the traditional philosophical goal of imperative normative ethics. Philosophers over the last hundred years have established to their satisfaction that the search for logically or analytically justified moral oughts is futile. Whatever ultimate norms we choose to live by are the result of presumptive or logically unjustified choices. This view I accept, as I believe Ebling did (10) in his introduction to an earlier conference on the subject of this workshop. What I do *not* accept is the nihilism in ethical and moral theory which philosophers often derived from these conclusions. Many textbooks and courses on ethics became totally preoccupied with efforts to prove that no moral standards can be justified. Moral and ethical values came to be regarded as expressions of idiosyncratic preferences or as emotive or exclamatory rather than normative (13).

Parallel philosophical developments in epistemology correctly arrived at the conclusion that certain descriptive

knowledge is impossible and that scientific truths are logically unjustifiable. But within epistemology there is now
emerging a point of view which, while agreeing with this
analysis, shows a willingness to pay the cost in assumptions, such as the assumption of the existence of an external
physical world, and to then reundertake the problems of
epistemology more nearly in the mode of science. Quine
(25) has spoken of "epistemology naturalized," Shimony (26)
of "Copernician epistemology," (and Konrad Lorenz (18, 21),
and I (2, 4, 5) of hypothetical and descriptive epistemology).
Agreeing that certain knowledge is impossible, these philosophers identify the assumptions that are being made in
science and show how within these assumptions (including
the normative assumptions underlying the decision rules
utilized in the choice of one scientific theory over another)
scientific knowledge can be *presumptively* justified. This is
a substantial movement, although still a minority position
within philosophy of science. (The very general relaxation
of standards as to what constitutes "justification," "good reasons," "rational choice," and so forth, amounts to a similar
shift). We need something similar in the philosophy of ethics
and morals, and it is this approach that I mean to indicate
by the heading "a scientific mediational normative ethics."
There are two words in this heading that make this a
much more modest quest than the philosopher's classic
search for ultimate justified norms. The word *mediational* is
obviously one. The quest is for *intermediate* ethical rules for
implementation of previously chosen ultimate values. The
word *scientific* adds further modesty, implying presump-
tiveness, contingency, and corrigibility, rather than entailed
truth or norms. Once any set of ultimate goals has been de-
cided on by any person or group, a scientific analysis of the
status of the world and man's nature can be used to derive
mediational ethical and moral rules that are normative,
that tell people how to behave, contingent on the assumed
ultimate values and on the validity of the scientific analysis
of the human condition. I believe that this is the source of the
norms that we employ in preaching against such modern
sins as overpopulation, nuclear warfare, radiation hazards,
destruction of the ozone layer, and air and water pollution.
It is the search for normative ethics of this modest, media-

tional, scientific kind which underlies the hundred-year-old tradition of naturalistic and evolutionary ethics and morality. Quillian (24) and Flew (12) have produced relatively recent philosophical reviews of the extensive evolutionary ethics literature, both biological and social. These are excellent and useful reviews, although from the present perspective, misleadingly negative because they accuse evolutionary ethical systems of failing to provide imperative entailed moral norms, a failing shared with all other ethical theories. (See also Toulmin (29).)

Scientific mediational normative ethics could be developed for any ultimate goal, but such development is obviously of little social or practical moral use unless the ultimate goals to which they are directed enjoy considerable popular consensus. Here evolutionary theory can enter in a reflexive way. From the neo-Darwinian version of evolutionary theory it would follow that all organisms, including humans, have as a built-in goal the survival of their own genes in future generations. But if we also consider the variety of human moral concerns, we can no doubt expand the set of goals. I feel certain that it includes more than future survival of the human genome. The set no doubt includes a preference that the present hedonic levels be retained, increased, or at least reduced as little as possible. Moreover, it probably includes the goal that we continue urban civilizations rather than reduce our population to what the world would support in terms of scattered family units gathering, hunting, or even tilling the soil. I suspect that the ultimate value package for most of us also includes the elimination of war, genocide, and even the reduction of poverty differentials. The borderline between ultimate goals and mediational values readily becomes blurred. I also suspect that we may end up with an "ultimate" set of goals in which no single value (not even a human life) is regarded as absolutely ultimate but in which there is a desire to optimize all values with differing levels of priority. It is not my purpose in this paper to propose such a set of goals, but rather to assert rather vaguely that we probably share one and that on the grounds of this sharing we can proceed with discussing scientific mediational ethics in a biological and evolutionary context.

NORMATIVE BIOLOGISM

This uncouth phrase has been chosen to designate the one aspect of the so-called naturalistic fallacy which I find fallacious. Under naturalistic fallacy and similar allusions to naturalism, philosophers refer to such a surprising and varied set of standpoints in ethical theory (see Gewirth (13) for an overview) that natural scientists who enter this discussion will communicate more clearly with philosophers if they avoid the term *naturalistic fallacy*. (My own interests and tools in moral theory are clearly naturalistic in the general sense, and also in ways overlapping philosophical usage, although I see moral oughts as independent of individual pleasures, pains, or natural intuitions.)

Most of those at this workshop admire the tremendous wisdom which biological evolution has built into the minds and behaviors of animals. This admiration and awe extend into the expectations that there is a great deal more such wisdom than we yet comprehend scientifically. This awe I share. However, there can result from this admiration a point of view that I specifically want to reject: the view that what is biologically natural is normatively good. Such a normative biologism underlies much of the current enthusiasm for sociobiology. It is implied, for example, even in E. O. Wilson's popular accounts of sociobiology (e.g., (37)) in spite of explicit disavowals in his more formal presentations ((36) pp. 563–564). A recent educational film entitled, "Sociobiology: Doing What Comes Naturally," clearly embraces normative biologism. (Wilson, DeVore, and Trivers, who appear in it, have expressed disapproval of the film for this and other reasons (9).) It was the implied normative biologism that made people fearful of Konrad Lorenz's title, *Das sogennante Böse* (19), (or, in the English translation, the chapter entitled, "What Aggression is Good for") even though that book explicitly denied the goodness of aggression when it leads to murder, warfare, and genocide. Normative biologism is shown through Lorenz's continual reference to our ultimate normative dependence on our innate "nonrational sense of values" ((20) and (22) p. 128) and on the ethical and aesthetic tastes we all share or that are epitomized by the noblest among us. (Later in this paper, I present an argument showing how an innate ethical sense might have evolved and give it great importance in ethical theory, but not incorrigible status.) In Teilhard de Chardin's (28) evolutionary perspective on morality, normative biologism is intensified by his teleological and God-guided view of biological evolution. Wickler's (31) *The Biology of the Ten Commandments* shows normative biologism in a form with which this paper will explicitly disagree. Pugh's (23) *The Biological Origin of Human Values* provides a pulpit for scolding the sins of modern society, but only at the expense of normative biologism.

There is no need, however, to single out ethology and sociobiology for blame for these trends. Normative biologism has also been implicit in the 100-year-old effort of psychology to emancipate itself from the restraints of philosophy and tradition, and in particular in its teachings against cultural repression and in favor of the individualistic hedonism of the erogenous zones (Campbell (6)). The predominant goal of psychotherapy in both psychiatry and psychology is the liberation of narcissism. So widespread has become the acceptance of normative biologism and of its accompanying normative individualism that even when sociobiology intends no such message, it is taken as such. Thus, on the U.S. political scene, to tell even the devout Catholic race rioters in South Boston that such rioting is biologically natural is to justify such rioting, giving it a positive moral value.

If we accept human survival as an ultimate value, either alone or as a part of an expanded ultimate set of goals, and if we accept the best current scientific analysis of the environment that human beings now exist in and will have to adapt to in the future, there result several formal considerations which provide a *scientific, mediational, normative, ethical justification for designating certain innate human behavioral tendencies as sinful or nonoptimal.* One such consideration is that the environment to which man has now to adapt has changed from the environment in which these basic behavioral tendencies evolved. This can occur because human beings have recently migrated into a new environment in which some of the old biological adaptations to the prior ecology are no longer adaptive. (The human migration into urban and technological ecologies provide examples. As a trivial but concrete instance, the innate human taste for sweets has ceased to be adaptive and is now maladaptive in the context of abundant refined sugar in the food supply and sedentary rather than physical labor. There results an innate "temptation to sin" as far as the candy box is concerned). This first type of discrepancy between our innate biological behavior predispositions and the environment in which we now live is sufficient to justify the recent antibiological scientific mediational normative ethics involved in the zero population growth movement, in the ecology movement, and in the world peace movement. Let us be careful that no normative biologism robs us of the moral stance from which we are able to preach against these new modern sins. Sharing with the evolutionary process since time immemorial the goal of human genetic survival as an ultimate value, we can identify certain products of the past biological evolutionary process as now sinful rather than good.

THE MORAL IMPLICATIONS OF GENETIC COMPETITION AMONG THE COOPERATORS

Whereas this first source of discrepancy between innate human behavioral tendencies and the behavior recommended by a scientific mediational normative ethic serves to present the issue clearly, this is not what I wish to concentrate on. Instead, I wish to deal with a source of discrepancy between such normative ethics and biological behavioral tendencies that has presumably existed ever since man started banding together for cooperative endeavors in social units larger than a single family. This is the puzzle known in the modern statistical evolutionary theory of population genetics under the labels "group selection" or "the genetics of altruism." Since I have recently (3, 6) written extensive reviews of the implications of this problem for human moralizing, I will be brief and dogmatic here, except insofar as I have extended or modified my position.

First, a sharp distinction needs to be made between the innate behavior of social mammals such as wolves, baboons, and humans, for which there is genetic competition among the cooperators, and that of the social insects. It is noteworthy that in E. O. Wilson's treatise (36) for every aspect of sociality, be it communication effectiveness, sharing information about sources of foodstuffs, mutual defense, or self-sacrificial bravery, the social insects are shown to be much more social than the nonhuman social mammals. In the social insects the cooperating castes are generally sterile, and hence there is essentially no genetic competition among the cooperators (even though in some species there exist exceptions to this rule, such as workers becoming fertile in the absence of the queen). Moreover, in evolutionary history the appearance of sterile castes *preceded* the specialized structure and behavior of the differentiated castes. At the initial stages of social insect evolution, sterile workers are morphologically and behaviorally otherwise undifferentiated from the queen. Once the sterile worker caste has been established, and if its sterility can be preserved, then in subsequent evolution the elaborate, specialized castes and the high degree of complex social interdependence emerge. This includes a full-fledged division of labor, with such highly specialized castes as soldiers whose jaws are so adapted for biting enemy ants and termites that they cannot feed themselves, and other castes that also do no food gathering and have to be fed by other workers, such as wine vat and ventilator fan castes. Any dispassionate *functional* analysis must find these social insects far and away more social than the most social of the baboons or apes. Undoubtedly, it is the elimination of the genetic competition for progeny both within a single caste, and between castes that makes possible the evolution of highly self-sacrificial altruism, through natural selection operating on queens.

In contrast, in social vertebrates there is a genetic competition among the cooperators, which, according to Haldane (16) and Williams (32), precludes high degrees of self-sacrificial altruism. Any socially useful self-sacrificial behavior benefits both the "altruists" and the nonaltruists in the group, the *net* benefit being greater to the nonaltruists because the gains to the altruists are reduced by the self-sacrificial risk costs they bear. Group selection may counter this temporarily for very small groups where chance might produce homozygous altruism, but for large groups, where differences in allele frequency only arise through individual selection within the group, the selection of a generally high degree of self-sacrificial altruism is precluded. And even if group selection under specialized conditions were to produce a population high in altruist allele frequency, this preponderance would tend to be eroded through the net selective advantage to the nonaltruistic free-riders, an advantage which is greater the higher the frequency of altruists.

In the recent literature of population genetics models have been put forward that allow for a higher degree of genetically based altruism for vertebrates. Of these, perhaps the most impressive model is that presented by David S. Wilson (33, 34, 35). His theory of deme selection attends to the implications modifying the simplifying assumption of random mating within an interbreeding group that population geneticists have previously employed. By substituting for random mating the assumption of a spatially autocorrelated similarity in mating pair genotype, Wilson finds much more favorable conditions for the selection of individually self-sacrificial altruism beneficial to the deme. Although his model may, in fact, be equivalent to Hamilton's kin selection (Maynard Smith, personal communication) if Williams (32), Ghiselin (14), Dawkins, *The Selfish Gene* (8), and my essays were to be written today, we would have to qualify our simple dogmatic emphasis on selection solely at the individual level. Even so, the alleles conferring altruistic traits permitted under these newer mathematical models would never exceed a frequency of 50 percent because they would increasingly be subject to counter selection as their frequency increased. Thus, under our best models of natural selection, vertebrates are precluded from achieving the extreme degree of innate self-sacrificial altruism found among the social insects.

Early humankind at the small hunting band stage might have existed under selective conditions supporting more innate altruism than that found among baboons and the other social primates. Features supporting this possibility would include: frequent colonization of new isolated areas by small inbred groups with a high rate of total colony extinction, long life, good memory, ability to discriminate group members from strangers, and genocidal behavior toward other groups. But by the time humankind entered multifamily social systems with urban settlements, incest taboos, and rules of exogamy, its selective conditions would have been *less favorable* for the retention of altruistic traits than the selective condition of the most social of other social primates, such as the baboons. We *cannot* explain human complex social interdependence on genetic grounds insofar as it goes beyond that achieved by other primates, and approaches or exceeds that of the social insects, in full-time division of labor, stored nonspoiling foodstuffs, apartment-house living, and self-sacrificial altruism.

Instead, human urban social complexity has been made possible by *social* evolution rather than biological evolution. This social evolution has had to counter selfish individualistic and familistic tendencies which biological evolution has selected, and continues to select, as a product of the genetic competition among the cooperators.

SOCIAL EVOLUTION

The social evolution I have in mind is often called Lamarckian because it involves the social inheritance of learned behavior (or taught behavior or socially acquired adaptations). This is a distracting usage for those of us to whom Lamarckianism also connotes self-conscious purposiveness and insightful knowledge on the part of the organism as to what it needs, which we deny as essential. The social evolution that I envisage holds to the fundamental paradigm of adaptation underlying individual learning and biological evolution: variation, selection, retention, and reproduction. For human social evolution the variation can be intelligent (Boehm (1)) or it can be stupid. The slogan perhaps should not be *blind* or *random* variation and selective retention, but it certainly should be *even-if-blind-or-random-variation* and selective retention. It shares the neo-Darwinian feature of biological evolution, in that the source of the fitness is attributed to the systematic effects of selection and not to the foresighted intelligence of the variations except as these have been winnowed by approximately valid vicarious variation and selection processes. While holding to this basic paradigm, there is not a one-to-one analogy to biological evolution. For example, there is no counterpart to bisexuality, and cross-lineage borrowing, precluded in biological evolution, becomes an important selective and reproductive process in social evolution.

For the present argument, it is not enough to point to the social evolution of tools and weapons, but rather the case must be made for a social evolution of attributes favoring social system effectiveness at the multifamily level. As I discuss in more detail elsewhere (6), this becomes problematic because of weakness in the retention and duplication systems (unstable selective conditions, too few elements for the stochastic processes to effectively operate on, positive feedbacks from variations, etc.). Nonetheless, an increasing number of anthropologists and sociologists believe that such a social evolution has taken place in human history. With laws of social organization operating as a part of the selective system, such a social evolution can account for the archaic independent development in the valleys of the Nile, Tigris, Euphrates, Indus, Ganges, Yangtze and Yellow rivers, and in Mexico, Yucatan, and Peru, of complex urban civilizations sharing many features with each other and some important features with social insects.

BIOLOGICAL SUPPORTS FOR THE SOCIAL EVOLUTION OF MORAL DOCTRINES

Whereas the predicament of genetic competition among the cooperators precludes the biological evolution for any strong innate tendencies toward self-sacrificial altruism in the group's benefit, there are a number of other possible biological dispositions supporting human social morality systems that are not precluded. First, an innate preference for altruistic, dependable, and socially constructive behavior *on the part of others* does not bear the genetic costs that altruistic behavior on one's own part does. (This could be the innate ethical sense of which Lorenz speaks.) An innate preference for joining a social group made up of predictable, dependable persons with inhibited selfishness, as opposed to joining a group made up of unpredictable, opportunistic persons, would likewise fit in with a model of individual selection on the basis of long-term procreational advantage. Going beyond this one runs into a series of borderline dispositions, probably less costly than one's own altruism, but carrying some genetic costs, indirect or otherwise, which require testing by detailed mathematical and computer simulation models. For example, are the superior survival advantages of joining an orderly, cooperative self-inhibited group sufficient to make it a progeny-furthering choice for one to be willing to join such a group at the cost of adopting such an overt behavioral pattern oneself?

Another borderline possibility is an innate tendency to praise and socially reward others who are conspicuously self-sacrificial altruists. Does such reward and adulation redistribute the economic and psychic resource within the group to one's own disadvantage so slightly that the gains in the survival potential of the group of which the individual is a part outweigh the costs? At a first level we can think of these as innate dispositions that modify the learning, acculturation, and emulation opportunities of others: innate tendencies that manipulate the learning environment of others. At a second level we can think of an innate tendency to provide increased procreational opportunities to altruists. In a brief comment, Ghiselin (15) has reversed the emphasis on individualistic selfishness of his 1974 volume (14) by suggesting that social man breeds altruists by "artificial selection," that is, by providing for the surviving altruists' increased procreational opportunities that more than make up for the genetic costs they bear. It seems clear that if such altruists are few in number, such an innate tendency would have relatively small individual costs compared to the group gains and to the individual gains from the increased group effectiveness. Even though it would favor alien altruistic genes in the competition for survival, this cost would be much less than would be altruistic behavior on one's own part, particularly if the social pool of persons were large and the number of altruists small.

Still more genetically costly, but perhaps not as costly as being homozygous for self-sacrificial altruism oneself, would be a tendency to be sexually attracted by surviving, heroic, self-sacrificial altruists, producing offspring that would be heterozygous for this trait. It would seem an important direction of development for the genetic theory of group selection and altruism to add these complications to the newer models that are producing increased possibilities for the selection of self-sacrificial altruism.

Robert Trivers (30) has called attention to two important genetic tendencies that avoid the cost of individual altruism, but support a group altruism. One of these is moralistic aggression, a biologically innate tendency for rage and aggressive behavior when others behave in violation of group norms or socially obligatory altruistic behavior. His second concept is that of an innate tendency to be predisposed to the creation of reciprocal altruism contracts with other persons, an innate tendency for what I would call "clique-selfishness," and along with this the tendency for moralistic aggression in the form of murderous rage toward those partners in reciprocal altruistic contracts who fail to live up to their commitments.

These concepts can be related to the profound insights contained within the concept of *pseudospeciation* as developed by Erik Erikson (11) and Konrad Lorenz (19, 20). Pseudospeciation refers to the tendency for tribal or nationalistic groups to socially organize in terms of in-groups versus out-groups, treating out-groups as though they were members of another species and were hence open targets for predation, hostility, and genocide (i.e., "ethnocentrism," Sumner (27); LeVine and Campbell (17)). In-group membership may be regarded as a socially inherited membership in a multi-person reciprocal altruism pact (a socially inherited clique membership for clique-selfishness), thus saving the risks involved in negotiating reciprocal altruism pacts with strangers. A biologically based tendency for punitive hostility against traitors to such an in-group pact would be equivalent to Trivers's moralistic aggression. (It is noteworthy that membership in such ethnocentric in-group pacts is usually not limited to kinsmen, but is often readily extended to those of different genetic heritage who are willing to join. However, an innate social tendency toward social speciation would produce an important genetic isolation if accompanied by endogamy. Evolutionary genetics should predict that large tribes should be endogamous, smaller ones exogamous as endogamy approximates the genetic costs of incest.)

If such innate tendencies exist, they support a social equivalent of "group selection," and predispose social customs enforcing self-sacrificial altruism on reluctant selfish individuals, just as would a purely social evolution of beliefs in transcendent social purposes, rewards and punishments after death, and social organizational features optimizing organizational survival.

(All this is based on the reasonable assumption that life in cooperating social groups increases one's inclusive fitness so greatly over solitary or single-family human existence that there are innate longings for group membership, innate fears of social ostracism, and innate conformity tendencies such as those that favor both the absorption and perpetuation of culture and the coordination of group action.)

OPTIMIZATION OF THE SOCIAL SYSTEM VERSUS INDIVIDUAL OR GENE SYSTEM

It is hypothesized that the socially evolved moralizing in each complex society is focused on those behavioral tendencies for which the optimization of the social system and the optimization of own-gene prevalence are in conflict. It is probably so that, on most options, the behavioral dispositions that further inclusive genetic fitness also optimize social system effectiveness. These behavioral tendencies would not require social system preaching, as people would spontaneously adopt them on the basis of their innate tendencies. In Moses' day, as in ours, a scientific mediational normative ethic would have supported the commandment: "Look out for your own interests." But it was left off of Moses' short list of the Ten Commandments which needed continual reiteration because in those days people were remembering to live by it without his prompting, unlike other commandments such as "Thou shalt not covet."

If we were to (a) achieve a formal theory of social organization that would specify the individual behavioral tendencies that were optimal for maintaining the social complexity of the ancient urban societies of Egypt, Mexico, China, and others; (b) apply the best of modern population genetics to describe the innate behavioral tendencies that biological evolution was probably producing in those settings; and (c) to compare these two sets of predicted behavioral dispositions, we would then have *in the differences* a theoretical basis for predicting the content of the folk moralizings, moral law, proverbs, commandments, temptations, and sins for each of those ancient high civilizations. Insofar as similar ecologies and laws of social organization were involved, there would emerge predictions of common content to these moralizings. Even in advance of the formal development of these theories, it becomes of interest to compare the recorded moralizings of these ancient civilizations. While very little of this research has been done, sketchy, preliminary searches show that cowardice and selfishness are probably universally scolded and group loyalty universally commended. Stinginess, greed, gluttony, envy, self-serving dishonesty, theft, lust, promiscuity, pride, and anger may also be universally proscribed. There are also puzzling universals and omissions.

NORMATIVE SOCIOLOGISM

Just as we must reject normative biologism, in spite of our recognition of much moral wisdom in the genome, so too must we reject a normative sociologism, which would posit an absolute normative dependence on social-evolutionary products such as the great religions. These too no doubt contain great wisdom where the relevant ecology has remained the same. But where the ecology has changed, what was once normatively moral may now be judged immoral in terms of a scientific mediational normative ethic. The wisdom of any evolutionary process, biological or social, is wisdom about past worlds.

Take, for example, that universal social evolutionary product: nationalistic military patriotism. There probably has been more widespread convergent evolution of it than for any other moralizing system (LeVine and Campbell (17)). It no doubt contained great adaptive value in past social and biological ecologies. Yet I share with Konrad Lorenz (19, 20) and many others the belief that nuclear weapons and other developments have now made this old virtue suicidal for modern man.

REFERENCES

(1) Boehm, C. 1978. Rational pre-selection from Hamadryas to Homo Sapiens: The place of decisions in adaptive process. Amer. Anthro., in press.

(2) Campbell, D. T. 1959. Methodological suggestions from a comparative psychology of knowledge processes. Inquiry 2: 152–182.

(3) ———. 1972. On the genetics of altruism and the counter-hedonic components in human culture. J. Social Issues. 28: 21–37. Reprinted In Sympathy, Altruism and Helping, ed. L. G. Wispé. New York: Academic Press, in press.

(4) ———. 1974a. Evolutionary epistemology. In The Philosophy

of Karl Popper, ed. P. A. Schilpp, vol. 14 I. The library of living philosophers. LaSalle, Ill.: Open Court Publishers.

(5) ———. 1974b. Unjustified variation and selective retention in scientific discovery. *In* Studies in the Philosophy of Biology, eds. T. Dobzhansky and F. J. Ayala. London: Macmillan; Berkeley and Los Angeles: University of California Press.

(6) ———. 1975a. On the conflicts between biological and social evolution and between psychology and moral tradition. Amer. Psychol. *30*: 1103–1126.

(7) ———. 1975b. Reintroducing Konrad Lorenz to psychology. *In* Konrad Lorenz: The Man and His Ideas, ed. R. I. Evans. New York: Harcourt Brace Jovanovich.

(8) Dawkins, R. 1976. The Selfish Gene. New York: Oxford University Press.

(9) DeVore, I. 1977. DeVore explains sociobiology film interviews. Anthro. Newsletter *18*: 2. (American Anthropological Association, 1703 New Hampshire Ave., N.W., Washington, D.C. 20009).

(10) Ebling, F. J., ed. 1969. Biology of Ethics: Institute of Biology Symposia: Number 18. New York: Academic Press.

(11) Erikson, E. 1966. Ontogeny of ritualization in man. *In* Philosophical Transactions of the Royal Society in London. Series B, 772, 251: 337–349.

(12) Flew, A. 1967. Evolutionary Ethics. London: Macmillan.

(13) Gewirth, A. 1974. Ethics. Encyclopaedia Britannica, 15th ed., Macropaedia 6: 976–998. Chicago: Encyclopaedia Britannica.

(14) Ghiselin, M. T. 1974. The Economy of Nature and the Evolution of Sex. Berkeley, Los Angeles, London: University of California Press.

(15) ———. 1976. (Comment) Amer. Psychol. *31*: 358–9.

(16) Haldane, J. B. S. 1932. The Causes of Evolution. London: Longmans.

(17) LeVine, R. A., and Campbell, D. T. 1972. Ethnocentrism: Theories of Conflict, Ethnic Attitudes and Group Behavior. New York: Wiley.

(18) Lorenz, K. A. 1941. Kant's Lehre vom Apriorischen im Lichte gegenwärtiger Biologie. Blätter für Deutsche Philosophie *15*: 94–125.

(19) ———. 1963. Das sogennante Böse. Vienna: Dr. G. Borotha-Schoeler Verlag.

(20) ———. 1973a. Civilized Man's Eight Deadly Sins. New York: Harcourt Brace Jovanovich.

(21) ———. 1973b. Die Rückseite des Spiegels. Munich: Piper-verlag.

(22) ———. 1975. Konrad Lorenz responds. In Konrad Lorenz: The Man and His Ideas, ed. R. I. Evans, pp. 119–127. New York: Harcourt Brace Jovanovich.

(23) Pugh, G. E. 1977. The Biological Origin of Human Values. New York: Basic Books.

(24) Quillian, W. S. 1945. The Moral Theory of Evolutionary Naturalism. New Haven, Conn.: Yale University Press.

(25) Quine, W. V. 1969. Ontological Relativity. New York: Columbia University Press.

(26) Shimony, A. 1970. Scientific inference. In Pittsburgh Studies in the Philosophy of Science, ed. R. Colodny. 4: 79–172. Pittsburgh.

(27) Sumner, W. G. 1906. Folkways. Boston: Ginn.

(28) Teilhard de Chardin, P. 1973. L'évolution de la chasteté. In Les directions de l'avenir. Paris: Editions du Seuil.

(29) Toulmin, S. 1957. Contemporary scientific mythology. In Metaphysical Beliefs, eds. S. Toulmin. R. W. Hepburn and A. MacIntyre. London: SCM Press.

(30) Trivers, R. L. 1971. The evolution of reciprocal altruism. Q. Rev. Biol. 46(4): 35–57.

(31) Wickler, W. 1972. The Biology of the Ten Commandments. New York: McGraw-Hill.

(32) Williams, G. C. 1966. Adaptation and Natural Selection. Princeton, N. J.: Princeton University Press.

(33) Wilson, D. S. 1975. A theory of group selection. Proceedings of the National Academy of Sciences USA. 72(1): 779–807.

(34) ———. Structured demes and the evolution of group-advantageous traits. The Amer. Natur. 110(975): 779–807.

(35) ———. Evolution on the Level of Populations and Communities, forthcoming.

(36) Wilson, E. O. 1975a. Sociobiology: The New Synthesis. Cambridge, Mass.: Belknap Press of Harvard University Press.

(37) ———. 1975b. Human decency is animal. The New York Times Magazine, Oct. 12, pp. 38–50.

THE BIOLOGY OF MORALS FROM A PSYCHOLOGICAL PERSPECTIVE

P. H. Wolff

In the context of a scientific approach to human morals, biologists apply the same rules of evidence they use to investigate the biochemical, metabolic, and neurophysiological processes of living organisms. The purpose of biologists in this endeavor is to identify the causal mechanisms for human behavior that have direct or indirect social consequences for other humans. However, their purpose is not to identify the intentions that motivate individuals to act morally.

Like other natural scientists, biologists are guided by an ethical code of procedure, but they usually take for granted the values implicit in the scientific method. The scientific study of human morals, however, makes values themselves the subject matter for investigation, and therefore requires an explicit definition of morality and of the criteria by which various behavior patterns can be categorized as moral. The ultimate criterion applied by biologists to evaluate the moral relevance of social behavior is survival of the genotype. Natural selection operates on social behaviors that promote reproductive advantage, whereas the individuals whose moral behavior has evolved are not, or need not be, aware of the reasons for the selective fitness of their behavioral genotype.

By contrast, moral philosophers, and at least some psychological theorists of morality, consider as moral only those forms of human behavior for which intention, deliberate choice among equally determined actions, and awareness of the social consequences of alternative actions can be assumed. Social behavior that is so rigidly determined by biological mechanisms as to be involuntary is considered to have no more moral content than the human sucking reflex or the gaping response of the herring gull. Yet, from a rigorous biological perspective, both reflex behaviors would have moral relevance. The biological and psychological approaches to human morals may therefore diverge so greatly as to be irreconcilable.

By positing survival of the genotype as a necessary and sufficient criterion of moral behavior, the biological approach either trivializes the central problems of human morals, or dismisses them as irrelevant epiphenomena. It does not distinguish between the prosocial behavior of soldier and worker bees which are genetically programmed to commit self-sacrificial acts, and the altruistic acts of a Mahatma Gandhi, whose life is defined by conscious moral choices. On the other hand, a psychological approach to morality that posits total autonomy of choice as a necessary condition for moral behavior may lead to absurd conclusions. For example, individuals committing antisocial or immoral acts, who suffer from temporal lobe epilepsy, chromosomal abnormality, or metabolic disorder are generally judged to have no moral responsibility if their transgressions are physiologically determined and, therefore, outside the realm of autonomous choice. We are inclined to absolve transgressions of responsibility when medical diagnosis identifies the physiological causes of antisocial behavior, but we insist on moral responsibility when no such causes can be demonstrated. Thus, we arrive at a classification of human morals under which only social behavior is considered to have moral content for which no causal mechanisms can be demonstrated. Should progress in biological research eventually explain all varieties of pro- and antisocial behavior in terms of metabolic and genetic processes, the belief in moral autonomy and freedom of choice would itself be shown to have genetic determinants, and the traditional views of human morality would evaporate as historical curiosities.

Within psychology, three comprehensive theories that retain some tie to biology have addressed the question of human morals. Social learning theory, which evolved historically from the concept of the conditioned reflex (2), investigates the environmental contingencies that shape socially relevant behavior. At present, it is nearly impossible to characterize the boundaries of contemporary social learning theory under a unitary set of hypotheses. Many hybrid versions of the original formulation have evolved from the incorporation of concepts from theories of cognition, perception, social perception, and personality. At the risk of doing injustice to such modifications, it therefore seemed most economical to return to the original formulation as it was derived from concepts of operant conditioning for purposes of this discussion.

"Pure" versions of learning theory equate human morals with forms of social behavior that are reinforced by social acceptance. The theory solves what it considers to be purely empirical questions by describing the stimulus conditions that assure social conformity, and it treats human moral behavior as simply another manifestation of the infinite varieties in which the behavior of all animals can be shaped through conditioning and schedules of reinforcement. It assumes that all programs of social conditioning are equally possible but does not explain what constitutes the society that either grants or withholds social acceptance, or how different societies adopt alternative codes of moral conduct. Learning theorists probably do not differ significantly from other psychologists and biologists in their moral rectitude or personal beliefs concerning good and evil. However, the theory to which learning theorists subscribe does not discriminate between social conditioning for mass murder in the national interest and moral training for nonviolent civil disobedience. Nor does the theory consider the long-range consequences for human welfare that result from alternative programs of social reinforcement to be relevant. The apparent advantage which social learning theory gains by a posture of value-free objectivity has to be paid for by a loss of relevance for the study of human morals.

In contrast to learning theory, Piaget's cognitive developmental theory of intellectual development and its elaboration as a theory of moral reasoning by Kohlberg (4) start from the assumption that morality is fundamentally a philosophical concern. The study of human morals must, therefore, begin with an a priori definition of the ethical systems to be explained by developmental analysis, the value system itself not being susceptible to empirical validation. After sampling the prevailing ethical codes of diverse cultures, Kohlberg concludes that distributive justice is the ultimate developmental endpoint of moral reasoning. Applying Piaget's method of clinical inquiry, he then describes the stage progression by which children in various cultures eventually acquire the notion of distributive justice. Whether distributive justice is, indeed, a universal or even the most commonly encountered ethical principle in diverse cultures remains a question that deserves more detailed investigation by social anthropologists than it has received so far.

Inherent to Kohlberg's investigations is the assumption that moral reasoning is a necessary although not sufficient condition for moral action. A persuasive demonstration of this assertion would argue strongly against the claims of learning theory. The theory's purpose is to demonstrate that moral actions are guided by ideas or theories which the child constructs from encounters with the physical and social world, and that such personal theories result from continuous developmental transformations determined jointly by brain maturation, experience, and a quasi-biological factor of "equilibration," or a general biological tendency to organize isolated elements into structured wholes. A demonstration that moral actions are determined by ethical concepts, and that such concepts are elaborated by biological mechanisms operating on individual experience would also militate against the sociobiological claim that humans are genetically programmed to behave in fixed social action patterns.

There is, however, at present no persuasive evidence that a person's capacity for moral reasoning reliably predicts his moral action in concrete situations that jeopardize personal comfort or physical welfare. The empirical evidence for a necessary relation between moral reasons and moral actions is derived primarily from situations that involve relatively little risk to the subject. As Kohlberg points out, moral reasoning is never a sufficient condition for moral action. Indeed, it remains to be demonstrated whether moral reasoning is even a necessary condition for moral acts, or simply a rationalization for actions that are caused or motivated by entirely different psychological but nonmoral factors. A systematic study of emotional development in the child that examines how humans acquire the capacity for empathy, compassion, and devotion to the welfare of others might provide the missing factor that links the development of moral thought to moral action.

While neither Piaget nor Kohlberg have systematically investigated emotional development in the child or its possible relevance for the development of moral judgment, psychoanalytic theory discusses the social-emotional development of the child in detail. The theory explains the ontogenesis of human morals in terms of inherent conflict between instinctual drives or their representations as wishes, and the restraints imposed on drive discharge by parental prohibitions and social conventions. The child incorporates the prevailing rules of moral conduct because of his emotional ties to the parent, and transforms these rules in the course of mental development as ego ideals or autonomous value systems. To the extent that the psychoanalytic theory traces the origin of moral standards to parental prohibitions reinforced by threats of disapproval, it resembles the formulations of social learning theory. However, to the extent that it envisages the instinctual drives as translating experience into private symbolisms, the theory conceptualizes the individual's moral norms, not as direct copies of parental prohibitions, but as symbolic representations of such norms modified by individual mental development.

Psychoanalytic theory is formulated in biological terms, but its developmental propositions are not susceptible to empirical refutation, and its clinical observations do not qualify as empirical data. Moreover, the theory's primary interest is clinical, and its general account of moral development is secondary to clinical considerations. In keeping with a clinical orientation, the theory emphasizes those aspects of deviant thought and social or antisocial behavior that (it assumes) are unconsciously determined and should be diagnosed as neurotic disorders, rather than judged as immoral acts. Among the neurotic disturbances that come to the attention of the psychoanalysts are disorders manifested as compulsive moralism and a crippling inhibition of sexual or aggressive behavior. Both critics and adherents to the theory have accused the clinical application of psychoanalytic theory of advocating antisocial or immoral behavior because it appears to equate mental health with a free expression of drive motivated behavior, and to regard social conventions that frustrate such expression as contrary to human interest. Yet, psychoanalytic ego psychology equates emotional maturity with the capacity for delay of drive discharge, for restraint and self-reflection. The stated aims of psychoanalytic treatment are not to rid the patient of all drive-restraining inhibitions, but to liberate the patient from a compulsion to respond to unconscious motivations, whether these produce neurotic promiscuity or compulsive abstinence. Successful treatment implies that the patient should be able to choose deliberately among alternative actions (3). By setting the psychological capacity for autonomous choices as one therapeutic goal, clinical psychoanalysis can be said to imply a prescriptive as well as a descriptive theory of human morals. However, the theory offers no formal account of moral norms that should be adopted by emotionally healthy adults.

The ethological proposition that biological evolution selects for the prosocial behavior of humans, as well as of other animal species, has attracted considerable attention among psychologists. From the perspective of human psychology, at least two distinct formulations of contemporary ethology can be identified. The first, or narrow version, postulates that those human behavior patterns which regulate courtship, mating, care of the young, appeasement of aggression, friendship, and similar social interactions are genetically programmed, physiologically mediated, and not significantly modified by experience. Environmental factors may control the time of emergence of social behavior, but experience neither produces nor significantly alters the pattern. By emphasizing the contribution of specific biological factors to socially relevant behavior, the ethological approach has rescued the study of human psychology from its earlier single-minded commitment to environmental determinism. The approach has, for example, motivated studies on the prefunctional organization of behavior patterns by which infants elicit care-giving and affectional behavior from their social partner and monitor the partner's social responses. However, the claims made by this psychological version of ethology extend far beyond the crib, to include assumptions about fixed action patterns that control human group cooperation, protection of the family, defense of national boundaries and altruistic self-sacrifice.

The general claim that all behavior is always determined by both genetic and environmental factors is obviously true and cannot be refuted. This truism does not define the limits of a natural science approach to human morals, since it fails to discriminate between moral, immoral, and amoral action, or between cognitive, perceptual, and social affective behavior. Only the more specific claim that particular genetic factors determine particular patterns of moral behavior would be of direct interest in the present context. As far as I know, there is no evidence showing that mature forms of morally relevant human behavior appear as universals in all members of our species, or that such behavior is sufficiently fixed by genetic factors to undergo an invariant development in grossly divergent environmental contexts. The sociobiological claims for the existence of genetic factors rest on certain formal similarities between the social behavior patterns of humans and nonhuman animals (for which evidence of genetic determination may be available).

Yet, ethology, the parent discipline of sociobiology, categorically rejects cross-species generalizations based on analogies of form that have not been confirmed by an analysis of species differences in the form-function relationship. It is, therefore, surprising, to say the least, that the sociobiological case for the genetic determination of human morals should rest on untested cross-species analogies. As long as the guidelines for distinguishing between legitimate and false cross-species analogies do not exist or are ignored, examples of genetically determined behavior patterns observed in animals cannot be adduced as evidence to support claims about the genetic determination of human social relations.

Plausible biological models of human morality should not be rejected for lack of empirical evidence. Yet, this version of sociobiology must be scrutinized with special care because it has been misused by all power aristocracies in the past to justify their position of privilege. Any dominant social group can find illustrations in the social behavior of insects, fish, birds, and baboons to rationalize its exploitation of other human groups on grounds of biological necessity. While sociobiologists may oppose the political misuse of their theories, a narrow version of sociobiology that postulates inflexible genetic contributions to specific forms of moral conduct should be challenged on moral, as well as on scientific grounds.

Some contradictions between the biological and psychological perspectives on human morality may be resolved by a more flexible approach to sociobiology. One such formulation begins with the premise that the organization of human cerebral functions which eventually govern behavior is not fixed at the time of birth, but is modified throughout postnatal ontogenesis by maturational changes in brain structure. This formulation posits that natural selection has equipped the human infant, not only with fixed action patterns for socially significant affectional and sensory motor behavior but also with species-specific programs for development along certain pathways and not others (Waddington's "creodes"). What emerges as social or moral behavior in the mature human will, therefore, depend on genetically determined epigenetic pathways that direct mental development toward the distinctly human faculties of language, cognition, perception, and perhaps moral conduct without, however, excluding the contribution of latent moral dispositions for social interaction present in the naive infant. At present, we do not possess even the basic terms needed to formulate a biological theory of such ethical dispositions, or to specify the range of alternative moral norms compatible with evolutionary fitness. We can only speculate that the ontogenetic programs guiding moral development probably differ qualitatively from programs guiding the development of cognitive and affective behavior, so that the development of human morals should be studied as a distinct psychobiological phenomenon before its functional interactions with cognition and affectivity can be fruitfully examined.

The more flexible formulation of a sociobiological approach to morality does not postulate that mature forms of moral conduct are themselves fixed by the genome. Whereas the biological constraints on moral development admit alternative outcomes, the range of extant ethical systems compatible with evolutionary fitness is limited. Natural selection operates on the boundaries within which ethical systems can develop and it buffers humans against arbitrary indoctrination by capricious ideologies or programs of reinforcement that would work against the long-range survival of the human genotype. However, the moral content of ethical systems adopted by an individual or group is not predetermined either genetically or by social convention.

The evolution of a brain capable of creating and transmitting historically stable cultures (1, 5) has added a qualitatively new dimension to the social behavior of humans, as compared to nonhuman species. Whereas the human capacity to create cultures is biologically determined, the products of that creation are no longer subject to natural selection at the biological level, since cultures evolve their own rates and rules of transformation. In the course of historical evolution, the moral values adopted by some societies may come into direct conflict with the biological goal of maximizing reproductive advantage. This appears to be the case for the use of nuclear weapons to implement the "territorial imperative," and for unlimited mating to maximize reproductive advantage. When the inexorable process of natural selection no longer serves human interest, the biologically evolved capacity to make intentional choices among alternative actions itself becomes the necessary condition for survival.

The capacity to reflect on and choose among alternative outcomes is inherent to mature human intelligence. Since neither human infants nor animals are, as far as we know, capable of evaluating the potential consequences of their choices, we must assume that such capacities are acquired in the course of human psychological development. The more flexible formulation of sociobiology might then suggest that the human brain has evolved the neurological mechanisms necessary for making self-conscious choices and that such mechanisms selected for in biological evolution have become essential for the survival of a species that is capable of creating its own culture. Biological evolution does not specify what forms of social action regulate moral conduct, but it defines the boundaries of ethical behavior compatible with species survival. Biology does not specify the choices made, but it prepares the structural conditions without which there can be neither intention or deliberate choice.

REFERENCES

(1) Campbell, D. T. 1975. On the conflicts between biological and social evolution and between psychology and moral tradition. Amer. Psychol. *30*: 1108–1126.

(2) Eysenck, H. J. 1976. The biology of morality. *In* Moral Development and Behavior, ed. T. Lickona. New York: Holt Rinehardt and Winston.

(3) Knight, R. P. 1954. Determinism, "freedom," and psychotherapy. *In* Psychoanalytic Psychiatry and Psychology, eds. R. P. Knight and C. R. Friedman. New York: International Universities Press.

(4) Kohlberg, L. 1971. From is to ought: how to commit the naturalistic fallacy and get away with it in the study of moral development. *In* Cognitive Development and Epistemology, ed. T. Mischel. New York: Academic Press.

(5) Waddington, C. H. 1960. The Ethical Animal. London: Allen and Unwin.

PROSOCIAL BEHAVIOR OF THE VERY YOUNG

H. L. Rheingold and D. F. Hay

INTRODUCTION

In this paper we present the early manifestations of a class of behaviors labeled positive, or prosocial. From these manifestations we derive a theoretical account of the development of prosocial behavior, outlining the processes by which the behaviors are acquired. After brief statements of directions for further research we present a conception of the infant's social behavior that contrasts with current developmental theories.

The account is limited to the behavior of normal children under three years of age. Although as a topic of investigation prosocial behavior is receiving increasing attention, its study in children under three has been scant, and only seldom has it been the primary focus of attention.

THE PROSOCIAL BEHAVIORS

We define prosocial behaviors as those that promote and maintain harmonious and satisfying interactions between the children and other persons. As examples of prosocial behavior we present evidence on sharing, caregiving, taking turns, friendliness and affection, empathy and sympathy, helping and cooperating, and obedience and conscience. For each we supply a definition that seems as appropriate for infants as for older children and adults. The definitions represent a combination of those given by the dictionary, those proposed by others, and those based on our own intuitions—but no fast claim is made for them. Although we treat the behaviors as separate, and define them as different, alternative and overlapping definitions can be entertained, and the distinctions probably should not be pressed.

The presentation is limited to occurrences of behaviors without recourse to conjectures about the infant's feelings, intentions, or motives. The review of the behaviors is selective and not exhaustive. By drawing on different types of sources—field observations, experimental findings, and reviews of the old and the current literature—a considerable measure of generality results. For much of the data we turned to the earlier astute observers of children; these data possess the authenticity of real life and obviate the need to generalize from the contrived procedures of much of the work with older children and adults.

Sharing

Sharing is defined as the granting by the original holder to another "the partial use, enjoyment, or possession of a thing though it may merely imply a mutual use or possession" (31). Children, as they pass their first birthday, commonly show and give objects to other people on their own initiative, without prompting, direction, or praise. These activities have been reported in the literature at least since Tiedemann's observations in 1787 (13).

In a series of laboratory studies children at eighteen months of age drew the attention of their mothers, fathers, and unfamiliar persons to toys by pointing to them and by holding them up for the other persons to view (20). The infants also brought toys to their companions, released them in the hands or laps of these persons, and then proceeded to engage the persons in play with the toys. Field observations corroborated these findings. Other studies (6, 17) indicated that both younger (twelve-month-old) and older (two- and three-year-old) children also displayed the behaviors, with the two- and three-year-olds also talking to their mothers about the toys in addition to the other behaviors.

A more detailed study in our laboratory of the ontogeny of pointing showed that as early as twelve months of age a majority of infants pointed out objects of interest to their mothers. The communicative function of the gesture was demonstrated by the infants' looking at and vocalizing to the mother while pointing, and by the mothers' vocalizing or looking at the object in response. It would seem then that the infants had already learned that others would find of interest what they themselves found noteworthy.

Sharing also occurs among siblings (29), children in a nursery (9), and even between unacquainted one-year-olds in the laboratory (7).

Caregiving

Caregiving is defined as the behaviors which parents perform for their young children: feeding, rocking, grooming, putting to bed, instructing, disciplining, and so on. The earliest evidence in our files describes how an eight-month-old girl fed zwieback to a dog. Boys and girls from the age of eleven months feed dolls with bottles and imaginary food (30). Children in the second year of life washed their dolls and put them to bed (29). Children not only attended to the "physical needs" of dolls but showed pictures to them and to teddy bears (30). Children in the third year of life also instructed their dolls: A boy sat a doll next to him, saying "Look, now, how I can build" (29, pp. 307–308), and a girl showed her doll various objects, asking "See? See?" "Say fish? Fish," "Can you say cupcake?" and so on for each of the objects (8).

In a laboratory playroom designed to promote caregiving, containing dolls, toy animals, a highchair, a cradle, dishes and baby bottles, a comb and brush, soap, and so on, we recently observed caregiving by two girls and three boys about twenty-four months of age. The boys as well as the girls held the dolls and toy animals, patted them, fed, bathed, groomed, and put them to bed. They instructed the dolls in how to behave, one boy spanking a doll for behavior for which his parents had disciplined him. An average of forty-six (range, forty-two to fifty) caregiving behaviors occurred in the thirty-minute sessions. The children carried out these acts with intentness and apparent seriousness.

Very young children also direct caregiving to persons. For example, children assist one another in everyday tasks: A girl of twenty-one months fed a fifteen-month-old boy; a boy of twenty-three months put a sock on a twenty-one-month-old girl; and a girl of twenty-four months helped a boy out of bed by opening the net, adjusting the stepladder, holding his hand, and saying "Not fall down" (9, p. 43). Young children also express concern for the well-being of adults (29). A two-year-old girl told her mother at various times to put on mittens before going outdoors; advised her to watch her fingers as a toy train was set in motion; tried to trim her mother's fingernails after having her own trimmed; brushed the mother's hair; kissed the mother's sore finger, offering to get a wet cloth for it, and finally putting a bandage on it; spread a blanket over her mother when the mother said "I'm cold," and then placed a pillow under the mother's head (8). Thus, care is given not only to dolls and teddy bears and should not be dismissed as just "pretend play."

Taking Turns

Taking turns with another person appears early in life. In its earliest form, turn-taking is illustrated by infants' vocalizing after other persons vocalized to them in a series of some length. On Day 49 of his son's life, Valentine reported that the infant started cooing in response to his own, "one coo to each of mine for 6 or 7 times" (30, p. 188). Experimental studies demonstrated that three-month-old infants vocalized after the experimenter's social response to each of the infant's vocalizations (e.g., 2). At the very early ages the partner probably makes the major contribution. These early verbal interchanges are honored by the term "dialogue" (24), and, as the essence of communication, play an important role in the development of language (4). By two and three years of age, children already converse with adults and children on a common topic of discourse.

Taking turns need not be limited to vocal and verbal dialogues. It occurs in numerous nonvocal interchanges between the infant and others, being especially common in such early games as peek-a-boo. Year-old toddlers in their play already act, then pause and watch while the other acts (21). Thus, taking turns, both in conversation and in the course of other activities, is a precocious manifestation of prosocial behavior that continues to be of service throughout life.

Friendliness and Affection

Friendliness and affection are related behaviors; the first may be defined as "kind interest, pleasant warmth, or familiar sociability"; the second as "tender attachment and love" (31). The behaviors denoting friendliness include smiles, cooing and babbling, and approaches; those denoting affection include cries of joy, hugs, kisses, patting, nestling, and eventually verbal declarations of love.

Human infants for many months during the first year of life smile readily to all who approach them. Toward the end of the first year they may be less likely to smile to unfamiliar persons, but the so-called fear of the stranger, although dramatic when it occurs, has been shown not to be characteristic of most infants and young children (19).

Affectionate behaviors to members of the family appear as early as three months of life (27) and are commonly reported in the succeeding months, as has been documented by K. M. Bridges. The recipients specifically named include the parents, grandparents, an aunt, baby brothers and sisters, and playmates (5, 9, 30).

Empathy and Sympathy

Empathy is here defined as the *capacity* for participating in or experiencing another's emotions. Sympathy, in contrast, is defined as *behavior* to alleviate the discomfort of another.

When confronted with the distress of another, children accord it close attention. The crying of newborns in response to the cries of other newborns (23) may indeed index empathy, although children may also on occasion cry in response to the laughter of others (30). With the onset of language, little children verbalize the distress of another, real or imagined. A twenty-six-month-old girl, watching her mother use scissors in making a cornhusk doll, said "Ow," as though the doll were being hurt (8). And Scupin's son at thirty-two months, on seeing the cook pluck a turkey's breast, said "O, Anna, you mustn't tear off poor turkey-cock's little shirt—he will be so cold" (29, p. 524).

In addition to these responses to another's real or imagined distress, young children show sympathy by consoling, distracting, or entertaining the sufferer (32). For example, a thirteen-month-old boy brought his own mother to comfort a crying friend; and a fifteen-month-old boy brought first his teddy bear to a crying friend, and when that did not help, finally stopped the crying by getting the friend's security blanket from the next room (12). Many accounts of sympathetic behavior are reported of children between nineteen and thirty-six months of age comforting their peers who were crying or hurt, by patting them, giving them toys, by clowning and laughing, and in one instance by putting one's own finger in the mouth of a hurt child (9, 14). A thirty-two-month-old boy, when told of a child who had no toys, of his own volition gave away four of his own (30).

Helping and Cooperating

Helping is defined as giving aid or support to another person, and cooperating as acting with another to a common end or to produce an effect jointly (31).

Little children help their parents in housekeeping and other tasks. A nine-month-old girl "appears at bedside to 'help' make the bed most mornings—pulls and pats blankets, swats the pillow" (5, p. 37). The same child, at eighteen months, was described by her mother as eager to help: "She works alongside me in the garden, manages to rake or use a trowel fairly well. . . . She helps put weeds in the basket. . . . In the house, she helps push the vacuum or mop, finds a sponge and 'dusts' the furniture, anticipates her father's needs in dressing or in building a fire in the fireplace, insists on helping to wipe spoons, 'sets' the table by carrying flatware to the table and scattering it about the periphery, continues to put most toys away spontaneously, finds various bits of dog fur or other fluff on the floor and puts them either in the ashtray or a wastebasket" (5, pp. 71–72). Valentine reported of his son at thirty-one months, "Very thoughtful nowadays. When I came in this morning he said, 'Daddy want slippers,' and ran off to get them" (30, p. 321).

Little children also help one another. Of many examples we report two. At twenty-one months of age a girl helped a boy of the same age build a structure by collecting all the blocks in the playroom and handing them to him one by one in succession (9). On occasion, help takes the form of direct verbal instruction: A thirty-six-month-old boy told a girl who could not go down the slide, "Yes, you can. Go down like this with your feet" (14, p. 98).

Unfamiliar adults are helped as well as parents and peers: A girl of twenty-six months brought a stool from another room for an observer in the home who was kneeling as she took notes (8), and a thirty-five-month-old boy brought a peer's mother a folding chair, opened it, and invited her to sit down (14).

Examples of cooperation may also be found among these very young children. Cooperating with an adult in being dressed qualifies as normative at twelve months of age on a developmental scale (11). Two nineteen-month-old children, a boy and a girl, were described as "founding a building society"; "whenever one of them started building, the other joined in quickly, and then they built in turns, each putting a brick carefully on the tower and then waiting until the other had put his brick on" (9, p. 49). Coordinating play to perform a common task or elaborate a social game was observed in infants at the end of the second year of life (7). In these examples we are inferring a "common end" based on the appropriateness of the children's actions, recognizing of course the speculative nature of such inferences.

Obedience and Conscience

Obedience is defined as the child's according with direct commands at the time they are given, conscience as the child's according with past prohibitions.

"Obeys simple commands" constitutes an achievement placed at twelve months of age on scales of infant development (11). A majority of infants between nine and twelve months of age obeyed such commands as "Come," "Sit," "Give it to me," "No, no," and "Don't touch," and about a fifth of them spontaneously arrested an act punished or forbidden in the past (28). Stern's eighteen-month-old son carried messages from his mother to the maid in another part of the house and his daughter at the same age carried out a difficult command with "real joy" (29).

In any infant's household, certain commands are given over and over again. To the extent that children refrain from these acts in the absence of explicit reminders, we may speak of conscience. A seventeen-month-old girl commanded herself "Don't touch" after her father prohibited her touching a floor lamp (26), and Scupin's son talked to himself while eating a roll: "'Bubi don't lick down the butter from the roll—big children don't do that, only quite little children do; that is very ugly, you know'" (29, p. 449).

Directions for Research

At present investigators of prosocial behavior in persons of different ages use different categories and definitions. A first task should be to work toward a common language. In the process of refining definitions, it will become clear that different behaviors may serve more than one function: Giving something to another person may qualify as sharing, caregiving, helping, or even cooperating, depending on antecedent and current events. Precision of definition, however, should not be sought at the expense of external validity.

Controlled observational studies are required. Anecdotes have a place but provide too limited a base for so heavy a freight. Studies are needed of the occurrence of the prosocial behaviors not only in homes and daycare centers but also in laboratory settings designed to increase the likelihood of the behaviors' appearing. Furthermore, once the prosocial behaviors of very young children become the focus of study, other behaviors may well be discovered. Just as some of the behaviors here categorized tended to escape attention, others may yet go unremarked; for example, what about recompense, retribution, a sense of justice?

How are the prosocial behaviors related among themselves? Are there prosocial children? Similar questions can be asked about the relations of prosocial behavior to other classes of behavior, such as agonistic behavior. Much more needs to be known about the psychometric properties of different classes of behavior before these questions can be answered. Frequency counts provide only limited data: How weigh a word of sympathy against a deed? How distinguish a conflict that is settled amicably from one that results in tears for both contestants (22)? Also, more sophisticated techniques should be employed than the tabulating of correlation matrices.

To trace the ontogeny of the prosocial behaviors, longitudinal studies should supplement cross-sectional ones. Such studies could determine the earliest occurrence, as well as the contributions of language and new motor and cognitive skills to the development of the behaviors. Both types of studies should seek also to weigh the effects of the child's sex and birth order, subject variables of considerable interest in this area.

THE ACQUISITION OF THE BEHAVIORS

Aside from possibly emphatic responses to the powerful emotional behavior of others (which may themselves be attributable to respondent conditioning), we propose that the prosocial behaviors result from experience; they are learned. It goes without saying that learning is viewed as an interaction with the natural biological characteristics of the human infant, preeminent among which is the predisposition to learn. Similarly, learning depends on the progressive maturing of motor and cognitive skills.

The behaviors are learned through reinforcement of the infants' own acts and through their observation and imitation of the acts of others. Learning through reinforcement comprises the capacity to distinguish between rewarding and nonrewarding events and the ability to modify one's behavior in terms of its consequences. The events following the occurrence of an act may be positive or negative, rewarding or aversive, and may stem from a variety of sources, including the responses of other persons and the sensory-motor feedback of the infants' own behavior. Reinforcement serves to regulate behavior, not only to determine the probability of its future occurrence but also to modulate and shape it. By itself, however, reinforcement does not account for the emergence of new behaviors (1). For most if not all of the prosocial behaviors, it seems likely that infants learn them by observing the behaviors of other people, as they are performed both for themselves and for others.

Imitation refers to the child's reproducing the behavior of others, who are termed *models*. The young child's copying of a modeled behavior has been amply documented (e.g., 30). At least by the beginning of the second year of life, infants imitate behaviors observed days or weeks before, thus displaying the ability to remember even in the absence of verbal prompting. In the process, the infants make the behaviors their own; they do not imitate slavishly. As in their use of language, they generate variations and compose new sequences of behavior.

Who are the models whose behaviors the infants imitate?

Among those who exhibit prosocial behaviors are first the parents, then other adults, relatives, and friends, then siblings and older children, and children of the infants' own age. These different persons of course model different classes of prosocial behaviors. Further, their responses to the infants' imitating a behavior serve to "fine-tune" its next manifestation. The words of other persons deserve special attention. They not only reinforce but, of even greater consequence, prompt, explain, and instruct.

The performance of any prosocial behavior obviously depends on the skills the children have acquired. But even at an age when the performance may still be fragmentary, children are capable of directing the behavior to a variety of persons and in a variety of settings, at the same time distinguishing among those persons and settings. They generalize and discriminate, and thus begin to display the prosocial behaviors at once freely and appropriately.

Sharing as an Illustration

How in any one child does sharing begin? In the first instance, because of the human infants' slow development, almost everything they need for survival must be brought to them. As the children mature, more and more things are brought to them for their comfort and amusement. Parents soon begin explicitly to show infants what they bring them. They hold the bottle and the bright object for the infants to see. They begin to accompany the showing with words: "Here's your bottle," "Look at the pretty toy." A few months later, even before the children understand the words, parents point to objects, saying "See the car," and so on.

Each behavior enumerated as a component of sharing by children has often been exhibited toward them by parents, siblings, relatives, and babysitters. Long before they are a year old they have had countless opportunities not only to observe other people modeling the behaviors but have been rewarded by them. As they acquire the motor skills, they reciprocate the sharing of others. But imitation need not carry the whole burden. Their sharing meets with responses from recipients, who, at the least, turn to look and often name the object. When given objects, recipients often smile and say thank you. This rich social response contributes to learning to share. By the differences in the responses of different people, sharing is modulated and refined (18).

In summary, infants have ample opportunities to learn to share by imitating the behaviors of others and by the responses of others to their own behavior. As a consequence from being only recipients, they now become actors.

Directions for Research

Because the acquisition of the prosocial behaviors depends so much on the behavior of models, it is to their behavior that we now turn attention. Let us consider the example of parents as models. Parental behavior is governed in part by the individual characteristics of their infants, parental behavior being viewed as an interaction between parent and child. In part, also, parental behavior is influenced by the family's socioeconomic status and the norms of its culture, both constituting factors for future study.

We need, in particular, to explore the effect on children's prosocial behaviors of parental differences in the prosocial acts they perform for different recipients; the information they provide children, especially about the real feelings of others or imagined feelings of animals and inanimate objects; and their verbal instructions. We need similarly to learn how they respond to (reinforce) their children's prosocial behaviors, and the effect of their responses on the children's subsequent behaviors. These same questions can also be asked about the effects of the modeling and reinforcing behaviors of persons other than the parents, especially of other children.

Experimental manipulation of some of these variables would provide evidence of how the prosocial behaviors are acquired. Adults, both familiar and unfamiliar, can be trained to model desired behavior, to offer suggestions, to instruct the children about the feelings of others, or to direct the children. Similarly, they can be trained to respond in specified ways to a child's prosocial behavior.

TOWARD A NEW CONCEPTION OF THE INFANT

The evidence assembled here forces the conclusion that prosocial behavior develops in the human infant before the age of three. Prosocial behavior results from the interplay of several processes: the infants' early physical helplessness and consequent need for care at human hands, providing the infants with the experience of being cared for and with models of prosocial behavior; their seeking of new experiences that lead to interaction with people and things, both familiar and unfamiliar; and their capacity to modify their behavior as the result of experience. The prosocial behaviors then are predictable outcomes of infants' biological characteristics and the experiences afforded them in human homes. Yet typically, the behaviors have not been remarked; no current theory of social development—neither psychoanalytic (10), attachment theory (3), cognitive-developmental theory (15), nor even social learning theory (1)— would predict a prosocial infant. Hence the data warrant a new conception of infants and their social development.

The Nature of the Infant

Human infants are born into a social group with an organized structure. They belong to a family, usually composed of a mother and father, often one or more siblings, grandparents, aunts, uncles, and cousins. They are members of a community, an ethnic group, a culture, and a generation. From birth infants are capable of mutual and reciprocating interaction with other persons. Although their physical helplessness demands care, they are not just passive recipients: By their demands (e.g., cries) and responses (e.g., smiles and vocalizations) they teach their parents how to care for them (16). As their motor, perceptual, and cognitive skills grow, they become aware of differences among people and the situations in which the behavior of familiar persons changes; they make more reliable predictions regarding the effects of their own behavior, coming to discern order in the social world.

Human infants thus are active partners in interactions with others. The portrait of social, prosocial infants which emerges from these observations differs from that of passive, dependent, often fearful organisms, bound up in ties with their mothers, as described by psychoanalytic (10) and attachment theory (3). The evidence also does not support the cognitive-developmental theory's (15) characterization of young children as egocentric, as failing to distinguish between themselves and others, and unable to realize that others' points of view may differ from their own. When evidence such as the infant's pointing out an object for another to see, or bringing a security blanket to comfort a crying friend, is considered, early signs of nonegocentricity abound.

As infants are not necessarily egocentric, so they are not necessarily egoistic. Theories of dependency (25) portrayed infants and young children as attention-seeking, affection-seeking, help-seeking creatures. The observations of prosocial behavior indicate, in contrast, that infants freely *offer* their own attention, affection, sympathy, help, and possessions to others.

The young child's very real contribution to social life should not be denigrated by always being cast in terms of play. In particular, the suggestion that a child who is sharing, or caring for a doll, teddy bear, or other person, is *playing the role* of the parent adds nothing to the statement that infants imitate their parents' prosocial acts. Rather, the suggestion detracts from the real quality of the child's activity.

The Nature of Prosocial Development

The prosocial behaviors further confirm the infant's status as an active and able participant in social encounters; moreover, their occurrence suggests that prosocial development is best viewed as a set of continuous and cumulative experiences. Further, the principles of reinforcement and imitation, which emphasize the importance of cumulative experiences, are able to account for early prosocial development. To be sure, development consists of qualitative as well as quantitative change, and the prosocial behaviors of children differ from those of adults in a number of respects. But a stage theory (15) that sets precise limits on the behaviors expected at earlier stages does not seem necessary. With respect to the particular stage theories of moral development, they do not begin early enough; the child under six need not be consigned to an amoral category.

SUMMARY

Thus, we see the need to extend developmental theories to account for an active, social, and prosocial infant. We recognize of course that the human infant's abilities and capabilities are characteristic of its species, and that the infant's behavior evolved and is built on a biological substrate. We could speculate on the adaptiveness of the behaviors, but recognize the difficulty of obtaining data to support such speculations. Similarly, we turn to maturational theories for examples of the behaviors but not for a theoretical account of the responsible processes.

Although the acquisition of the behaviors has been worked out in terms of learning theory, the behaviors are not reflexive or mechanical. Cognitive abilities underlie them. To share, sympathize, help, and so on, demonstrates knowledge of the behaviors of others and the demands of the situation. Imitation of behaviors observed at some time in the past also attests to the requisite cognitive skills. Nevertheless the behaviors are not precluded from occurring at earlier periods in cognitive development, and accounts of their acquisition and developmental course can be offered without recourse to mentalistic speculation.

Thus, this conception allows us to predict a prosocial infant. It arises from the everyday observation of normal children. It incorporates principles of biological and cognitive development. It invokes principles of social learning, but subscribes neither to reinforcement by itself nor to imitation by itself. This interactional conception integrates the infant's status as an active social partner with the richness of human society as a setting that supports prosocial activity. Given this view, we propose that the prosocial behaviors are precursors to the prosocial, altruistic, and moral conduct of later life.

Acknowledgment

Supported in part by NIH research grants HD01107 and HD23620 from the National Institute of Child Health and Human Development to H. L. R.

REFERENCES

(1) Bandura, A. 1977. Social Learning Theory. Englewood Cliffs, N.J.: Prentice-Hall.

(2) Bloom, K. 1977. Patterning of infant vocal behavior. J. Exp. Child Psychol. 23: 367–377.

(3) Bowlby, J. 1969. Attachment and Loss (vol. 1: Attachment). London: Hogarth.

(4) Bruner, J. S. 1974/75. From communication to language—A psychological perspective. Cognition 3: 255–287.

(5) Church, J., ed. 1966. Three Babies: Biographies of Cognitive Development. New York: Random House.

(6) Cook, K. V. 1977. The Verbal and Nonverbal Sharing of Two-and Three-Year-Old Children. Master's Thesis, University of North Carolina.

(7) Eckerman, C. O.; Whatley, J. L.; and Kutz, S. L. 1975. Growth of social play with peers during the second year of life. Dev. Psychol. *11*: 42–49.

(8) Emery, G. N. 1977. Personal communication.

(9) Freud, A., and Burlingham, D. 1944. Infants Without Families: The Case For and Against Residential Nurseries. New York: International University Press.

(10) Freud, S. 1938. An Outline of Psychoanalysis. London: Hogarth.

(11) Gesell, A., and Amatruda, C. S. 1941. Developmental Diagnosis: Normal and Abnormal Child Development. New York: Hoeber.

(12) Hoffman, M. L. 1975. Developmental synthesis of affect and cognition and its implications for altruistic motivation. Dev. Psychol. *11*: 607–622.

(13) Murchison, C., and Langer, S., trans. 1927. Tiedemann's observations on the development of the mental faculties of children. Ped. Sem. and J. Genet. Psychol. *34*: 205–230.

(14) Murphy, L. B. 1937. Social Behavior and Child Personality: An Exploratory Study of Some Roots of Sympathy. New York: Columbia University Press.

(15) Piaget, J. 1932. The Moral Judgment of the Child. New York: Harcourt, Brace.

(16) Rheingold, H. L. 1969. The social and socializing infant. In Handbook of Socialization Theory and Research, ed. D. A. Goslin, pp. 779–790. Chicago: Rand McNally.

(17) ———. 1973. Independent behavior of the human infant. In Minnesota Symposia on Child Psychology, ed. A. D. Pick, vol. 7, pp. 178–203. Minneapolis: University of Minnesota Press.

(18) ———. 1977. Sharing at an early age. In New Developments in Behavioral Research: Theory, Method, and Application. In Honor of Sidney W. Bijou, ed. B. C. Etzel, J. M. LeBlanc, and D. M. Baer, pp. 489–502. Hillsdale, N.J.: Lawrence Erlbaum Associates.

(19) Rheingold, H. L., and Eckerman, C. O. 1973. Fear of the stranger: A critical examination. In Advances in Child Development and Behavior, ed. H. W. Reese, 8: 185–222. New York: Academic Press.

(20) Rheingold, H. L.; Hay, D. F.; and West, M. J. 1976. Sharing in the second year of life. Child Dev. 47: 1148–1158.

(21) Ross, H. S., and Goldman, B. D. 1977. Establishing new social relations in infancy. In Advances in the Study of Communication and Affect, ed. T. Alloway, P. Pliner and L. Krames, 3 (Attachment Behavior), 61–79. New York: Plenum.

(22) Ross, H. S., and Hay, D. F. 1977. Conflict and Conflict-Resolution Between 21-Month-Old Peers. Paper presented at the Biennial Meeting of the Society for Research in Child Development, New Orleans.

(23) Sagi, A., and Hoffman, M. L. 1976. Empathetic distress in the newborn. Dev. Psychol. 12: 175–176.

(24) Schaffer, H. R. Acquiring the concept of the dialogue. In Psychological Development From Infancy, ed. M. H. Bornstein and W. Kessen. Hillsdale, N. J.: Lawrence Erlbaum Associates, in press.

(25) Sears, R. R. 1963. Dependency motivation. In Nebraska Symposium on Motivation, ed. M. R. Jones, pp. 25–64. Lincoln: University of Nebraska Press.

(26) Sears, R. R.; Maccoby, E. E.; and Levin, H. 1957. Patterns of Child Rearing. Evanston, Ill.: Row, Peterson.

(27) Shinn, M. W. 1900. The Biography of a Baby. Boston: Houghton Mifflin.

(28) Stayton, D. J.; Hogan, R.; and Ainsworth, M. D. S. 1971. Infant obedience and maternal behavior: The origins of socialization reconsidered. Child Develop. 42: 1057–1069.

(29) Stern, W. 1924. Psychology of Early Childhood Up to the Sixth Year of Age. 3d ed., trans. A. Barwell. New York: Holt.

(30) Valentine, C. W. 1942. The Psychology of Early Childhood. London: Methuen.

(31) Webster's Third New International Dictionary of the English Language, Unabridged. 1965. Springfield, Mass.: G. & C. Merriam.

(32) Zahn-Waxler, C.; King, R. A.; and Radke-Yarrow, M. 1977. The Impact of the Affective Environment on Young Children. Paper presented at the Biennial Meeting of the Society for Research in Child Development, New Orleans.

THE DEVELOPMENT
OF MORAL CONCEPTS

E. Turiel

In considering the development of moral concepts as important for a psychological perspective on morality, I take the position that reasoning is at the core of the individual's moral functioning and that such reasoning undergoes a process of change in ontogenesis. Development, entailing transformations in the structure or organization of moral thought, is a constructive process stemming from the individual's actions upon the social environment. From a relatively young age the individual forms theories about morality; these are theories that are tested and applied and that become transformed. Over time there can be discernible development in the theories maintained by the individual: they may become more consistent, objective, and in greater equilibrium with the social environment.

In viewing morality as a judgmental process, it is necessary to distinguish it from other forms of judgment, and particularly from other forms of nonmoral social judgments. Most commonly, moral prescriptions have not been distinguished from the conventions of social systems. Social organizations have implicit or explicit nonmoral behavioral uniformities that serve to coordinate interactions within the system (32, 33). Such uniformities constitute shared knowledge and are determined by the social system in which they are formed. Social conventions are, therefore, relative to the societal context. In themselves, social-conventional acts are arbitrary, in that they do not have an intrinsically prescriptive basis: alternative courses of action can serve similar functions. That is, a conventional uniformity within one social system may serve the same function as a different uniformity in another social system. In contrast, within the moral domain actions are not arbitrary, and though moral prescriptions form part of social organization, their justification is not based on their status as conventionally determined implicit or explicit regulations. The individual's moral prescriptions (for instance, regarding the value of life) are not determined by convention, but by factors inherent to social relationships; thus morality is not specific to the societal context. This contrast between social convention and morality suggests that there are different experiential sources for the development of an understanding of each domain.

I will return to the issue of experiential origins and the morality-convention distinction. For now, it should be noted that there are two separable questions requiring investigation: (1) how does the individual develop concepts of culture and social organization, and (2) how does the individual develop moral concepts. That is, moral judgments and concepts of social organization constitute two distinct aspects of social-conceptual development. In my view, the failure to distinguish between these two questions, between morality and social convention, has been a major obstacle in the social scientific study of morality.

There have been two main trends in social scientific analyses of moral development from at least the 1920s until the present time. One trend is represented by internalization and social psychological conformist theories (those maintaining that the individual's moral knowledge and behavior represent internal replicas of environmental content) and the other is represented by structural-developmental theories (those maintaining that the individual's moral knowledge and behavior represent internal structures constructed through interaction with the environment). In the 1920s and 1930s some of the prominent social scientists maintaining internalization positions were Durkheim (8), Freud (10, 11), and Hartshorne and May (13). At the time, the structural view was represented by Piaget (23). More recently, the new-behaviorists (28, 36) and social learning theorists (1, 2) have maintained the internalization position, while followers of Piaget have extended his explanation of moral development (16, 17, 26, 30). Though doing so in rather different ways, both approaches have assumed that convention and morality are part of one domain and that they do not develop independently of each other. Internalization theorists, on the one hand, have proposed that moral development is the learning of socially acceptable behavior and the incorporation of transmitted values. In viewing social behaviors and values as the incorporation of externally determined and imposed content, theorists taking this view make no conceptual distinction between different social behaviors. Structural theorists, on the other hand, have maintained that moral development is not an internalization of values, but the construction of universal judgments of right and wrong. However, the specific structural formulations proposed have been based on the presumption that moral judgments apply to all forms of social behavior. As a consequence, convention has been treated as a subclass of the moral.

Furthermore, in empirical research, insufficient attention is given to the appropriateness of the events used to study moral behavior or judgments. This point can be illustrated through an obvious example. Suppose that in order to investigate moral reasoning a researcher posed a series of mathematical problems to subjects of different ages. Of course, such a procedure would be questionable; we could not be at all confident that subjects in the study had engaged in moral reasoning. The inadequacy of using mathematical problems to study moral development would be quite apparent, and as far as I know no one has done so. However, the adequacy of certain types of social situations used by moral development researchers is open to question. As one example, in an experiment (29) on the role of imitation in moral development, children were assigned to do a boring task while a very attractive film was being shown in the same room. Children who left their assigned task to look at the film were considered to have violated a moral standard. The researcher classified "duty and responsibility in performing a job" as a moral standard on the grounds that such behavior reflects a moral value of the society.

But it is not self-evident that the performance of an assigned task is a valid measure of moral behavior. Does it reflect a moral standard or a nonmoral standard which relates to social and economic organization? More generally, it can be asked if all societal values and prohibitions should be categorized as part of the same domain. Consider as examples norms or regulations regarding murder and theft or the values of equality, rights and respect for persons. Also consider norms and regulations regarding sexual behavior, family living arrangements, forms of address or modes of greeting. Are all the various norms and values we could list to be classified within the moral domain and can they all be appropriately used in the study of moral behavior and judgment?

A concrete illustration of the theoretical and methodological problems being raised is provided by the fact that in a rather large number of cases children's acquisition of moral behavior has been studied through experiments in which the behavior measured is whether or not (or the extent to which) the child learns to adhere to a prohibition against playing with some toys available in the experimental room (e.g., pairs of toys are available and the prohibition is against playing with the more attractive of each pair presented). The assumption underlying these studies is that the prohibition and the experimental manipulations, such as administration of rewards and punishments, simulate the naturalistic conditions in which moral behaviors are internalized by children.

The important point regarding this approach is that the action required of the child—to refrain from playing with a designated toy—is an arbitrary one, labeled as "moral" by the researcher. Therefore, such investigations cannot be said to be dealing with moral behavior, unless one assumes that moral behaviors are merely arbitrary acts that become behaviorally nonarbitrary for the individual through the appropriate psychological engineering. That is, a moral behavior is any behavior conditioned or internalized through rewards and punishments. Of course, any such learned moral behavior can just as well be made arbitrary again through its deconditioning (extinction).

The use of arbitrary acts, such as a restriction upon playing with a designated toy, is consistent with the behavioristic view that morality is convention, with convention being defined as conformity to external norms. Moral development is the incorporation of external values and norms of behavior imposed upon the child by socializing agents and/or "society." In behavioristic accounts two basic mechanisms have been proposed to explain how the socialization process is accomplished. One mechanism is the direct conditioning of behavior through the rewards and punishments experienced by the child (1, 20). Because of their rearing function, the parents are most likely to have opportunities to reward and punish the child for socially acceptable and socially unacceptable behavior. A second basic socialization mechanism proposed by behavioristic theorists (2) is the direct copying (imitation) on the part of the child of others' values and behaviors.

It is thus not surprising that morality has been defined as "evaluations of actions generally believed by the members of a given society to be either 'right' or 'wrong'" (3 p. 44). According to this definition morality is relative to the culture; different groups may choose different actions to be designated as morally right or wrong. Moreover, if morality is merely conventional it follows that those who most strongly conform to the group's values, *whichever they might be*, would be considered the most moral individuals in that society: "a person has strong moral values if he shares in the cultural consensus; he agrees with most of the other people in his society as to whether certain acts are 'right' or 'wrong'" (3 p. 44).

Behavioristic theories have assumed a dichotomy between the individual and the group, such that group interests are initially opposed to individual interests and through socialization behaviors are transformed to be consonant with group interests. Another example of this approach can be seen in psychoanalytic explanations of moral development. Psychoanalytic theory is also based on a presumed dichotomy between the individual and society, although relative to behavioristic accounts a more dynamic conflict is posited. According to Freud (11), moral prohibitions of individual aggressive and sexual instincts serve the function of maintaining the social system. The socialization of the child occurs through superego formation, which is the resolution of the inevitable conflict between instinctual impulses and the environmental demands that stem from society's needs to temper and control those impulses. The superego is essentially a largely unconscious incorporation of parental values (ego-ideal) and their regulation by the internalized sanction of guilt (conscience). Given the intensity of individual interests, the regulation of internalized standards must be through forceful means: guilt is aggressive instinctual energies redirected toward the self. As in behaviorism, moral values are seen to be directly derived (through identification with a socializing agent) from the social environment and thus morality is defined as culturally relative convention.

A contrasting approach to the relation of the individual to the social system is based on the assumption that children engage in cognitive activities (an assumption with much empirical support), and that therefore moral development is not reducible to conformity to societal standards. In this view, the developing child is not shaped by the group, but rather forms conceptions about the social environment. As stated at the outset, individuals form prescriptive and descriptive concepts regarding their social world. As a rational process, moral development involves a gradual and continual construction from early childhood—a construction that is based on the child's constant interactions with the social environment. The interaction is a reciprocal one through which the environment is cognitively transformed and cognition is reorganized. Moreover, the individual's relation to nonmoral aspects of social organization is not merely one of conformity, but also entails the conceptualization of conventions.

This view of the development of moral reasoning and concepts of social organization is based on the epistemological and developmental assumptions of "structural-developmental" theory. The basic assumptions, now well known through Piaget's work on cognitive development (24, 25), are that (a) thought is structured in organized systems, (b) structural development is the product of interactions between the individual and the environment, and (c) developmental changes are reflected in progressive restructuring of systems of cognitive organization. The constructivist and interactional thesis, as summarized by Piaget, is that (24 p. 704) "in order to know objects, the subject must act upon them, and therefore transform them: he must displace, connect, combine, take apart, and reassemble them. From the most elementary sensori-motor actions to the most sophisticated intellectual operations, which are interiorized actions, carried out mentally . . . , knowledge is constantly linked with actions or operations, that is, with transformations."

Extensive work on logical-mathematical reasoning and concepts about physical phenomena has shown that development progresses through a lawful sequence of stages. Whereas there is individual and cross-cultural variability in the rate of change and ultimate extent of development, the sequence of stages has been found to be the same in a large number of cultural settings (7). Research on moral reasoning has been less extensive and at the present time our knowledge of moral development is more tentative. Nevertheless, there is a growing body of evidence indicating that individuals systematically progress through a series of structural transformations in the moral domain as well (6, 16, 17, 23, 30, 31). Such transformations refer to structures of thought and are descriptive of *how* moral judgments are made. That is, the surface content of responses or knowledge of cultural values, in themselves, do not provide an understanding of how moral judgments are made (the structure of thought) nor of how development occurs (the sequence of structures of thought).

Research into children's moral judgments was first conducted by Piaget (23) over forty years ago and recently extended by Kohlberg (16, 17). In that early work, Piaget proposed that following a premoral phase, moral development proceeds through two stages: the first being labeled *heteronomous* (generally corresponding to ages 3 to 8) and the second *autonomous*. According to Piaget, the child's moral orientation develops from an attitude of unilateral respect for adult authority to relationships of mutual respect among equals. At the heteronomous level, morality is based on a nonmutual but unilateral respect the child feels toward adults (regarded as authority). At this level, rules are viewed as fixed and unalterable. In turn, the social order and its adult authorities are regarded as sacred.

Developmentally, the young child's morality of unilateral respect becomes reorganized into a morality of cooperation and mutual respect. The basis for this autonomous stage is the emergence of concepts of reciprocity and equality. At this level rules are no longer regarded as fixed or sacred, but are viewed as products of mutual agreement, serving the aims of cooperation, and thus, are regarded as changeable.

Kohlberg has modified and extended Piaget's two-stage system into a six-stage system. The major modifications made in the stages formulated by Kohlberg are that at the earliest levels moral judgments are based not on respect for authority and rules but on an orientation to punishment, and that those early stages are followed in adolescence by an orientation toward maintaining the rules and laws of the social system. At the most advanced developmental levels moral judgments are autonomous and based on principles of justice.

A number of studies based on these stage formulations have been conducted in various cultures. Studies were done with children and adults in Kenya (9), Mexico (16), Honduras (12), the Bahamas (35), India (22), and Turkey (34). The findings of these studies paralleled the cross-cultural studies of nonsocial cognitive development mentioned earlier: the same sequence of development was observed in all those settings, though the rates and extent of development did vary.

The systematic process of construction in development is evidenced in a series of studies, which show that stage transitions involve gradual reorganization of one structure into the next. Direct instruction of moral content is not successful in producing changes in children's thinking. In both short-term experiments (15, 30) and long-term (6 to 12 months) educational interventions (4), it was only possible to stimulate very small amounts of change toward the next developmental stage. Moreover, it has been found (26, 27) that children and adolescents are able, at best, to comprehend only the reasoning corresponding to the stage directly above their own; they are unable to comprehend reasoning at any of the levels more distant from their own. It appears from the results of these studies that there is an inherent directionality in development, and that the child's existing stage defines the way he interacts with the environment. Thus the existing form of reasoning sets limits upon the type of change that can be stimulated.

Whereas the stages formulated by Piaget and Kohlberg, as well as the related experimental, educational, and cross-cultural research support a structural interpretation of moral development, it should not be assumed that the extant descriptions of moral judgment are fully adequate. Quite to the contrary, it is my view that those stage descriptions are formulated in too global a fashion, encompassing more than the moral domain. As stated earlier, these stage descriptions have also failed to distinguish between individuals' moral prescriptions and their descriptive understanding of culture and social organization.

Piaget and Kohlberg have relied on a "differentiation" model that assumes moral reasoning emerges out of its separation from nonmoral processes. Such a model has been widely used in psychology (18, 19) and sometimes in anthropological explanations of the moral evolution of social systems (14): presumably, less developed moral systems are based on conformity to conventionally defined rules, whereas more advanced systems are based on principles distinct from conventional rules. In the Piaget and Kohlberg formulations of ontogenesis, social-convention is treated as part of *moral* development and relegated to early developmental states. That is, it is assumed that development progresses from a state of conformity to the conventions of the social system, to a state of autonomous and principled moral reasoning; the most advanced forms of moral judgment are defined as those in which concepts of justice *displace* concepts of convention and social organization.

The basis for these differentiation models seems to be that societal rules and conventions are deemed simpler than more complex moral principles. This assumption needs to be questioned, however. If we focus on the phenomena of culture and social organization in themselves (i.e., independent of moral issues), it becomes apparent that these are not simple to comprehend. Indeed, anthropologists and sociologists provide complex and abstract theories in efforts to explain cultural systems. Social scientists are not the only ones who seek to understand and explain social organizations and their conventional regularities. It is plausible to suppose that members of a social system, like social scientists, engage in efforts to explain its structure and form a comprehension of the functions of convention in social interactions. It is also plausible to suppose that by at least early childhood, when the individual is already engaging in group activities, concepts of social convention and social organization would begin to develop.

Indeed, my own studies (32) show that children, adolescents, and young adults form concepts of social organization which structure their thinking about such conventional issues. It has been found that there is an age-related sequence, in which concepts of social convention are closely tied to the individual's conception of social organization. In ontogenesis there is a systematic sequence of change in the conceptualization of social systems and in the understanding of the connections between convention and social structure. Other research indicates that as early as infancy social conventions are used in consistently organized ways. For instance, infants begin to use conventions in communication and games (5).

Recent research shows that children as young as three or four years of age make distinctively moral judgments (6). Furthermore, another series of studies (21, 33) support the proposition that social-conventional and moral concepts develop in parallel fashion: young children, as well as older children and adolescents, do distinguish the two domains. In these studies concepts of social regulations were examined. One of the important distinguishing features between morality and convention, from the point of view of the individual's concepts, is that moral acts are justified on the basis of factors intrinsic to actions, whereas conventional acts are justified by their relation to implicit or explicit regulations.

Accordingly, in the moral domain the existence of a social regulation is not necessary for a child to view an event as a transgression. If, for example, one hits another and, thereby, causes physical harm, a child's perception of that event as a transgression would stem from features intrinsic to the event (e.g., from a perception of the consequences to the victim). In such cases a rule would stem from the act to which it pertains; it is only violations of implicit or explicit regulations that can be considered transgressions. For a child to regard a particular act as a transgression, he would have to possess culture-specific information about the act's status as a socially determined regularity.

This type of distinction is understood by four and five-year-olds. As an example, in one study systematic observations were made in a number of preschool settings of social behaviors that could be classified as either social-conventional or moral according to preestablished criteria. Children were asked questions about some of these events, which they had witnessed. Through this procedure we were able to determine that the large majority of those children discriminated between the two types of events. The children's evaluations of social-conventional acts were tied to the existence of regulations in the school, while evaluations about the moral events were not based on the presence or absence of regulations. As indicated by similar findings from studies with subjects from six to nineteen years of age, the morality-convention distinction is made across development levels.

It appears, therefore, that concepts of social organization and moral concepts develop in parallel fashion. Within each domain there is a long-term ontogenetic sequence entailing cognitive constructions generated through individual-environment interactions. Moreover, the finding that young children are able to discriminate between the two domains is further indication that reasoning is at the core of moral functioning. If individuals' values and behaviors reflected social conformity, it is unlikely that they would distinguish between different types of societal regulations. The conceptual discriminations made by children between moral and conventional regulation are the result of abstractions from experience. Finally, these findings also show that for an adequate analysis of individuals' moral judgments, it is necessary that social convention be distinguished from morality.

At the outset I stated that traditionally social scientists have assumed that the individual's moral behavior is environmentally determined. According to those views, moral regulations exist by convention and thus differ from setting to setting. If morality is convention, it follows that it is relative to the culture and that there is no rational basis for evaluating moral systems. Among some social scientists there now appears to be a shift from environmentalism to the view that morality is biologically determined. It may be that such a shift is due to a recognition of the inadequacies in reducing morality to convention. The search for nonarbitrary and universal features in moral behavior has led some to explain it as a function of innate behaviors and ideas. While nativism may be a parsimonious way of explaining universality in human thought, it is not necessarily the most correct. A rejection of a cognitively passive-to-the-environment organism should not result in the assertion of a cognitively passive-to-biological-structures organism. Morality and convention are different aspects of social regulation, and each conceptual domain emerges out of individual-environment interactions. Social concepts are neither direct copies of environmental content nor direct products of biological maturation. In attempting to understand the social world the developing child engages in intellectual activities.

REFERENCES

(1) Aronfreed, J. 1968. Conduct and Conscience: The Socialization of Internalized Control Over Behavior. New York: Academic Press.

(2) Bandura, A., and Walters, R. H. 1963. Social Learning and Personality Development. New York: Holt, Rinehart, and Winston.

(3) Berkowitz, L. 1964. Development of Motives and Values in a Child. New York: Basic Books.

(4) Blatt, M., and Kohlberg, L. 1975. The effects of classroom moral discussion on the development of moral judgment. J. Moral Educ. 2: 129–161.

(5) Bruner, J. S. 1974/1975. From communication to language: a psychological perspective. Cognition. 3: 255–287.

(6) Damon, W. 1977. The Social World of the Child. San Francisco: Jossey-Bass.

(7) Dasen, R. P. 1972. Cross-cultural Piagetian research: A summary. J. Cross-Cult. Psychol. *3*: 23–40.

(8) Durkheim, E. 1925. Moral Education. Glencoe, Ill.: The Free Press.

(9) Edwards, C. P. 1975. Societal complexity and moral development: a Kenyan study. Ethos. *3*: 505–527.

(10) Freud, S. 1923. The Ego and the Id. New York: W. W. Norton.

(11) ———. 1930. Civilization and its Discontents. New York: W. W. Norton.

(12) Gorsuch, R. L., and Barnes, M. L. 1973. Stages of ethical reasoning and moral norms of Carib youths. J. Cross-Cult. Psychol. *4*: 283–301.

(13) Hartshorne, H., and May, M. S. 1928–1930. Studies in the Nature of Character: Studies in Deceit, Vol. I; Studies in Self-control, Vol. II; Studies in the Organization of Character, Vol. III. New York: Macmillan.

(14) Hobhouse, L. T. 1906. Morals in Evolution. London: Chapman and Hall.

(15) Keasey, C. B. 1973. Experimentally induced changes in moral principles and reasoning. J. Person. and Soc. Psychol. *26*: 30–38.

(16) Kohlberg, L. 1969. Stage and Sequence: The cognitive developmental approach to socialization. *In* Handbook of Socialization Theory and Research. Ed. D. Goslin, pp. 347–480. Chicago: Rand McNally and Co.

(17) ———. 1976. Moral stages and moralization: the cognitive-developmental approach. *In* Moral Development and Behavior: Theory, Research and Social Issues, ed. T. Lickona, pp. 31–53. New York: Holt, Rinehart, and Winston.

(18) Loevinger, J. 1976. Ego Development: Conceptions and Theories. San Francisco: Jossey-Bass.

(19) McDougall, W. 1908. An Introduction to Social Psychology. London: Methuen.

(20) Miller, N. E., and Dollard, J. 1941. Social Learning and Imitation. New Haven: Yale University Press.

(21) Nucci, L., and Turiel, E. 1978. Social interactions and the development of social concepts in pre-school children. Child Dev., in press.

(22) Parikh, B. 1975. Moral Judgment and Development and Its Re-

lation to Family Environmental Factors in Indian and American Upper-Middle Class Families. Ph.D. Boston University.

(23) Piaget, J. 1932. The Moral Judgment of the Child. Glencoe, Ill.: Free Press.

(24) Piaget, J. 1970a. Piaget's theory. In Carmichael's Manual of Child Psychology. Ed. P. H. Mussen, pp. 703–732. New York: Wiley.

(25) Piaget, J. 1970b. Structuralism. New York: Basic Books.

(26) Rest, J. R. 1976. New approaches in the assessment of moral judgment. In Moral Development: Theory, Research and Social Issues. Ed. T. Lickona, pp. 198–218. New York: Holt, Rinehart, and Winston.

(27) Rest, J., Turiel, E., and Kohlberg, L. 1969. Level of moral development as a determinant of preference and comprehension of moral judgments made by others. J. Person. 37: 225–252.

(28) Sears, R. R., Maccoby, E. E., and Leven, H. 1957. Patterns of Child Rearing. Evanston, Ill.: Row, Peterson.

(29) Stein, A. 1967. Imitation of resistance to temptation. Child Dev. 38: 157–169.

(30) Turiel, E. 1969. Developmental processes in the child's moral thinking. In Trends and Issues in Developmental Psychology. Ed. P. H. Mussen, J. Langer, and M. Covington, pp. 92–133. New York: Holt, Rinehart, and Winston.

(31) Turiel, E. 1974. Conflict and transition in adolescent moral development. Child Dev. 45: 14–29.

(32) ———. The development of concepts of social structure: social-convention. In Personality and Social Development. Ed. J. Glick and A. Clarke-Stewart, vol. 3. New York: Gardner Press, in press.

(33) ———. 1978b. Distinct conceptual and developmental domains: social-convention and morality. In Nebraska Symposium on Motivation, 1977. Lincoln: Nebraska University Press, in press.

(34) Turiel, E., Edwards, C. P., and Kohlberg, L. 1978. Moral development in Turkish children, adolescents and young adults. J. Cross-Cult. Psychol.

(35) White, C. B. 1975. Moral development in Bahamian school children. A cross-cultural examination of Kohlberg's stages of moral reasoning. Dev. Psychol. 11: 535–536.

(36) Whiting, J. W. M. 1960. Resource mediation and learning by identification. *In* Personality Development in Children, eds. I. Iscoe and H. W. Stevenson, pp. 112–126. Austin: University of Texas Press.

PSYCHIATRY, BIOLOGY
AND MORALS

F. A. Jenner

"Moral behavior" in this paper will usually refer to behavior that is intentionally compassionate. It is axiomatic that one's ego ideal is satisfied by such behavior. Hence moral behavior could be viewed as satisfying a "higher" selfishness and therefore lacking moral worth. Regardless of this apparent terminological paradox, the problem to be approached here is how far can a clinical psychiatrist feel content with a naturalistic approach to morality defined in terms of compassionate intent. The term *naturalistic* is taken here to imply mechanistic and predictable; the term *biological* to imply chemical, physical, or sociobiological and genetic.

We can concede at the outset that a totally biological explanation of man could conceivably be achieved. But the clinician can ask only how much has been explained and with what degree of confidence that explanation can be accepted. A particular problem arises for the clinician from explanations in terms of natural selection, since, given sufficient ingenuity, it seems possible to produce a selective hypothesis for the origin of any biological feature, especially since any feature may be selected as a consequence of a "package deal" as a necessary concomitant of another highly adaptive feature of the individual or his behavior. Our problem is thus to grasp the reasons for changing the status of a hypothesis from the conceivably to the probably valid.

In accord with the philosophical body-mind dualism, psychiatric discussions take place at two distinct levels: (a) the anthropological, sociological, psychodynamic, and cultural; and (b) neurophysiological, genetic, ethological, and sociobiological. At level (a), functional and purposive explanations are more obviously appropriate than at level (b), at which the aim is to reduce functional to causal explanations. For that reason, mental processes invoked at level (a) necessarily become brain processes. What we will ultimately accept as an explanation usually involves both functional and causal concepts at level (b). We inflict so much on our language and our reality that the most important metaphysical questions are complicated mixtures of linguistic and psychodynamic problems. I take this viewpoint to be quasi neo-Kantian.

A completely mechanistic explanation of man would be deterministic and, while not necessarily a case of *reductio ad absurdum*, it would nevertheless seem strange. Clinical psychiatry would, of course, be compatible with such an explanation and classical psychoanalytical theory actually espouses it. Such an explanation would allow one to grasp the consequences of one's acts and to know oneself. It brings us close to the Hegelian notion of the emergence of the spirit, or to the notion of the Way as conceived by Far Eastern moral philosophy. In day-to-day psychiatric practice such a level of Freudian psychodeterminism is usually taken for granted. Within that deterministic framework, there is adequate room for compassionate intentions, and perhaps even a hope for the emergence of a "better man." To see the right way is the cause of its espousal.

In general, psychodynamic theories do not, however, see therapy at such an intellectual level; catharsis and other emotional experiences with the therapist, rather than self-knowledge, are thought to be necessary to release the patient from his neurosis. Only after discharge of pent-up affects would he be free to be himself, let alone to be truly moral. In any case, the goal of both psychotherapeutic approaches is to free the patient to be himself, so that he can be freed *from* himself. As Alan Watts (38) observed, Western psychotherapy and Far Eastern philosophy have much in common. Both lead to the discovery (made belatedly in the West by Hume) that the self is an illusion. By and large (but not always) it seems to be good to release people from the consequences of their selfhood, such as high levels of anxiety, jealousy, delusion, and depression. That is the ethic of the clinician.

Self, however, and selfishness are concepts for the proper use of which clinical psychiatry requires philosophical assistance. Selfhood evidently depends on memory and on neural circuits with negative feedback loops, notions that follow from Claude Bernard's recognition that the body must keep the internal milieu invariant in the face of a variable environment. It is almost tautological therefore to allege that such circuits are "selfish." The conscious element of the circuits, however, does add a new dimension: grasping mutuality and seeing that there are fates worse than death raises the paradoxical possibility that the self is not, after all, selfish.

In psychiatry, biological hypotheses (which often turn out to be mistaken) influence treatment regimes and reduce therapeutic optimism before they are tested. Indeed in many cases it is almost impossible to test them fully. Moreover, in many cases intelligent concern is not of value for treatment and genetic explanations, though interesting, are usually therapeutically irrelevant. We cannot know the limits which they impose or the possibilities which they open. The genetic contribution to the susceptibility to schizophrenia is an obvious example. Despite the apparently biological basis of schizophrenia, it has been possible recently to free the patient from the iron grip of a genetically determined, hopeless prognosis, because drugs and changes of the human environment have both been shown to be therapeutically effective.

The excitement engendered by sociobiology arises from its possible application to man. The danger implicit in that application is that here too hypotheses of man's genetic limitations are taken too seriously, and that meanwhile other more direct approaches to the relief of difficulties in the human condition are neglected. Moreover, if it is true that in the study of human behavior we tend to get the answers that are inherent in our questions, the criticism to be leveled at sociobiology is not just tactical. There is likely to be associated with sociobiology a distortion of reality, possibly involving the discovery of an ethically neutral world, and the denial of the conflict of interests often characteristic of mental illness and other psychopathological behavior.

From my personal position, the need to focus discussion of the moral on the mentalistic is central. Intentions could be epiphenomena, and sometimes probably are, but one is bound to believe otherwise. That belief is the essential dualism of body and mind, without which the evolution of consciousness is not easily explained by Darwinism. The body-mind correspondence needed for a plausible Darwinistic account of man must therefore be bought at the price of a nonparsimonious, incoherent theory of psychophysical parallelism. Rejection of dualism in favor of a coherent outlook probably leads to panpsychicism, which would radically alter chemistry and physics, but not psychology and psychiatry.

I have given what seems to me a necessary statement of a possible working position for a clinical psychiatrist. Admittedly, most human behavior, as seen in psychiatric clinics, does seem to be egotistical, or controlled by a conventional restrictive superego, into which the sentiments of a social group have been introjected. Nevertheless, compassion can and does arise for another person's experiences. This could have originated as part of a package deal in evolution. Our ability to formulate norms may have given rise to the capacity for compassion. But the capacity for compassion may have arisen evolutionarily; it seems more valuable to learn how to develop its realization ontogenetically. Of course, the development of compassion without intelligence has great dangers too. As envisaged by Nietzsche, it may produce chaos and squalor, which authoritarian elitism can avoid. Can democracy?

Even if we grant humans "pure curiosity," we can hardly deny that they (we) still do particular things for particular reasons, and that our reasons are our real values. The choice of subject to be explored and the level at which we study it are therefore topics for psychodynamic inquiries, which are bound to reveal that unconscious motives play a part. For instance, subtle, cynical selfishness with a veneer of social skills is common among scientists. This personality trait is consistent with the way that they set out to explain the world mechanically. It can, using an analog of the super-ego—the introjected parent figure—partially explain the scientists' own and other people's deluded morality. Were these other people to see the truth, they too would be as cynical as the scientists, but wise enough not to show it. They might lead to a general belief that "compassion is foolish," but the psychiatrist must then ask "foolish for whom?"

For the adamant, there is no discernible logical limit to a possible naturalistic explanation of man; the degree of success of such an explanation at any period of history marks simply how far we have traveled toward that goal. It is precarious to generalize from what has been explained to what has not yet been explained, and confidence in the (Kuhnian) paradigm used for such generalization is faith, but the degree of success brought to the attempts to explain man by use of nonteleological, amoral arguments using concepts such as change and randomness (but also cause when convenient) is remarkable. No philosophy or psychodynamic theory that fails to grasp and grapple with this fact is worthy of much attention.

What then is raised for a psychiatrist by the question of whether morality is a biological phenomenon? It is not whether man was produced by evolutionary forces, for as Leonardo wrote: "Naturally Nature has so disposed me." Rather the question is ontological: what exactly are these evolutionary forces and what does their role imply clinically? How much scope for freedom is there in man? Was Durkheim (6) correct to separate sociology from psychology, for example, and how far must the other levels of discourse also be treated separately, at least for practical purposes? Should we accept two apparently inconsistent formulations of human behavior because for practical purposes both are useful at their own levels of explanation?

The problems of the psychiatric clinic do not lie outside the scope of a unified biology. To claim that they do would be to deny a tautology. Indeed, psychiatry itself is among the biological phenomena to be explained.

But in psychiatry the word *biological* currently designates the intellectual allegiances of clinicians convinced of the limited value of such "soft" disciplines as psychoanalysis, sociology, and phenomenology. Moreover, and more acceptably, the biological psychiatrist can use biological terms to define his field of interest. Who is to have drugs, rather than his time? Otherwise the couplet Biological Psychiatry is a pleonasm.

There is, though, a hidden question raised by biological psychiatry: to what degree should extrapolation from, or application of, other subjects (such as neurophysiology, animal behavior, biochemistry, genetics, and ethology) as they are currently developed, influence the clinician or the psychopathologist in his attempt to produce a theoretical basis for the arbitrarily defined profession of psychiatry? This question must be posed for a limited time span. We cannot profitably discuss what could conceivably happen in future centuries, when each of these subjects might have changed into a discipline quite beyond our present ken.

Another related question that distinguishes the problem of the reduction of psychiatry to biology from that of the reduction of biology to physics and chemistry is connected with human understanding—the *Verstehen* of Brentano (4), Weber (39), and Jaspers (16), namely: Is the way of thinking about people different from thinking about anything else because one knows "What it is to be a man"? If the answer is affirmative, then Existential Psychiatry or the Phenomenological Psychiatry of Binswanger (2) leads to "quasi- or nonscientific knowledge," which is analogous to literature and quite clearly valid, but inappropriately called "biological."

The limitations of what has been "explained" so far in human behavior become apparent when experience suggests that given enough time much of the behavior of most individuals can be "understood." There is something very strange about molecules as we think of them as producing meaning and moral sentiments. What works in the clinic (not all that much, I am afraid) has its own claim for serious consideration. Theories corroborated in humans are the only ones on which the clinician can rely, and he knows that his own moral concern is part of the equations he has to solve.

Animals show such social behavior as cooperative grooming and maternal and family care, but we do not learn from that fact that human beings are social animals. Moreover, the human use of a formal language brings a qualitative difference to social intercourse. For instance, language extends the tacit nonverbal assumption that A would be cross with B if aware that B is consciously misleading him: though one may decide to react overtly to false expression, one inevitably implies in conversations that indifference to honesty is inappropriate. The possibility of using language to mislead rather than to inform can only develop secondarily. Without a general practice of teaching the agreed upon words for things to children, language could not exist. This may not be a very important point, but it illustrates that human behavior is primarily social and only secondarily antisocial. Furthermore, it shows that honesty is high in the hierarchy of virtues: honesty is a general habit. This point can be used also to identify what behavior "usually" causes guilt feelings in some of us and shame in even more of us. It perhaps refines the concept of selfishness and defines the normal limits of brutish indifference. To modify Hobbes's (13) dictum, it is only during war that enmity and cheating are virtues; for even if Hobbes were right in saying that a commonwealth is required to give the concept of justice meaning, there is in fact no "state of nature" for man. The helplessness of the human infant and its dependence on maternal instinctive care sets the lifelong scene for mutual trust.

Unrestrained moral optimism, uninformed by any experience, is a folly of the young. But has biology a conceptual framework adequate to explain the culturally emergent? The emphasis one suspects in much scientific discussion belies even the emergent evolution before one's eyes. If so much has already been achieved, what is still possible? The natural selection of humans, if not their genetic variability, is also under conscious control.

Behavior itself determines what will survive, in the forests, in the mountains, in the north, or in the south. Conscious behavior can even more severely restrict who shall be allowed to copulate and with whom. Difficulties sometimes arise in discussions of psychiatrists with biologists from explaining behavior in terms of reasons rather than of causes. We sweat to reduce our body temperature, and in that case it is not too difficult to translate reasons into causes. Taylor (33), however, suggests that it is more difficult to explain the behavior of a man driving slowly over ice by reason of the risks involved in causal terms. It is not intrinsically impossible to do so, and allowing for a sufficiently complex theory, even a Skinnerian (Stimulus-Response) approach might provide a complete causal explanation. Having found such an explanation, one would have explained his behavior, but not have understood the man. Might an evolutionary explanation of the development of morals not also be similarly limited? Under such an explanation the experiences humans have, their breakfasts, the way they construe and their moral sentiments would appear to be so much alike that we could not understand them as moral agents. Hence moral development would still be better accounted for in sociological and purposive terms, though the biological explanation might be "really the true one." Or is the biological explanation just the "best one for some purposes or for someone's point of view"? An affect like love that encourages sex and staying together for the sake of the children is after all the biological basis of the family. The family though is currently on trial as a social institution. One needs to be mindful of one's personal prejudice in predicting the outcome of that trial. The family may be saved yet by the embourgeoisement of the Western superego (25) that has produced inertia in the social system and guilt about moral transgressions. The psychiatrist probably feels unable to discern his patients' discontent with their family-forming genes, regardless of the social arrangements noted in other primates. Left on their own, single parent families manage, but their ability to cope depends on such social institutions as the income tax, the family allowance system and nurseries. The environment, as well as the genes, are important for the survival of the family. My own prejudice is based on the acceptance of anthropological studies that show man to be a moderately reluctant monogamous incest-avoiding animal, whose genetic tendencies need a lot of social reinforcement to express themselves fully. The guilt felt by previous generations over premarital sex has virtually disappeared, and with it much sexual shame. Female fear of pregnancy, and some male feeling of responsibility, account for much of the earlier attitudes but not genes. Freud, in fact, published only just in time to still be relevant as re-

gards sexuality; and a sociobiological neo-Darwinism based
on his material would be as parochial and as passé as
Freud himself now seems.

Biological explanations of behavior present no difficulties
when they invoke demonstrated stochastic relations between definable events, and if it admitted that extrapolation
from experimental conditions to the real world is precarious, especially extrapolation that implies that a is nothing
but b, or that x is caused by a y, or that d is analogous to e.
Nevertheless, one must question the merits of a sociobiology
for which it is so confidently claimed that the hypothalamic
and limbic systems "evolved by natural selection. That simple biological statement must be pursued to explain ethics
and ethical philosophers, if not epistemology and epistemologists, at all depths" (42). How do the hypothalamic and
limbic systems come into the picture anyhow? Because
"these centres flood our consciousness with all emotions—
hate, love, guilt, fear, and others." This statement, in gloss-
ing over the problem of dualism that it tacitly raises, reveals
a lack of appreciation of the actual difficulties presented by
biological explanations of the human mind. It underplays
the fact that consciousness does not produce society; instead society forms much of the content of consciousness (1).

The shortcomings of biological explanations of the evolution of consciousness, as demonstrated by James (15), and of
the contribution of consciousness to social and moral behavior of man (and animals), can be too easily obscured.
Few persons would wish to be treated by a psychiatrist
whose approach implies that what they actually feel is not
important for what they do.

Perhaps the communication theory concept of noise is
also relevant for an appreciation of explanations in evolutionary terms. Even a hardheaded neo-Darwinian knows
that the most adapted genotypes do not necessarily survive,
since the hazards of life are so unpredictable. There now
seem to exist grounds for questioning the rigor with which
natural selection can explain even the structure of protein
molecules. Many variant protein molecules appear to have
arisen which presented no increase in adaptive value; but
nevertheless they direct evolution. Noise is, of course, only
variability unexplained by the theory; but if the unexplained variability is high, then the adequacy of the theory

is low, or the factor identified by the theory plays only a minor role in the phenomenon. With these reservations in mind, the psychiatrist is very wary of genetic explanations of human morality. Indeed, he suspects that much of the noise in sociobiological theory is the information that he should discern for his work with people, and that the complexity of the phenomena to be analyzed is too high to hope soon for much reliable knowledge.

Psychiatry, like everyday communication, is based on flimsy intuitive commonsense. But that commonsense perceives that the answers to some questions affect the politics and morals of the profession. This is especially true for questions that the psychiatrist cannot answer about the relative effects on his patient of nature and nurture, of biological and sociological factors, of the patient's remote past and his present environment, and of his cerebral chemistry and interpersonal relations. These existential dilemmas warrant caution in basing treatment on extrapolations from findings on primate behavior, Marxist theory, psychoanalysis, neurophysiology, neo-Darwinianism, and anthropology. Treatment, rather, demands statements of many of the problems of people in terms of conflicts of interest that require diplomatic resolution and a pluralistic acceptance of different value systems and views of reality.

Dawkins (5) sets the scene for this discussion when he writes: "This chapter [The Battle of the Generations] and the next, in which we discuss conflict between mates, could seem horribly cynical and might even be distressing to parents devoted as they are to their children, and to each other. Once again, I must emphasise that I am not talking about conscious motives. Nobody is suggesting children deliberately and consciously deceive their parents because of the selfish genes within them. And I must repeat that when I say something like 'A child should lose no opportunity of cheating . . . lying, deceiving, exploiting . . .' I am using the word 'should' in a special way. I am simply saying that natural selection will tend to favour children who do act in this way, and therefore when we look at wild populations we may expect to see cheating and selfishness within families. The phrase 'the child should cheat' means that genes which tend to make children cheat have an advantage in the gene pool. If there is a human moral to be drawn it is we must teach our children altruism, for we cannot expect it to be part of their biological nature." No one could explain more clearly why a psychiatrist feels that moral behavior is not a biological phenomenon.

The limitations of biological explanations of morality emerge also from the statement by T. H. Huxley (14): "Let us understand once and for all that ethical progress of society depends not on imitating the cosmic process, still less in running away from it, but in combating it."

The psychoanalyst might remark: if we do not interact with our children they die; if we do, we compel them to learn about a world with interpersonal values, and they develop a superego which will act on them rather like their parents have done. Children cannot have things quite their own way, not even, as Melanie Klein (20) says, at the breast. There and elsewhere children have a problem of adapting (a) to the physical environment with which they, by and large, learn not to be cross—that achieves nothing, and (b) by other people, who, as they soon learn, can be manipulated by moral arguments, who coerce them by their own moral arguments but who can also react negatively. Of course, id, superego, ego, and the like, are a mere *façon de parler*, concepts that are less valuable for a generalized theory of the universe than, for example, even Dalton's atoms. But like Dalton's atoms they will do for some purposes, but require alteration for others. Is psychoanalytic language less explanatory of the cheating, blushing, guilt, love, hate, and jealousy of children than the molecular-biological, neo-Darwinian parlance of the natural selection of DNA?

In the living world, the capacity to develop almost any feature is genetically determined. I say almost, because such achievements of space age progress as spare-part surgery and genetic engineering seem to transcend that determination. Nevertheless, currently to be a human being still means to have started life with human DNA. Without a cytoplasmic or uterine environment, a parent or substitute, an education, the DNA's moral capacity is limited. The relative contribution of DNA to the realization of that capacity seems very difficult to assess, the problem being difficult because the concept of capacity is not totally free of "capacity under such and such conditions." Part of the problem is linguistic.

A dog develops a "superego" and seems to feel guilty if trained. Equally, when domesticated he shows jealousy. There is a limited way of understanding canine pleasure, anger, jealousy, hatred, and aggression. There are, however, undoubtedly innate canine tendencies to be faithful and welcoming. They are quite different from the innate feline indifference. "And it isn't any use for you to doubt it: for he will do as he do do and there's no doing anything about it!" (8). Are human personalities equally determined innately? Anthropology suggests that they are not, but the biological approach to morality attempts to affirm that they are.

Trivers (35) sees guilt as an unpleasant emotion that can arise from exploiting others. Dogs seem capable of having it, less so cats. Guilt acts to help one avoid some situations and also often leads to reparation. The income tax service learns the latter fact from anonymous souls who suddenly pay their taxes (depressed patients with unusual guilt and no debit?). Moralistic anger, Trivers implies, stops others from putting one on. Gratitude is the opposite: it rewards Altruism.

Pride, he suggests, is the ability to accept rewards for acceptable behavior; it is the ability to enjoy social status. However, Trivers (35) also points out that gratitude can be an unpleasant feeling—one prefers not to be beholden and therefore obligated, since obligation affects the peck order. The analogies between these affects and animal behavior are, of course, striking. Humans and animals do have much in common, but this recognition is mainly a rediscovery by ethologists of psychodynamics; and its extrapolation to animals is a contribution of psychiatry to the study of animal behavior. It is perhaps reminiscent of the dilemma that surfaced when Pavlovian conditioning seemed inadequate to explain psychodynamics and psychotherapy. The Russian resolution of this paradox is enshrined in Platonov's (28) book: the word is a conditional stimulus. This comparison may be unfair to the worthy attempt to explore the similarities between human and animal moral behavior. We risk offending by not attempting to take man out of his evolutionary context, and to suggest rather that we may explain animal behavior in human terms we grasped long since. However, we must add that it is humans who matter most to us. We know the function of guilt, shame, gratitude, and the dominance-submissive position games of human intercourse. Novelists make their living out of helping us to relive in fantasy the strategies we use. Psychiatrists tire of hearing about them. They can see that it might be interesting to develop comprehensive theories of primate, mammalian, or metazoan behavior but human morality and behavior are still best studied at close quarters. The results of such studies are more reliable if they are still deeply embedded in the social context, since we are bound to live in the world of human politics.

Just as is the case for cerebral metabolism and the distribution of cerebral amines, interspecies behavioral analogies are obvious. But their validation for men requires studies of man. Hence we can only argue that, in view of what is the case for gibbon, rhesus, and marmoset, might it not be also the case in man? The need for human-specific validation is less true for tautologies such as natural selection, and presumably for the general chemistry of human DNA, which, just as the human Kreb's cycle, seems to be shared across the animal kingdom. But these biological universals seem quite remote from the processes of man's morality.

Fairbanks (10) points out that gibbon and rhesus monkeys have very similar mother-infant bonds until sexual maturity, but after that stage the mother rejects the offspring in one species and maintains with it a special relationship for life in the other species. Fairbanks suggests that this ethological finding should make psychiatrists aware that some human "problems in adult behavior (e.g., adjusting to parenthood) may be caused as much by difficulties encountered in maturing from adolescence to adulthood as from patterns that appeared at an earlier stage of development." Of course, they may be so caused, but Fairbanks has a cumbersome way of discovering this homely truth.

The same must be said for Pavlov's demonstration that dogs become "neurotic" and aggressive if they are given impossible discriminatory tasks. This observation certainly confirms the insights into human aggression that inspired it and the fascinating special grandmother-granddaughter relationship of the baboon (10) certainly resembles that often seen in human families, especially in the USSR where Babushka is the only person at home.

Trivers (35) claims that the weaning conflict in animals between mother and offspring arises because the mother cannot conceive while lactating, and she has as much interest (genetic involvement) in the next litter as in the present one. Thus, the offspring's and the mother's real interests are in conflict. This example, according to Weisfeld (41), "demonstrates both the power of ethology to explain an otherwise mystifying behaviour pattern and by contrast the inadequacy of behaviouristic and psychoanalytical explanations not based on biological considerations."

The difficulty with resorting to such theories in a psychiatric context arises from the uncertainty of the extent to which human weaning behavior is genetically influenced. Thus, social influences on weaning human infants are obviously enormous: in some societies breastfeeding is prolonged; in ours it might disappear. Perhaps the structure of the mother's DNA can in some meaningful sense explain her feeling that enough is enough of a good thing, but in humans one must take into account also the social inconvenience, modesty, and the mother's desire to do things other than to have the next litter. How far is she deluded about her own motives? Precisely because humans have developed a conscious grasp of what is needed and involved, we can envisage a future society in which breastfeeding is considered an anachronism, a crude atavism carried on right to the end of the twentieth century.

There is, in some sense, an innate tendency for mothers to want to breastfeed their children; perhaps genes govern behavior in that sort of way. But in humans there arises also the conscious question of the purpose of one's behavior, which questioning may have other evolutionary functions, and which in turns influences behavior. This is how the genetic governance may work.

Whereas innate mechanisms undoubtedly play a role in breastfeeding, the actual behavior in humans is too crudely explained in that way. Calling attention to innate mechanisms may be helpful and promising in terms of suitable advice to mothers. But sociobiology notwithstanding, it is still reasonable, if we want to know what mothers want to do, to ask them or to watch them. It is less illuminating to watch gorillas instead. Some women give breastfeeding up when the child's teeth develop! Eventually, artificial insemination, abortion, euthanasia, test tube babies, and genetic engineering will be the big problems with which human intelligence and morality must grapple. Are they just the sort of developments that show how far man can transcend his genes? How, in this sense, do the memes (Dawkins's (5) word for self-replicating ideas) take over the governance of behavior from the genes? As for moral behavior, Dawkins refers us to the description by Turnbull (36) of the utterly selfish Ik, and in contrast with the gentle altruism of the Arapesh described by Mead (26). This is not a genetic difference. Waddington (37) presumably would have thought that given time it might partially become genetic, in that mutations accentuating sexual advantage in a given cultural context would be favored. The kinematics of adaptation of genes to culture is of course problematic. According to Lowentin (23), mutation rates cannot possibly keep up with cultural and racial changes in behavior.

No one would want to deny the stimulating effects of Lorenz's (22) concept of innate releasing mechanisms, nor Tinbergen's (34) concepts of displaced behavior. The latter is very well illustrated in obsessional neurosis; the patient seems to have the problem of unacceptably aggressive or sexual urges and a fear of their consequences if he gives them full rein. Displaced behavior is the basis of the psychoanalytical model of intrapsychic conflict—id versus superego—and for this case much better ethologically demonstrated in Eckman's (7) intriguing transcultural study of facial expressions in men. These expressions, fairly innate, we clearly share with animals and they deserve further study. The psychiatrist's question is: how do most of us cope with our innate urges so acceptably?

Violence in our society is increasing, as is crime everywhere (30). One suspects that a comparative study of identical and nonidentical twins might possibly show a statistically higher concordance in the monozygotic pairs for operationally defined football hooliganism, and undoubtedly the presence of many different kinds of gene combinations is a necessary condition for violent behavior. But it is hardly a sufficient cause and probably not a very interesting cause for the task of reducing the level of violence. Anyone who has worked with violent persons knows that there are very few of them with whom it is not possible to make friends. Prisoners lend money to fellow inmates, even to strangers, and trust them with as much, if not more, confidence than strangers trust each other on the outside. Prisoners have allegiance on the inside. This allegiance is reflected in their behavior and might be an important therapeutic clue for the therapist and penologist. In fact, the innate capacity for allegiance might be a suitable topic even for the sociobiologist. Allegiance may depend on some innate human bonding.

Apparently, "Detroit, with much the same population size as Northern Ireland, has even in these grim days five times the murders" (30). But the rate of homicide in the United States is now ten to twelve times higher for the black than for the white population. For the latter it is at present not very different from the rate of homicide in Western Europe. Now even if there existed genetic factors responsible for racial differences in intelligence (9, 19) and other aspects of personality, it is rather unlikely that the rate of criminal homicide in a given ethnic group reflects a hereditarily determined tendency. Radzinowicz and King (30) point out that Jewish, Irish, English, and German immigrants to the United States all had, at some time, higher crime rates than the general American population. In England, Irish immigrants have a high crime rate, whereas Pakistani immigrants have a low crime rate, not above that of the English themselves.

The danger of using the current social distribution of crime and morality for drawing facile racial or genetic conclusions is very real and explains the psychiatrist's antipathy to sociobiology. Another source of danger at the opposite end of the ideological spectrum is the New Criminology of Taylor, Walton, and Young (31) which sees moral deviance as normal, in the sense that "men are now consciously involved (in the prison that is contemporary society and in the real prisons) in asserting their human diversity." This is a politically overromanticized way of agreeing with Durkheim (6) that a normal society has a normal crime rate.

These extreme anticonformists nevertheless declared that: "Close reading of the classical social theorists reveals a basic agreement; the abolition of crime is possible under certain social arrangements. Even Durkheim, with his notion of human nature as a fixed biological given, was able to allow for the substantial diminution of crime under conditions of a free division of labor, untrammelled by the inequalities of inherited wealth and the entrenchment of interests of power and authority (by those who were not deserving of it)." However great may be their antipathy to sociobiological conservatism, few psychiatrists would be as unbiologically Utopian as the New Criminologists.

Certainly, as under Rawls's (31) Theory of Justice, so it follows from my remarks about the social contract implicit in conversation that inequality can be justified only to a dispossessed if he perceives it to be in his interest, at least, if he perceives that his interests are being taken seriously. However, a sociobiologist could rightly retort that the human genotype might not be so socially adjustable as to permit honesty; more likely than not, that some persons cannot help deceiving and others cannot help getting cross when they find that they have been deceived.

The growing concern for the current rise in violence must take into account that there is evidence that the crime rate is increasing because, owing to the bulge in the birth rate, the percentage of the population of the age at which social deviance is most marked has recently increased. It is possible, therefore, that the crime rate will now begin to drop continuously regardless of any other social factors.

This problem of violence and crime requires a great deal of thought. Scientific thinking and experimentation is probably the only way to consensus of opinion, but scientism, that is, the overplaying of biological or sociological explanations, though necessary outside the academy where existential decisions are imperative, is to be avoided. The psychiatrist would guess that any generally acceptable view of the criminal would be explicable in a psychoanalysis of the man, his vested interests, his needs, and his superego that does not let him escape from the need to appear to be good.

For the hope of arriving at a general theory of man, the evidence cited by Blakemore's (3) showing that early experience even influences the cat's ability to distinguish vertical from horizontal lines is important. It follows from this evidence that neural connections are not rigidly determined by genetic factors, but like so much in man, depend on the ontogenetic environment (32). The nature of the experientially induced synaptic changes still eludes us, though. It is possible that development begins with an initial superabundance of innate neural pathways and connections. Maturation and learning would then depend on their selection, and about this we still know very little. The possibilities for selection might be determined genetically and limited, as might the structures needed for language development. Indeed, "social maturity" is "an integrated electrophysiology of the brain"; what else could it be? The objects designated by the terms "integrated and mature person" and "brain" are interchangeable. Both evolved in nature and are therefore biological. Both display moral behavior and the avoidance of guilt and shame. Still, the clinician would feel bound to be careful of using the evidence from psychometric measures of maturity or electroencephalographic tracings in preference to talking to the patient, in order to get *zu den Sachen*. Nevertheless, the idea that moral behavior equals mature and thoughtful behavior, certainly dependent on the highest hierarchical level of integration of the inhibitory systems of the frontal lobes, seems undeniable. Stupid, aggressive, and uninhibited behavior results from damage to these systems, and leucotomies release patients excessively constrained to fit in with society from the excessive guilt, inhibition, and tension.

But the crudity of neurophysiological models currently available to explain moral behavior is gross. They amount to little more than the following précis. There are pleasure centers in the brain that are activated in situations of biological gratification, or put in a different way, the activity of which *is* biological gratification (24, 29, 32, 40). The pleasure centers are possibly located in the limbic system, and memory of affective consequences is conceivably stored in their vicinity (24), whereas objective knowledge of the facts seems to be stored holographically in the cerebral cortex.

To illustrate the crudity of neurophysiological models of morality, we may consider a hypothetical but plausible electrical machine with a limited capacity for learning facts for a purpose (to turn on "pleasure centers"). Such a machine requires an internal system able to abstract and represent features of the environment. If able to alter its behavior in the light of experience and to interact with similar machines, this machine would build up knowledge of the others and of its environment. Different interacting groups of such machines would tend to evolve different social rules depending on the contingencies of learning about each other. Different extant machine "cultures" would be explicable in terms of the history of their past interactions.

Moderately complicated machines might learn how to stimulate their model pleasure centers by behavior other than that which satisfied the analog of their biological need (e.g., feeding). Such behavior would necessarily be "studied" and developed and repeated; it would have something of the "aesthetic" about it. By definition it would be highly satisfying, but not "utilitarian." It would have something in common with human opiate addiction, which produces pleasure pharmacologically. A group of such machines would be analogous to modern countercultures preaching the value of drugs to expand consciousness. The discovery of enkephalins opens new vistas in that direction.

It is not difficult to envisage how our machines could be made able to communicate their knowledge, and also how to color it in terms of the perceived effects of such calculated communicating. There are no insuperable difficulties for postulating internalization (largely in the frontal lobes) of inhibitory systems acting on the pleasure centers in terms of previously achieved rewards and punishments. The interacting machines produce a set of social norms, some of which are inevitable because of unavoidable mutual needs, but others of which are contingent, depending on the actual experiences of interaction. We would thus have realized an electrical model of morality.

The design of the required electronics for such machines is not difficult and there does not seem to be anything which humans or animals do that could not be in principle simulated. But the complexity of the real brain makes these models ludicrously simple.

These models can be understood without postulating or referring to "consciousness." We know some necessary conditions for generating consciousness; currently we produce new conscious beings by sexual intercourse and there seems little reason to doubt that eventually other methods of procreation could be found, if we want them. We cannot deny animals consciousness, while granting it to humans, nor avoid the conclusion that the conscious self can be bisected by a split brain operation. Many persons now believe that even computers could be conscious. The fact that certain physical conglomerations are or could be conscious makes most of us hesitate either in using or in avoiding words like *responsibility*, *moral*, and *choice* which presuppose the conscious state.

In French and other Romance languages, the term *conscious* is itself ambiguous, as it is in Shakespeare: "Our conscience doth make cowards of us." It does not distinguish clearly between modern English conscience (German *Gewissen*) and modern English consciousness (German *Bewusstsein*). Its etymology is the Latin, *conscientia* (i.e., joint knowledge), a literal translation of the Greek συνειδηοιφ. The classical terms connote moral complicity, or conniving with. It does not require overwhelmingly convincing scientific evidence to infer that this ambiguity indicates, as do the early chapters of Genesis, an ancient intuitive grasp of the obvious fact that awareness is the prerequisite of morality.

We cannot live in everyday life without acting as though morality depends on intention. For an act to have moral content, it is fairly important that the agent could have acted differently, but that he performed it with the hope that it would have an effect on another person's, or animal's, experience is vital. This is the kind of language that phenomenological psychiatrists wish to reserve for moral discourse, without necessarily etherealizing morality. But it would certainly be foolish to deny outright the possibility of some contribution to our understanding of morality in the languages of molecules, natural selection, and neurophysiology, even if so far that contribution has been rather limited.

In attempting to work within a "nineteenth century" paradigm of mental illness as an abnormal physiochemical process leading to psychosis, I spent many years studying periodic psychoses (17). This group of psychoses is arbitrarily considered as a clinical entity by workers (including myself) who are interested in finding a psychopathological phenomenon for which sociologically and personally meaningful events seem minimally relevant. One of our male patients was in mania every other day for a decade or so, depressed on the days between, and predictably changing mental state and EEG between 00.00 and 02.00 hours. Evidently, he seemed to be suffering from a genuine "illness." Though such patients are rare, an explanation of the pathology of even one such case would be an important demonstration that a scientific, and certainly naturalistic, biological approach to mental processes is, in fact, possible. Our patient responded to lithium and relapsed with placebo, and three years later, after remaining quite well while taking lithium, again relapsed with a placebo (12).

The patient had boxed and, just as other forty-eight hour cycle psychotic patients reported in the literature, possibly had some brain damage (27). His wife said that before the onset of the illness he was "friendly, helpful and industrious; he made furniture the family all value and kept the garden beautifully." During the illness the marriage was in ruins; he was irresponsible, promiscuous, aggressive, drank excessively, and could not be trusted. After treatment, there was a remarkable reconciliation, a new honeymoon, and years later he cared for his wife through her terminal malignancy with every sign of concern and responsible maturity. He then adapted to the bereavement also without illness.

When ill and living in an experimental suite in an abnormal time regime (under an apparent day and night cycle of twenty-two hours), the forty-eight hour rhythm became a forty-four hour rhythm, twice the experienced day. Like the circadian rhythm, the periodic psychosis seemed environmentally entrainable (18).

The moral interest presented by this illness was that the patient felt guilty when depressed and self-righteous when manic. One day he would be overactive, hilarious, and generous if handled sympathetically, but if thwarted he would be violent and aggressive. The manic day's morality was, as in most manic patients, dependent on the environment. The drive is determinant, its direct contingent. Generosity or violent aggression seemed both dependent on the same manic factor. In mania an upper middle-class respectable woman might enjoy sexual relations with a previously unknown lorry driver or she might take out a group of deprived children for the day. Some days later, in depression, she might feel guilty about a minor indiscretion committed twenty years earlier. This erratic behavior pattern can sometimes disappear upon taking lithium salts, a fact of which marriage counselors ought to be aware.

Unfortunately, from symptoms alone one cannot predict which patients will respond to lithium salts; neither is precise periodicity of the psychosis or family history necessarily an adequate indication. Some periodic catatonic patients respond very strikingly to lithium. In our results to date, the symptoms of the catatonic group are susceptible to personally meaningful environmental factors. Thus, the cycle of psychosis is disrupted under the stress of a strange social environment, for example, in another hospital. Affective disorders are less obviously influenced by personally meaningful factors. Another complicating difficulty in treatment arises from some patients being made well by taking lithium salts, and once stabilized remain in remission for long periods without further treatment (in our current series, one to two years); they then relapse. Other patients need sustained treatment to remain in remission. Or, patients made well simply by moves to new hospitals or wards relapse once they become familiar with the new environment.

The difficulties in understanding these phenomena are enormous, both pharmacologically and psychologically, and we cannot even fathom the nature of an explanation that would be adequate to cover social meaning, entrainable rhythm, pharmacology, genetics, and fathoming the possible previous experience releasing the syndrome, or making it possible, is beyond us. Nevertheless, these periodic psychoses illustrate the degree of complexity with which an adequate "biology of morality" must cope. Guilt, shame, aggression, and violence, as well as generosity, drive, and concern, are here discernibly dependent on biological rhythms, changing drive, and optimism. Morality seems low in the etiological hierarchy, or a word useful only in discourses other than the therapeutic.

Freud's (11) concept of the superego being in alliance with the ego in mania sees this alliance as giving uninhibited powers to the manic personality, possibly by an ego defense—denial of depression. Conversely, Freud sees depression, and the blame the person places upon himself, as the tyranny of the superego. We know mania, as well as depression, can follow bereavement and their relation is one of the core constructs of psychiatry, certainly known since Aretaeus ca. A.D. 100. We can see how denial of the limitations of one's own ability may solve many problems by overlooking them, and so dissipate guilt. At the biological level we know that adrenal secretions and other stress responses tend to be inhibited during the manic phase with its successful denial of any problem. The stress responses are raised in the depressive phase, when the patient feels guilty and responsible. On entering his nth manic phase, the patient will explain that his problems are now over after all these years. They are obviously not, and he eventually enters the ntlst depressive phase. We are capable of deluding ourselves, and cerebral mechanisms do underlie both delusions and guilt.

How could one explain an intermittently oscillating superego, susceptible to influence by lithium salts? Psychiatry does not present many such clear questions, but perhaps this question gives an idea of the dimensions of the problem, and accounts for the belief that such rare examples might help to produce heuristically valuable questions, even if not answers.

Psychiatrists commonly encounter unusual or abnormal guilt in affective and obsessional disorders. Shame can be profound in schizophrenia. The psychiatrist, himself encumbered by values produced by his own social context, spends much of his time helping patients to be less morally restricted, while at the same time despairing of their sociopathic behavior. It is sociopathic, not because the patients lack guilt feelings but because they lack social skills. That is why the psychiatrist sees them.

As an agent for the individual, the psychiatrist has little time for moralizing. His values must be adult. His aim is to help people to have the courage or sense to do what will work for them. He certainly notes that the satisfaction of most individuals he sees depends on the respect that others have for them and, ultimately, that they have for themselves. It is the fact that to survive individuals need a good image of themselves, in the introjected eyes of their parents and of others, that makes them moral agents. They often learn to play their cards well. It is, however, important to ask what utility there could be in the sociobiological wisdom that man is really selfish, since he has to be tricked by his superego and education into altruism. Whether or not humans are innately amoral, they need a good image of themselves; without it they become ineffective; and they live in their own perception of other people's views of themselves (21). Much wealth and most learning is to impress others. Few persons rise beyond that level of morality.

Psychiatry has much to learn from biology; in return it can offer an estimate of its real present value. If biologists do their work with compassionate intention, they act morally. If they lack that intention, a biological explanation of morality would be adequate.

REFERENCES

(1) Berger, P. L., and Luckmann, T. 1967. The Social Construction of Reality. Harmondsworth: Penguin.

(2) Binswanger, L. 1942. Grundformen und Erkenntnis menschlichen Daseins. Zürich.

(3) Blakemore, C. 1977. Genetic instructions and developmental plasticity in the kitten's visual cortex. Phil. Trans. R. Soc. Lond. B. *278*: 425–434.

(4) Brentano, F. 1973. Psychology from an Empirical Standpoint. London: Routledge and Kegan Paul.

(5) Dawkins, R. 1976. The Selfish Gene. London: Oxford University Press.

(6) Durkheim, E. 1915. The Elementary Forms of the Religious Life. London: George Allen and Unwin.

(7) Eckman, P., and Friesen, W. V. 1974. The Psychology of Depression: Theory and Research. Washington: Winston.

(8) Eliot, T. S. 1969. The Complete Poems and Plays of T. S. Eliot. London: Faber and Faber.

(9) Eysenck, H. 1973. The Inequality of Man. London: Maurice Temple Smith.

(10) Fairbanks, L. A. 1977. Animal and human behaviour. Guidelines for generalisation across species. *In* Ethology and Psychiatry. London: Grune and Stratton.

(11) Freud, S. 1940. Gesammelte Werke Bd. 13. London: Imago.

(12) Hanna, S. M.; Jenner, F. A.; Pearson, I. B.; Sampson, G. A.; and Thompson, E. A. 1972. The therapeutic effect of lithium carbonate on a patient with a 48 hour periodic psychoses. Brit. J. Psychiat. *121*: 271–280.

(13) Hobbes, T. 1651. Leviathan. (See, for example, the edition edited by M. Oakeshott.) London: Oxford University Press.

(14) Huxley, T. H., and Huxley, J. 1947. Evolution and Ethics 1893–1943. London: Pilot Press.

(15) James, W. 1890. Principles of Psychology. New York: Holt.

(16) Jaspers, K. 1959. Allgemeine Psychopathologie. 7th ed. Berlin: Springer.

(17) Jenner, F. A. 1968. Periodic psychoses in the light of biological rhythm research. Int. Rev. Neurobiol. *11*: 129–169.

(18) Jenner, F. A.; Goodwin, J. C.; Sheridan, M.; Tauber, I. J.; and Lobban, M. 1968. The effect of an altered time regime on biological rhythms in a 48 hour periodic psychosis. Brit. J. Psychiat. *114*: 215–224.

(19) Jensen, A. R. 1973. Educability and Group Differences. London: Methuen.

(20) Klein, M. 1952. Developments in Psychoanalysis. Ed. J. Riviere. London: Hogarth Press.

(21) Laing, R. D.; Phillipson, H.; and Lee, A. R. 1966. Interpersonal Perception. London: Tavistock.

(22) Lorenz, K. Z. 1966. Evolution and Modification of Behaviour. London: Methuen.

(23) Lowentin, R. C. 1976. Sociobiology—a caricature of Darwinism. J. Phil. Sci. Ass. *3*: 11–19.

(24) Luria, A. R. 1973. The Working Brain. London: Penguin Modern Psychological Texts.

(25) Marcuse, H. 1955. Eros and Civilisation. London: Sphere Books.

(26) Mead, M. 1950. Male and Female. London: Gollanz.

(27) Menninger-Lechenthal, E. 1960. Periodizität in der Psychopathologie. Vienna: Wilhelm-Maudrich.

(28) Platonov, K. 1959. The Word as a Physiological and Therapeutic Factor. Moscow: Foreign Languages Publishing House.

(29) Pribram, K. H. 1971. Languages of the Brain. London: Prentice Hall.

(30) Radzinowicz, L., and King, J. 1977. The Growth of Crime. London: Hamish Hamilton.

(31) Rawls, J. 1972. A Theory of Justice. Oxford: Clarendon Press.

(32) Rose, S. 1973. The Conscious Brain. London: Weidenfeld and Nicholson.

(33) Taylor, C. 1964. The Explanation of Behaviour. London: Routledge and Kegan Paul.

(34) Tinbergen, N. 1953. Social Behaviour in Animals. London: Methuen.

(35) Trivers, R. L. 1958. The evolution of reciprocal altruism. Q. Rev. Biol. 46: 35–57.

(36) Turnbull, C. 1972. The Mountain People. London: Jonathan Cape.

(37) Waddington, C. H. 1975. The Evolution of an Evolutionist. Edinburgh: University Press.

(38) Watts, A. W. 1973. Psychotherapy East and West. Harmondsworth: Penguin.

(39) Weber, M. 1930. The Protestant Ethic and the Spirit of Capitalism. London: George Allen and Unwin.

(40) Weil, J. L. 1974. A Neurophysiological Model of Emotional and Intentional Behaviour. Springfield: Thomas.

(41) Weisfeld, G. E. 1977. A sociobiological basis for psychotherapy. In Ethology and Psychiatry. London: Grune and Stratton.

(42) Wilson, E. O. 1975. Sociobiology. The New Synthesis. London: Belknap Press.

(43) Young, J. Z. 1977. Concluding Remarks. Phil. Trans. R. Soc. Lond. B. 278: 435–436.

PART
2

IN SEARCH OF
SOCIAL
UNIVERSALS

LITERACY AND MORAL RATIONALITY

J. Goody

INTRODUCTION

On the surface this paper may appear to have little to do with the theme of the Workshop. I see the link in the following way. To deal with biological elements in morality (e.g., sexual mores, such as prohibitions on "incest") we have to isolate universals, or at least features that crosscut cultures. The response of many social scientists to the efforts to "biologize" social theory is often to stress cultural differences that therefore require a specific cultural explanation (in terms of the fit of meanings or functions). While not wishing to deny the relevance of such an explanation at some level, it seems important to stress two factors. The first is that even universals of morality (and we think that some exist) may have social explanations, that they may be related to organizational prerequisites, as Parsons and others have argued for the prohibition on incest. The second is that differences in moral systems are not only a matter of the "choice" of individual "cultures" (the extreme relativist position) but can sometimes be associated with other differences across a number of human societies, which are themselves linked by spatial, socioeconomic, or developmental factors. Indeed we recognize the importance of evolutionary factors in moral systems, but in the context of social rather than genetic evolution. And the specific factor with which we are here concerned is the influence of the means of communication (and specifically, literacy) on moral norms and on the "rationality" of those norms.

Even those convinced of their own rationality (as against someone else's irrationality or nonrationality) are vague about what this quality entails, or even when it was acquired. Aristotle viewed rationality as exclusively human, indeed as defining humanity (19). Others have seen rationality as characteristic of literate man, the art of writing, setting up a boundary not between man and animal but between savage and civilized, while yet another school locates the Great Divide at the time when writing was mechanized by the introduction of print and the rise of modern science.

Anthropologists of liberal persuasion have tended to take the Aristotelian view and their work has leaned toward the position that if all men are not rational, at least all mankind is. They have rejected the nonrationality of the savage (irrationality is a characteristic of us all) and concerned themselves with explicating the relationship that he assumes between his ends and his means. In this way, they have, in a substantive sense, made intelligible the unintelligible and explained the inexplicable.

Other writers have phrased the difference between "us" and "them" as a matter of logic rather than rationality, though the distinction is frequently of a rather casual kind. Once again the cultural relativist, as represented by Evans-Pritchard (5), steps forward to dismiss the Grand Dichotomy of Lévy-Bruhl (17) between "us," the logical, and "them," the prelogical (or nonlogical). As in Pareto, the logical appears to be identified with the rational and it is this very logic that the Azande people are shown to have in abundance (see also Gluckman (7, 8) and for other discussions (29)).

This weak use of the concept of rationality really comes down to intelligibility, the test being that a belief possessing it can be understood and explained. But once again we are faced with the question of "understood by whom" and "in whose terms." A sympathetic observer may empathize with the objects of his inquiries in a process of *verstehen*. Or an analytic observer may render a belief intelligible in terms of a particular schema, such as the logic from Aristotle's *Organon*. For rationality clearly cannot be confined to the application of our procedural rules of logic; and it follows that it is perfectly possible, as Lévy-Bruhl maintained and Evans-Pritchard denied, for a set of beliefs to be rational but nonlogical (or even prelogical), although the implications of this statement are certainly not those drawn by Lévy-Bruhl.

Other anthropologists have adopted a stronger use of rationality, the weaker one being taken as universal. Nadel discusses the situation with characteristic incisiveness. It will not do to specify rational action solely in terms of understanding "the 'subjective' purpose of the actions and their conception of one mode of an action as a 'means' and of another as the 'end.'" Neither can the "objective" determination in terms of needs or functions not consciously pursued by the actors serve as the sole specification of rational action. Rational relations are those in which the "nexus of subjective intentions coincides with that of an 'objective' purpose intelligible to the observer" (20). Rationality is "purposiveness plus something else, namely, the fact that the steps taken to achieve the purposive appear by their nature appropriate and empirically sound" (20, 21).

The stronger concept of rationality, as used by (some) philosophers, is rather different from that of the social scientist. Warnock begins with the minimal definition; rationality is still connected with "some ability to perceive and consider alternative courses of action, to appreciate what is to be said for or against the alternatives, to make a choice or decision, and to act accordingly" (27). The exercise of rationality is seen as characterizing a language-using animal and is in practice confined to human beings. Besides this minimal use of rational, the ability is "in at least some degree to envisage practical alternatives, to deliberate, and to decide." And, there is yet the most exacting sense of "being regularly disposed to deliberate well and to act accordingly" (27). The additional criteria are no longer empirical (20), but evaluative. The process involves the differentiation of good from bad, of right from wrong, which, while the rules may differ from society to society, as historians and anthropologists may be concerned to point out, are in themselves universal as "moral concepts" (27). Being rational is not simply the process of judgment, but of making the right judgment, an end that is associated with the presence of goodwill, of humane intentions, of human sympathies. "Is not the case that much of the failure of human sympathy is itself the direct offspring of unreason? Racial hostility . . . is not merely . . . a gross defect of human sympathy; it is also . . . a gross deformation of rationality. If people were saner, their sympathies also would be less stunted and deformed" (27).

Morality and rationality, then, are both universal and universalistic. The medieval Scottish chieftain who "acted morally badly in slaughtering all the rival clansmen whom he had invited to a banquet, does not know . . . what morality is . . ." (27). Morality, then, in the sense that it is understood in this philosophical discourse, is universalistic, that is, as distinct from the particularism of earlier societies. The code of a headhunting tribe, Warnock claims, cannot be a morality. Closed systems are limited, bounded, whereas morality applies to everyone, to all rational beings. In a different context, Williams points out that the "appeal to the consequences of an *imagined* universalization is an essentially moral argument" (28).

"Universalism" was seen by Max Weber as characteristic of rational-legal societies, of those governed by bureaucratic rather than traditional authority. It is an idea much elaborated by Parsons (21) and by those influenced by him (e.g., Fallers) who have contrasted this pattern variable with the "particularism" of simpler social systems. The particularity of moral judgments consists essentially of what Southall (26) (following Durkheim, Radcliffe-Brown, Fortes, and Evans-Pritchard) has discussed as the segmental nature of morality. Adultery with the wife of a fellow member of a lineage or age-set is differently regarded, in prospect and in sanction, than the same act with an outsider. The point is more obviously true of homicide, which may remain unpunished in the family, the subject of compensation among close kin, of feud with nonkinsmen and war with outsiders. Clearly the segmentation of moral values is associated with the segmentary nature of Nuer or Alur society, the virtual absence of centralized judicial institutions that could impose a national code. (This statement is not a resort to reflex theory; one could claim that the two structures were isomorphic, but that would be to reify the "structures." More adequately, it can be held that the structure of moral rules is an intrinsic aspect of the structure of social relations.) All societies, however, even the most centralized, are segmented into subunits. We too judge acts differently depending upon the unit to which a man belongs, upon the social distance between the actors involved, or upon the context of social relations. The injunction "Thou shalt not kill" clearly does not apply when a man is dressed in a khaki uniform and Warnock's radical distinction between closed and open moralities is unacceptable, except as a matter of degree or in respect to norms of the highest order of generality.

But there is at least one other important factor in the distinction between universalism and particularism, namely, the intervention of writing and its effect on moral norms, indeed on all norms. It is perhaps easiest to approach this discussion by returning to the subject of logic, "our" logic, which has so often been confused with the wider problem of rationality, either in its weaker or its stronger forms (as Nadel sees them, not, for the moment, as Warnock does).

In a paper entitled "The Consequences of Literacy," Watt and I claimed that the kind of procedures associated with logic, that is, "our logic," was critically linked to the emergence of the alphabet in Greece (12). Most superficially there was its connection with letters as in the syllogism, but the problem goes much deeper. It is of central importance here to note that Vygotsky and other investigators have used the presence of "syllogistic reasoning" as a way of distinguishing between advanced and primitive populations, for example, between schooled and unschooled groups in central Asia and elsewhere (see esp. the works of M. Cole, and the discussion in Cole and Scribner (1)). While the specific form of the syllogism is clearly connected with letters, and hence with the appearance of the alphabet, there is a more fundamental sense in which this type of reasoning represents the kind of decontextualized procedures that are encouraged by all forms of writing and is foreshadowed in the prealphabetic activity of Mesopotamian scribes (10). These scribes developed such analytic forms as the list, the formula, the table, and the recipe. The same could be said of the kind of investigation into contradiction and similarity (17), into analogy and polarity (18), which is represented by

Aristotle's work on the nature of opposites. The kind of binary reductionism that these procedures so often entail is also linked to the reduction of speech to a graphic form, which in the extreme case produces the Pythagorean table of opposites. It is only necessary to refine the concept of opposition when you have reduced the world to incomprehension by placing "black" against "white" in a way that eliminates all context (i.e., in a simplified graphic form such as we encounter in the table).

The elimination of the complexity of differentiation was one of the two forms of category oversimplification that was so common in early Greek argumentation, where "opposites of any type tend to be taken as mutually exclusive and exhaustive alternatives" (18). The second was the tendency to assimilate the relationship of similarity to that of complete identity; analogy was seen as demonstration. Both Plato and Aristotle made important contributions to the analysis of types of opposition that had earlier been merged together. These included the discussion of division and dichotomy by Aristotle and were related to the development of the syllogistic method. But Lloyd notes that Plato continued to use arguments based upon inexhaustive alternatives while Aristotle expressly recommends the juxtaposition of contraries in the context of rhetorical arguments "as a means of securing admissions from an opponent" (18). In other words, the discriminations that Aristotle developed out of the simplifications of the earlier written mode are abandoned in the oral, rhetorical one (that is to say, an oral one much influenced by the presence of writing).

The decontextualization of speech by writing is, it would seem, a prerequisite for the kind of procedure we identify as logic. Such an assumption would explain, in a parsimonious manner, why it was that Lévy-Bruhl (rightly in a sense) found primitive (i.e., preliterate) man to be prelogical, as lacking in an appreciation of the "law of contradiction," and why Vygotsky and others have been unable to identify syllogistic reasoning among the unschooled. Perhaps it would also explain why attempts to apply Piaget's developmental schema in crosscultural settings have led to such tantalizing diverse results (2). Many of these procedures that we refer to as cognitive "skills" (for they are hardly to be regarded as characteristics of different mentalities, if by that we imply in-

nateness; indeed my argument runs counter to certain aspects of contemporary rationalism) are dependent upon the
"abstraction," the "decontextualization" which is promoted
by writing.

We do not find much difficulty in pointing to ways in
which "our" logic has been influenced by writing; the record makes it plain. What about "rationality"? Let us separate for one moment the actors' from the external observers'
view. Nadel's criteria of the empirical validation of the
means-ends relationship must involve the growth of universal (or widespread) methods and standards of assessment
associated with the cumulative growth of knowledge, especially scientific knowledge, which writing has done so
much to enhance. Here in the first place is a specific historical component to rationality. The same appears to be the
case with Warnock's evaluative criteria, since rationality involves judgments based upon universalistic ideas not available to tribal man. The subjects of the anthropologists, he
claims, simply do not know what moral notions are, so that
once again we are faced with a historical break. To this
position we will return later, but the more general ability to
assess the means for obtaining specific ends, often spoken
of as rationality, is certainly present in all societies, although it may not be employed in all circumstances. Nevertheless, means change, ends change, and the nature of
the rationalizing also changes. It would be difficult to account for the rapid adaptation of New Guinea highlanders
or Konkomba yam farmers to the rational conditions of the
market unless one's concepts of culture, society, and modes
of thought are sufficiently flexible to allow for a general underlying ability which flourishes in specific social conditions. Once again the admission of this possibility opens the
way, in a theoretical sense, to allow for the influence of the
means of communication.

I would tentatively suggest that even the calculation of the
means-end relationship by the actors themselves, the subjective purpose, the consideration of alternative courses of
action, that these procedures of assessing the profit and the
loss, the cost and the gain, are sharpened by the recourse
to writing. This possibility arises from two kinds of consideration. In the first place, the potentialities of planning
are greater when information can be stored in writing and

used at a later date; in written form it can be corrected, compared, and criticized—and the possibility of following through a plan is greater when one can turn to a check list (e.g., an itinerary or a shopping list). In the second place, consciousness of calculation is increased not only by these particular procedures but by the nature of the communicative act itself. In reading one is not simply engaging in indirect communication with another individual; the communication is at times anonymous, usually impersonal, always decontextualized. It is a communication on which one offers a continual commentary, for reading is not simply receiving, it is talking to oneself.

Such is more obviously the case with writing. Even more than in reading (which originally was often aloud), a significant component of writing is self-communication, a process that is analogous to what we often call thinking and one that increases the consciousness of what a person is doing and saying. To be caught speaking to oneself is a disturbing sign. But writing to oneself is greatly praised. At any rate, it appears to promote the organization of information, of thought, of behavior, in ways that are often described as rational.

Having considered the connection of logic and rationality with writing (though other features of the means of communication may also be relevant), let me now return to morality, specifically "moral rationality." We have noted, in many preliterate societies, how moral norms are linked to social distance. It is the external inquirer, the legal ethnologist, who demands a single answer to the question, What is the punishment (or treatment) for adultery? For such people the puzzle of the reactions to homicide in the Old Testament can only be resolved by placing the different treatments in a historical framework, thus neglecting the fact that different reactions might characterize different coexisting relationships (25). As I have suggested, this monolithic approach is a feature of highly centralized societies in which all are subject to one law, a national law that is applied from the center outward and downward. But it is also the case that once they are written down, moral as well as legal norms tend to get phrased in a national and even universalistic manner because they are communicated outside the context of particular social relations and hence, decontextualized made more abstract, more general in their application. In the courts and outside, these norms then have to be modified by the application of other sources of law and judgment, of equity, of legal fictions, of specific consideration of the relation of this man to that. It is as if the oral or segmentary process of judgment were turned on its head, starting from the most general and ending with the most particular.

Of course all rules (normative ones as distinct from statistical ones) are in a sense overgeneralized. The rule that "Englishmen do not marry their sisters" is applicable in some cases, but inapplicable in others; many doctors do just this. However, we are unlikely to be disturbed by this apparent inconsistency because we interpret the rule (more precisely, we interpret the word *sister*) in a contextual way, by excluding a certain range of possible meanings.

By rule in this sense, we mean a verbal statement of obligation, or prohibition. In oral societies and in oral situations, explicit rules are uncommon, in the sense that one rarely hears statements of this kind in natural situations except in response to an outsider's question. One situation in which we might hear such statements is the judicial context, where judgment is sought or offered about somebody's conduct. In literate societies, however, overgeneralized statements of this kind are the lifeblood of much written communication and the particular situation tends more readily to be interpreted in terms of some underlying principle, some universal criteria. "Thou shalt not kill" becomes a general axiom of behavior, in place of the more particularistic "Thou shalt not kill unless they have done you harm, or except in times of war, or unless they are Jews or Arabs, criminals, defectives, or the very old." Enshrined in the written word, passed down from century to century, from society to society, the generalized, decontextualized statement becomes the touchstone of moral rationality. It implies that all men should be treated in the same way, that status, relationship, age, and sex are irrelevant in making judgments about the conduct of mankind. Such a morality is promoted by the widening scope of social relations, by the centralization of decision making, and by the driving force of the written word itself, but it often rides roughshod over the more particularistic codes by which man controls and judges his own conduct. In this way, the concept of brotherhood or parenthood may get extended from lineage and clan, so that all men become brothers, or in any event, those that belong to the same trades union, masonic order, religious sect, or political party. But clearly the moral implications of the concept of fraternity get diluted as they get generalized. The decreasing specificity, on which I have commented, leads on the one hand to the elaboration of particular comprises and on the other to the formation of more general dissent groups that object to features of the abstract code, or are unable to reconcile the general statement (Thou shalt not kill) with the obligation to ignore the injunction under particular circumstances. Overgeneralization and decontextualization create problems for any rational morality that exists outside the covers of books, giving rise to conflict over the application, and even applicability, of high-level norms and ideologies which writing has helped to generate.

By saying that literacy promotes ideology, I do not of course mean that preliterate or illiterate peoples do not have ideas. I mean that their ideas are more likely to be embedded in reality, to be the kind of ideas that mark folk wisdom. Written forms of these ideas may alter the originals in a variety of ways, as we have seen. The position and personality of the writer himself can affect the situation, as in the case of programs of the German Peasants' war. The Twelve Articles were drafted by priests, town scribes, bishops' secretaries, and hence might not have been representative of the peasants' own views simply because they were put down by outsiders. Again the actual process of writing may itself transform, not only by generalizing the content and the audience but also because writing a report or a program means paying minute attention to the forms of expression. In this way writing serves to increase the self-consciousness of ideas, to open them up for a different kind of inspection and critique, as well as for a more deliberate and explicit statement—the kind associated with the words, plan, program, and ideology.

In this way, then, norms of conduct may vary from society to society, while on the most abstract level the written code of the New Testament or the Koran is taken as the ultimate source of right living. And in more secular societies, a battery of similar high-level abstractions provides the framework of our moral judgments and less frequently of our moral conduct.

In recent times anthropologists have tended to see logic, rationality, and moral rationality as universal characteristics of human society, whereas philosophers have tended to introduce more specific, society-bound (even ethnocentric) criteria. These views do little to clarify our understanding. Beginning with logic, I have suggested that the more specific procedures to which we often refer are influenced by social factors, particularly by changes in the means whereby man communicates with man, by the introduction of an easy system of writing. What is thought of as rationality in general, and moral rationality in particular, is also shown to have been influenced by the addition of a visuo-spacial dimension to language, which stresses the abstract and the generalized by decontextualizing speech from its particular framework of social relations, of A to B re X. In writing, the X achieves an independent life, material and cultural, of its own.

The rationalizing process encouraged by literacy is not of course confined to morality; it is present in the organization of the Sumerian lexicon, of Egyptian onamastica, of Euclidean geometry, and of Chaldean astronomy. It is a process that is heavily dependent upon the capacity to store and reorder information in the more systematic ways that writing provides (11). It is this reordering, as well as the generalizing, that is a component of moral rationality.

In suggesting that rationality (as some have defined it), and indeed morality itself (in the sense of a universalitic morality) is a function of the written formulation of moral norms, I do not of course imply that oral man was nonrational, nonmoral. I am rather pointing to the limitations of such concepts as often understood. At the same time, the written word *did* make a difference, just as the spoken word had done before. If on a wider definition of morality, actions such as altruism are governed by intention, then it is clear that language is critical to its discovery, its development, and its formulation (its formulation to the self as well as to others). Again this statement is not a denial of intent, planning, foresight to the behavior of animals without a *developed* language (i.e., nonhumans). However it does emphasize the important leap from prelinguistic to postlinguistic behavior, with its implications for what various authors have called normative, goal-oriented, intentional, rational, jural, and even moral behavior (or "action" as some would prefer). For it is important to recognize the differences as well as the similarities in the behavior of social animals and to link these differences to specific mechanisms, such as the way they communicate, the instrumentation of their learning. And where the process and the equipment involve the spoken or the written word, the genetic component must remain of marginal interest.

REFERENCES

(1) Cole, M., and Scribner, S. 1974. Culture and Thought. New York: Wiley.

(2) Dasen, P. R. 1972. Cross-cultural Piagetian research: a summary. Cross-Cultural Psychol. 3: 23–40.

(3) Derrida, J. 1967. L'Écriture et la différence. Paris: Editions du Seuil, Collection "Tel Quel."

(4) Edel, A. 1963. Method in Ethical Theory. London: Routledge & Kegan Paul.

(5) Evans-Pritchard, E. E. 1937. Witchcraft, Oracles and Magic among the Azande of the Anglo-Egyptian Sudan. Oxford: Clarendon Press.

(6) Fallers, T. n.d. Bantu Bureaucracy. Cambridge: Heffers.

(7) Gluckman, M. 1944. The logic of African science and witchcraft. Rhodes-Livingstone. 1: 61–71.

(8) ———. 1949–50. Social beliefs and individual thinking in primitive society. Transactions of the Manchester Literary and Philosophical Society 16.

(9) Goody, J. R., ed. 1968. Literacy in Traditional Societies. Cambridge: The University Press.

(10) Goody, J. R. 1977. The Domestication of the Savage Mind. Cambridge: The University Press.

(11) Goody, J. R.; Cole, M.; and Scribner, S. 1977. Writing and formal operations: a case study among the Vai. Africa, 47: 289–304.

(12) Goody, J. R., and Watt, I. P. 1963. The consequences of literacy. Comparative Studies in History and Society 5: 304–345; reprinted 1968.

(13) Hartshorn, H., and May, M. A. 1925–30. Studies in the Nature of Character. New York: Columbia University Teachers' College.

(14) Hobhouse, L. T. 1915. Morals in Evolution: A Study in Comparative Ethics. London: Chapman & Hall Ltd.

(15) Kohlberg, L. 1968. Moral Development. In International Encyclopedia of the Social Sciences. New York: Macmillian & Co. & The Free Press.

(16) Levi-Strauss, C. 1962. La Pensée sauvage. Paris: Plon. Eng. trans. London: Weidenfeld & Nicolson, 1966.

(17) Lévy-Bruhl, L. 1910. Les Fonctions mentales dans les sociétés inférieures. Paris: Librairie Felix Alcan, Eng. trans. London: Allen and Unwin., 1926.

(18) Lloyd, G. E. R. 1966. Polarity and Analogy. Cambridge: The University Press.

(19) MacIntyre, A. 1967. A Short History of Ethics. London: Routledge & Kegan Paul.

(20) Nadel, S. F. 1951. The Foundations of Social Anthropology. London: Cohen and West.

(21) Parsons, T. 1937. The Structure of Social Action. New York: The Free Press of Glencoe, A Division of the Crowell-Collier Publishing Company.

(22) ———. 1951. The Social System. Glencoe, Ill.: The Free Press.

(23) Piaget, J. (1932) 1948. The Moral Judgement of the Child. Glencoe, Ill.: The Free Press.

(24) Richards, D. A. J. 1971. A Theory of Reasons for Action. Oxford: Clarendon Press.

(25) Schapera, I. 1955. The sin of Cain. J. R. Anthrop. Inst. 85: 33–44.

(26) Southall, A. 1956. Alur Society: a Study in Processes and Types of Domination. Cambridge: W. Heffers & Sons Ltd.

(27) Warnock, G. J. 1971. The Object of Morality. London: Methuen & Co. Ltd.

(28) Williams, B. 1972. Morality: an introduction to Ethics. New York: Cambridge University Press, 1976.

(29) Wilson, B., ed. 1970. Rationality. Oxford: Blackwells (for articles by Horton, Beatie, Gellner, Lukes, Jarvie, Winch and MacIntyre).

THE "MORAL UNIVERSAL" FROM THE PERSPECTIVES OF EAST ASIAN THOUGHT

W. Tu

A defining characteristic of East Asian thought is its widely accepted proposition that human beings are perfectible through self-effort in ordinary daily existence. This proposition is based on two interrelated ideas: (1) The uniqueness of being human is an ethicoreligious question that cannot be properly answered if it is reduced to biological, psychological, or sociological considerations; and (2) the actual process of self-development, far from being a quest for pure mentality or spirituality, necessarily involves the biological, psychological, and sociological realities of human life. For the sake of convenience, the first idea will be referred to as an ontological postulate and the second as an experimental assertion. I will begin this paper with a few general observations on the proposition. After I have noted some of the salient features of the East Asian mode of thinking relevant to the present deliberation, I will proceed to a more focused investigation of the two basic ideas. For brevity, the discussion of East Asian thought will be confined to the Mencian line of Confucianism, the Chuang Tzu tradition of Taoism, and the Ch'an (Zen) interpretation of Buddhism.

It should be mentioned from the outset that the primary focus of the "Three Teachings" under study is self-knowledge. Since the conception of a Creator as the ultimate source of morality or spirituality is not even a rejected possibility, there is no appeal to the "wholly other," according to one theological tradition, as the real basis of human perfectibility. Rather, the emphasis is on learning to be human, a learning that is characterized by a ceaseless process of inner illumination and self-transformation. The Confucian ideal of sagehood, the Taoist quest for becoming a "true person," and the Buddhist concern for returning to one's "original mind" are all indications that to follow the path of knowledge backward, as it were, to the starting point of the true self is the aim of East Asian thought.

Knowledge so conceived is not a cognitive grasp of a given structure of objective truths; nor is it an acquisition of some internalized skills. It is basically an understanding of one's mental states and an appreciation of one's inner feelings. Since presumably a genuine knowledge of the self entails a transforming act upon the self, to know in this sense is not only to reflect and comprehend, but also to shape and create. For to know oneself is simultaneously to perfect oneself. This, I think, is the main reason that East Asian thought lays as much stress on how to cultivate oneself as on who and what the true self is. To the Confucians, Taoists, and Buddhists, self-knowledge is predominantly an ethicoreligious question, although it is inevitably laden with epistemological implications.

In a deeper sense, self-knowledge is neither "knowing that" nor "knowing how"; it is, in essence, an objectless awareness, a realization of the human possibility of "intellectual intuition." It is believed that self-knowledge is nothing other than the manifestation of one's real nature (inner sageliness in Confucianism and buddhahood in Ch'an), and that that real nature is not only a being to be known but also a self-creating and self-directing activity. However, although self-knowledge does not depend upon empirical knowledge, it is not incompatible with sense experience, or the "knowing of hearing and seeing." Thus the relation between self-knowledge and empirical knowledge can be either mutually contradictory or mutually complementary. In an extreme formulation, the Taoist maintains that in the pursuit of the Way one must first lose all that one has already acquired in order to embody the Tao. But it is one thing to lose the fragmented and confusing opinions of the world and quite another to lose a sense of reality by enclosing oneself in a totally narcissistic state. Generally speaking, East Asian thought takes empirical knowledge seriously, while focusing its attention on the supreme value of self-knowledge.

The idea of "intellectual intuition" needs some elaboration. For one thing, it is significantly different from either irrationalism or esoterics. To be sure, it does claim a direct knowledge of reality without logical reasoning or inference. But, unlike what is commonly associated with mysticism, it has very little to do with revelation. Actually, the whole tradition of contemplation as a way of coming to an immediate cognizance of the true essence of God without rational thought is alien to the East Asian mode of thinking. Rather, the possibility for each human being to have "intellectual intuition" is predicated on the presumption that since humanity forms an inseparable unity with heaven, earth, and the myriad things, its sensibility is in principle all-embracing. The theological distinction between Creator and creature, signifying an unbridgeable gap between divine wisdom and human rationality, is here transformed into what Joseph Needham characterizes as an organismic vision (10). Human beings are therefore thought to have as their birthright the potential power and insight to penetrate, so to speak, the things-in-themselves, or in Ch'an terminology, the suchness and thusness of *saṃsāra*. This resembles the Christian notion of divinity inherent in human nature. For, after all, in the prelapsarian state man is created in the image of God; and in the medieval Christian thought man is sometimes defined as divinity circumscribed.

It would be unfortunate if this organismic vision were understood as no more than a form of primitive animism, a doctrine that apparently conflicts with the scientific explanations of natural phenomena. Far from being an unexamined belief in the continued existence and mutual interaction of individual disembodied spirits, organismic vision here seems to have been the result of a philosophical anthropology which neither denies nor slights the uniqueness of being human. As a matter of fact, it subscribes to the nonevolutionary observation that human phylogeny has its own specific structure which cannot be fully explained in terms of some general laws governing the animal kingdom as a whole. Needless to say, it also rejects the attribution of a discrete indwelling spirit to any material form of reality. It is perhaps not farfetched to consider the organismic vision as an ecological insight, locating humanity in a highly complex web of interdependency.

It would be equally unfortunate if, instead of animism, the organismic vision is taken as a form of anthropocentrism. The human possibility of "intellectual intuition" must not be viewed as a license for manipulative imposition of the human will upon nature. Promethean defiance and Faustian restlessness are not at all compatible with the cherished value of harmony, as both societal goal and cosmic ideal, in East Asian thought. On the contrary, the authentic manifestation of the human will is thought to be ultimate self-transformation, a liberation rather than a conquest. To Confucians, Taoists, and Buddhists, knowledge is enlightenment, a power of self-illumination. And only in its corrupt form does knowledge become a power of conquest. According to this line of thinking, to be fully human requires the courage and wisdom of constantly harmonizing oneself with an ever-enlarging network of relationships, which necessitates a perspective going beyond the restrictions of anthropocentrism.

Yet the transcending perspective never allows a departure from the lived world here and now. This is part of the reason why all major spiritual traditions in East Asia emphasize inner experience as a basis for ethicoreligious deliberation, not only the abstract "inner experience" as a category of thought for systematic analysis but also the concrete inner experience of the thinker engaged in philosophizing. The line between religion and philosophy is inevitably blurred. And what is normally associated with the discipline of psychoanalysis becomes religiously and philosophically relevant and significant. The conscious refusal or, if you will, the inability of East Asian thought to submit itself to the academic compartmentalization characteristic of modern universities is not simply a sign of its lack of differentiation but also an indication of its wholeness with all of its fruitful ambiguities. Indeed, common experiences, such as eating and walking, are respected as having great symbolic significance for moral and spiritual self-development. For example, to the Confucian every human act is perceived as the reenactment of a time-honored ritual. Each gesture, such as eating, requires numerous practices before it takes the proper form. Only through socially recognized forms can one establish the communication necessary for self-cultivation. Human growth can thus be described as a process of ritualization. However, it is misleading to characterize Confucianism as a kind of ritualism. For a coercive imposition of well-established social norms upon the individual who cannot choose but adjust to the all-powerful society is at best the result of a highly politicized Confucian ideology of control. Confucian ethics, on the contrary, is built upon commonly shared human feelings, such as empathy. Ritual in this connection is not a fixed norm but a flexible and dynamic procedure by which self-realization as a concrete means for communal participation rather than as an isolated means for inner truth becomes possible. The Ch'an teaching of *satori* may on the surface seem diametrically opposed to the ritualized world, but as the Ch'an masters have never failed to note, the enlightening experience is a confirmation rather than a rejection of common sense because simple acts such as carrying water and chopping wood are the Way of Buddha. Taoism, too, for that matter, affirms the intrinsic value of ordinary human existence. They are all, in a sense, involved in the art of practical living.

It is vitally important to mention at this juncture that the East Asian concept of the human as a self-perfectible being in common ordinary existence without the intervention of a transcendent God is atheist only in a profoundly religious sense. The ultimate concern of self-realization actually necessitates a ceaseless process of inner moral and spiritual transformation. The purposefulness of life, however, is not a form of teleology in the sense of a preconceived cosmic design. In fact, human beings often remain tragically aimless and helpless, like "rudderless ships on restless waves." It is misleading to define sageliness or buddhahood in the language of entelechy. Surely human beings can become sages and buddhas because they are endowed with the "germinations" of morality or "seeds" of enlightenment, but it is highly problematical to perceive these germinations and seeds as the functional equivalents of what some vitalists claim to be the suppositiously immanent but immaterial agency responsible for the achievement of maturity in the human organism. For one thing, in either Confucianism or Buddhism, the duality of spirituality and materiality is meaningless. The Confucian *hsin*, which must be awkwardly rendered as "heart-mind," is a case in point. Intent on integrating the emotive aspects of human life with other dimensions of self-development, Mencius considers the fulfillment of the "bodily design" the highest manifestation of self-cultivation. In Ch'an, the assertion that *nirvāna* is saṃsāra, with all its ramifications, clearly rejects the artificial dichotomy between the body and the enlightened mind. Suggestively, the root metaphor shared by all Three Teachings in East Asian thought is the Way.

In the light of the above discussion, the rhetorical situation in which the East Asian Way is articulated has, at least, the following features: (1) the inquirer is as much an inside participant as an outside observer. It is inconceivable that the general question of self-knowledge can be completely independent of the questioner's own self-knowledge. Indeed, as the questioning process unfolds, the inquirer deepens and broadens his understanding of the general issue only to the extent that his personal transformation confirms it. However, (2) it would be mistaken to infer that the East Asian Way is subjectivistic because it lays much emphasis on inner experience. Actually, the idea of "intellectual intuition" does not give any particular individual a privileged access to truth. Indeed, the concept of individuality is not at all compatible with it. Rather, it is predicated on a strong sense of shareability and commonality. In other words, the experience that is considered truly personal is not at all private to the individual; self-knowledge is a form of inner experience precisely because it resonates with the inner experiences of the others. Accordingly, internality is not a solipsistic state but a concrete basis of communication, or, in the Taoist expression, of "spiritual communion."

It is in this sense that (3) the aforementioned organismic vision is the result of neither animism nor anthropocentrism but of a transcending perspective which seeks the ultimate meaning of life in ordinary human existence. Of course, it is often taken for granted that the ultimate meaning of life is never found in ordinary human existence. The commonly observed distinctions between soul and body or between sacredness and profanity are clear indications that this is so. Paradoxically, all Three Teachings of the East Asian Way endorse the view that everydayness is not only the point of departure but also the eventual return of any significant moral and spiritual journey. They believe that the true test of lasting values in any ethicoreligious tradition is common sense and good reasons. But they by no means glorify the trite and plain languages of every day. It is actually in what Herbert Fingarette calls the "secular as sacred" (3) that the spirit of their concern for ordinariness really lies.

Against this background, the ontological postulate can be introduced with one more observation. The uniqueness of being human must first transcend many familiar forms of reductionism. It is fallacious to define human nature merely in terms of biological, psychological, or sociological structures and functions because, viewed holistically, a more comprehensive grasp of its many-sidedness is required. However, an empirical enumeration of as many as practically feasible "human" traits is not satisfactory either. For one thing, it cannot address the question without in principle changing it in a fundamental way. To put it differently, the question about the uniqueness of being human will always be relegated to the background, as advances in biology, psychology, and sociology never intend to provide it with an answer.

The postulate about the perfectibility of human nature is thus empirically unprovable. And yet it is certainly not an unexamined faith in something beyond rational comprehension. Its status is ontological because it specifies a mode of understanding the being of the human. To be sure, perfectibility presupposes malleability and changeability. And ordinarily it is quite conceivable that malleation or change may not lead to the desired perfection. As a result, it seems that human nature can be seen as corruptible no less seriously than as perfectible. However, common to all Three Teachings is the further claim that inherent in human nature is the moral and spiritual propensity for self-development. Only when this original propensity is frustrated by a complexity of internal and external causes is human nature destroyed or led astray. It is in this connection that Mencius insists upon the goodness of human nature as the real basis for self-realization. The Mencian thesis deserves a brief exposition.

Each human being, Mencius seems to assert, is endowed with a "moral sense," also known as the sensibility of the *hsin*. Inherent in the hsin are the four germinations of the four basic human feelings: commiseration, shame and dislike, deference and compliance, and right and wrong. Although environment, both social and psychological, features prominently in human growth, the germinating power of these feelings is the structural reason for moral and spiritual self-development. In a strict sense, morality or spirituality is not internalized by but expressed through learning. The learning to be human in the Mencian tradition is therefore conceived as the "mutual nourishment" of inner morality and social norms rather than the imposition of external values upon an uncultured mind. Indeed, hsin is both a cognitive and an affective faculty, symbolizing the functions of conscience as well as consciousness. For it not only reflects upon realities but, in comprehending them, shapes and creates their meaningfulness for oneself.

Similarly, in the view of Taoism, the inner illumination of the mind is the real basis for self-liberation. Although Confucian values, such as humanity and righteousness, are rejected by Chuang Tzu as unnecessary and harmful social and cultural constraints detrimental to the spontaneity of nature, the pursuit of the Way requires a process of ultimate self-transformation which appeals to neither the immortality of the soul nor the existence of God but the "intellectual intuition" inherent in the true self. The *prajñā*, commonly rendered as "intuitive wisdom" or "nondual knowledge," in Ch'an also refers to an inalienable quality of the mind which manifests itself as the true buddha nature in each person.

Accordingly, despite divergent approaches to the actual process of moral and spiritual self-development, Confucianism, Taoism, and Buddhism all share the fundamental belief: although existentially human beings are not what they ought to be, they can be perfected through self-cultivation; and the reason that they can become fully realized is inherent in what they are. Therefore, the human condition here and now, rather than either the original position in the past or a utopian projection into the future, is the central concern. It is in this sense that the ontological postulate of human perfectibility must be supplemented by an experiential assertion about the concrete path by which one's own "germinations" and "seeds" can eventually be brought to fruition. This may account for some of the deceptively simple paradoxes in East Asian thought, such as:

(a) There is sageliness in every human being / Virtually no one, not even Confucius, can claim to be a sage.

(b) Every sentient being is endowed with buddhahood / Nirvana can never be attained except through Great Death.

(c) Tao is everywhere / Only the most sensitive and subtle mind can hear the Way.

It should be mentioned that germinations and seeds constitute only one of the many forms of the metaphorical language used in this connection. A frequently used analogy is the digging and drilling of a well, suggesting many degrees and layers of personal knowledge. Only after one has penetrated, as it were, the deepest ground of one's existence can one truly experience the "taste" of one's enlightening self, which significantly also provides the authentic possibility for communicating with others and understanding things as they really are. The self so conceived, far from being an isolated and enclosed individual, signifies a sharable commonality accessible to every member of the human community. However, it is vitally important to note that commonality here by no means implies sameness, for it inevitably assumes different shapes of meaning as it is perceived and manifested in different persons. The idealist's claim that all rational beings will finally agree is too restrictive a notion to account for the complex structure of common selfhood in East Asian thought. It is also in this sense that all Three Teachings assume that moral and spiritual self-development involves not only a convergence of stages to be perfected but also a multiplicity of ways to be pursued. Exclusivism in ethicoreligious thought is rejected mainly because by insisting upon a single path it would be incapable of accommodating the divergent interests and concerns of human beings as a whole. The recognition that the best way for me is not necessarily the best for my neighbor is a psychology essential for the peaceful coexistence of different and even conflicting beliefs in East Asian society and culture. The Confucian Golden Rule, for instance, is deliberately stated in a negative form: "Do not do to others what you would not want others to do to you."

The reluctance to impose one's own way on others is a consideration for the integrity of the other, and also a recognition that one can never fully comprehend another to the same extent and in the same degree as one can comprehend oneself. The veil of ignorance, however, must not prevent one from constantly trying to empathize with other human beings as an integral part of one's own quest for self-knowledge. Indeed, a sense of community, which is a manifestation of the organismic vision, is absolutely essential for moral and spiritual self-development. Surely, among the Three Teachings, only Confucianism unequivocally asserts that society is both necessary and intrinsically valuable for self-realization. Taoism and Ch'an do not seem to have attached much importance to human relations. But neither Taoism nor Ch'an belittles the lived world as a meaningful context in which ethicoreligious developments are assessed, as problems of afterlife, Heaven and Hell are deliberately relegated to the background. It is this sense of togetherness in the secular world, I suppose, that accounts much for the concerted efforts of the Three Teachings to eradicate the alleged fallacy of "individualism." The Confucian instructions on the falsehood of self-centeredness, the Ch'an warning against egoist attachments, and the Taoist advocacy of self-forgetfulness all seem to point to the necessity of going beyond the private in order to participate in a shared vision.

The underlying thesis, then, is equality without uniformity. To be sure, moral and spiritual self-development can be understood as a process toward an ever-deepening subjectivity, but this must not be taken as a quest for pure morality or spirituality. The idea that inner truth is mysteriously connected with a transcendent reality not accessible to the human community at large does not feature prominently in East Asian thought at all. The perfected self is never conceived as a depersonalized entity assuming a superhuman quality. This partly explains the absence of priesthood, presumably a spiritual elite mediating between the secular and the sacred, in any of the Three Teachings. Confucian, Taoist, and Ch'an masters are supposed to be exemplary teachers. They may try to instruct, discipline, and enlighten the student. But the purpose is always to inspire the self-effort of the student because the ultimate reason for self-realization is one's own inner strength.

The "Moral Universal," viewed from these perspectives, assumes a twofold significance: Human beings are moral because, as self-perfectible beings, they cannot be circumscribed merely by the instinctual demands for survival or, for that matter, by the necessities and needs for the solidarity of the group, or for the perpetuation of the species. The meaning of being human is so uniquely personal that functional explanations, no matter how broad the scope they attempt to encompass, rarely escape the danger of reductionism. Indeed, simple human acts such as eating and walking have profound symbolic significance, making them qualitatively different from similar "acts" in other animals. Human hunger, for example, may from a naturalistic point of view be no more than a common physiological condition in the animal kingdom, but symbolically it is a phenomenon sui generis. Human development, therefore, involves much more than the combination of biological growth, psychological maturation, and the continuous internalization of social norms.

However, human beings are also inescapably biological, psychological, and social; and in order to realize themselves they must transform these circumscriptions into necessary "instrumentalities" for self-development. To learn to become what one ought to be, far from being a total rejection of what one is, must begin with a critical self-examination, "a reflection on things at hand." Commonly experienced feelings are therefore the points of departure for cultivating personal knowledge. It is not asceticism but perhaps a balanced diet, and certainly not occultism but a disciplined mind that can really broaden one's vision and sharpen one's awareness. Methods of "quiet-sitting," "regulated breathing," or zazen, notwithstanding their varying degrees of seriousness in different traditions, all seem to suggest that the given "body and mind" is after all the concrete place where great ethicoreligious insights occur. Pure morality and spirituality, admitting no biological, psychological, or sociological factors, is a kind of formalism as unacceptable to the East Asian mode of thinking as an extreme kind of behavioral reductionism would be. Mencius may have a point when he claims that if we can fully extend the common experience of feeling unable to bear the sufferings of others, our humanity will become inexhaustibly abundant.

ADDENDUM

Having prepared a general statement on East Asian thought as a background paper for the Workshop and having participated in the discussions of its relevance to a critical examination of the "biological foundations of morality," I propose to offer in retrospect, especially in the light of Clifford Geertz's thought-provoking comments on my presentation, some observations that may have a direct bearing on the psychological and philosophical issues raised in our joint endeavor. For expediency, I would call our attention to the thought of Wang Yang-ming (1472–1529), which is said to have combined the wisdom of Ch'an Buddhism and the aesthetic sensitivity of Taoism with the humanist concerns of Confucianism. This may help us to focus more sharply on the salient features of the so-called Three Teachings. To begin, it should be remarked that Yang-ming, hailed as a most original and influential thinker in premodern China, was a distinguished scholar-official who consciously and conscientiously put into practice his metaphysical vision and demonstrated through his own personal spiritual development the beliefs he held. Indeed, his life history was an exemplification of the "unity of knowledge and action" idea which he advocated as a defining characteristic of his mode of thinking.

The Great Man Regards Heaven, Earth, and the Myriad Things as One Body. Thus begins the first line of Wang Yang-ming's "Inquiry on the *Great Learning,*" a synoptic view of the central theme he had been formulating throughout his life. What he intends to convey here is neither an intellectual ideal nor an ethical injunction but, as Geertz noted, primarily "a common experience of feeling that undergirds morality." This shared feeling is explicitly described as the "emotional inability to bear the sufferings of others." In Yang-ming's words:

That the great man can regard Heaven, Earth, and the myriad things as one body is not because he deliberately wants to do so, but because it is natural to the humanity of his heart that he do so. . . . [In fact, this is true with every human being.] Therefore when he [an ordinary person] sees a child about to fall into a well, he cannot help a feeling of alarm and commiseration. This shows that his humanity forms one body with the child. It may be objected that the child belongs to the same species. Again, when he observes the pitiful cries and frightened appearance of birds and animals about to be slaughtered, he cannot help feeling an "inability to bear" their suffering. This shows that his humanity forms one body with birds and animals. It may be objected that birds and animals are sentient beings as he is. But when he sees plants broken and destroyed, he cannot help a feeling of pity. This shows that his humanity forms one body with plants. It may be said that plants are living things as he is. Yet, even when he sees tiles and stones shattered and crushed, he cannot help a feeling of regret. This shows that his humanity forms one body with tiles and stones. [(1), p. 272]

Underlying these deceptively simple experiential assertions is an ontological claim about the "humanity of the heart." The reason that the great man can manifest his empathic and sympathetic feelings toward another (human being, animal, plant, or stone) in a genuine and spontaneous manner is thought to be in the structure of the heart itself. Indeed, following Mencius, Yang-ming maintained that the "emotional inability to bear the sufferings of others" is an inborn capacity, not acquired (although it must be enhanced and refined) through imitative learning. Of course this does not mean, to paraphrase P. H. Wolff (this volume), that human sensitivity "matures in isolation from specific socioenvironmental influences." On the contrary, from a developmental point of view, it is like a delicate bud which can be easily frustrated without proper nourishment.

The opposite of this kind of unpremeditated human sensitivity is often depicted as selfishness (or self-centeredness), a deliberate refusal to share with, care for, and show affection to another. Selfish acts are obviously in conflict with H. L. Rheingold and D. F. Hay's "prosocial behavior of the very young" [this volume]. Viewed from this perspective, the humane qualities of the infant as empirically identified by Rheingold and Hay are ontologically as well as ontogenetically inherent in the original capacity of the heart. Understandably the growth of a human being depends as much upon the active participation of the learner (the infant, for example) as a "partner," indeed a "socializer" (a sharing, caring, and feeling "great man" in process) as on what we commonly call "socialization" from outside. This middle path, as it were, must also reject both "normative biologism" and "normative sociologism" (D. T. Campbell, this volume).

It is vitally important to know that Yang-ming's interpretive position is actually predicated on a metaphysical vision. If properly understood, such a vision is in accord with the Aristotelian, and for that matter Kantian, assertion that what makes "reason" most valuable and essential to human beings is precisely the fact that it is beyond genetic constraints and thus "biologically irrelevant" (Group Report by R. C. Solomon et al., this volume). For one thing, the innateness of universalizable feelings shared by the human community is conceived as a manifestation of the same "principle" (*li*) which underlies Heaven, Earth, and the myriad things. Indeed, there is only one "principle" in all beings and that "principle" is inherently in and intrinsically knowable to the "humanity of the heart." Unlike the Platonic idea, the "principle" that is embodied in each concrete thing is the "principle" in its all-embracing fullness. There is no distinction here between man and animal, plant or stone. The uniqueness of man, however, lies in his ability to know and manifest through self-effort the "principle" in him.

Man has this ability because ontologically he is endowed with the "humanity of the heart" for self-realization which, in the tradition of *Chung-yung* (*Doctrine of the Mean*), necessitates a concomitant realization of the other. But, in practice, unless a consistent and strenuous effort at self-development is applied, man can in actuality become as insensitive as stone. This metaphor, widely used in Chinese literature, seems to imply that although man is the most sentient being that embodies the "principle" in the cosmos, what he is existentially may turn out to be a parody of what he can and ought to become. It is therefore not only man's right but also his duty to be moral. This reminds us of Kant. However, unlike Kant, Yang-ming believed that the "principle," which has also been rendered as "reason," is what human nature in the ultimate sense really means. As a result, the formalist approach in Kantianism is here replaced, so to speak, by an appeal to the universality of moral feelings which are biologically based but not genetically determined. For the "principle" and the "humanity of the heart" are one and the same reality.

The Preservation of the Heavenly Principle and the Elimination of Human Desires. Implicit in the claim that the "humanity of the heart" is universal and that the greatness of being human lies in the maximum development of this commonly shared feeling are two conflicting images of man. He can "embody" (*t'i*) the cosmos in his heart as a concretely lived experience rather than as merely an intellectual projection. Man so conceived symbolizes, in the words of Chou Tun-i (1017–1073), "the highest excellence" of the creative process of the universe. Unfortunately, it is also probable that man is so circumscribed and corrupted by his "human desires" (*jen-yü*), biologically rooted and socioenvironmentally conditioned as well, that he can in fact inflict inhumanity upon himself and his closest kin. Even without the myth of the Fall, the range of human possibility for morality and immorality is frightfully extensive. Man can go beyond anthropocentrism (let alone egoism and ethnocentrism) and serve as a guardian of nature; or he can exhibit an aggression toward himself as well as all other beings as the most destructive force in the universe.

The contrast between the "Heavenly Principle" and "human desires" is of great significance in the light of the above. Yang-ming took it for granted that what is truly human necessarily manifests the "principle" in its most generalized sense. Paradoxically "human desires," as limited and distorted expressions of the self, are detrimental to the original rhythm of the heart. This is why "human desires" are also described as "selfish desires" (*ssu-yü*). Just as selfishness endangers the authentic development of the self, "human desires" frustrate the true manifestation of humanity. Thus Yang-ming confidently stated that learning to become a great man "consists entirely in getting rid of the obscuration of selfish desires in order by his own efforts to make manifest his clear character, so as to restore the condition of forming one body with Heaven, Earth, and the myriad things, a condition that is originally so, that is all" ((1), p. 273).

Actually, the preservation of the Heavenly Principle and the elimination of human desires must be taken as a unitary

effort of self-cultivation, signifying a holistic process of ultimate personal transformation. A key concept in this connection is *i* (intention), especially an act of the will to manifest
one's "clear character" informed by the Heavenly Principle.
For without a continuous quest for self-knowledge by an
ever deepening psychology of purification, selfish desires
cannot be eliminated and the quality of one's life, so far as
the "principle" is concerned, remains obscure. This, I suppose, is the main reason why Yang-ming attached so much
importance to "establishing the will" (*li=chih*) as the first essential step in the ceaseless process of learning to be truly
human. This view seems remarkably similar to F. A. Jenner's concluding observation (this volume), in which he suggests that "we cannot live in everyday life without acting as
though the moral depends on intention, indeed intentionality." For Yang-ming, we can surmise, morality entails intend-
ing, both as a state of conscious knowing (directionality of
the mind) and as a process of conscientious acting (transforming effect of the heart). Perhaps in this sense we can follow E. Turiel's distinction between morality and convention
without necessarily committing ourselves to the claim that
they are "different aspects of social regulation" (E. Turiel,
this volume).

The Full Realization of Primordial Awareness. I mentioned earlier that the Confucian hsin must be glossed as
"heart-mind" because it involves both cognitive and affective dimensions of human awareness. This "fruitful ambiguity" is perhaps the result of a deliberate refusal rather than
an unintended failure to make a sharp distinction between
conscience and consciousness (F. A. Jenner, this volume). To
Yang-ming, consciousness as cognition and conscience
as affection are not two separable functions of the mind.
Rather, they are integral aspects of a dynamic process
whereby man becomes aware of himself as a moral being.
Indeed, the source of morality depends on their inseparabil-
ity in a prereflective faculty. Borrowing a classical term from
Mencius, Yang-ming defines this prereflective faculty as
liang-chih (commonly translated as "innate knowledge" but
here rendered as "primordial awareness"), signifying an in-
nermost state of human perception wherein knowledge and
action form a unity. For this primordial awareness, which
can also be understood as a more subtle way of characteriz-

ing the "humanity of the heart," creates values of human understanding as it encounters the world. Learning to be human, in this sense, involves a continuous development of one's "primordial awareness." The expression *chih liang-chih*, often translated as "the extension of innate knowledge," may be more appropriately interpreted here as the full realization of one's primordial awareness. I do not see any obvious conflict between this line of thinking and T. Nagel's analysis (this volume) that "a capacity to subject their prereflective or innate responses to criticism and revision, and to create new forms of understanding" is that unique quality that human beings have discovered in themselves. Yet I must admit that Yang-ming's "primordial awareness" is not merely a rational capacity; nor is it simply a perceptual and motivational starting point. Needless to say, it also has little to do with biological nativism. Rather, it is a mode of perceiving which I earlier noted as the function of "intellectual intuition." A feature of it is that, as a critical self-awareness, it can understand our true nature and apprehend the thing-in-itself, a capacity which Kant thought is humanly impossible.

The justification for this seemingly outrageous claim is relatively simple: "Knowing thyself" means to realize the "principle" inherent in one's nature. Since the same "principle" also underlies humans and things in general, the procedure by which other forms of understanding are created is, in the ultimate sense, identical to that of self-knowledge. But the assumption that the level of self-knowledge attained entails a comparable depth of knowledge about humans and things in general is not an expression of subjective idealism. For the true self so conceived is never an isolated entity. The solipsistic predicament (an extreme case of self-centeredness perhaps), so far as it may have a bearing on this, is rejected by a direct appeal to the common experience of feeling. The sense of cosmic togetherness, or in Chang Tsai's (1020–77) poetic expression that "Heaven is my father and Earth is my mother. . . . All people are my brothers and sisters, and all things are my companions" ((2), p. 497), is a primary background understanding in this tradition. As a result, the whole philosophical activity centered around the skeptic's questioning about the outside world and about other minds is never developed. Whether or not this mode of thinking will eventually lead to a form of pan-psychism is beyond the scope of our present discussion. It is clear, however, that the position introduced here is basically at odds with the view that biological or any physical structures can in themselves explain human morality.

The apparent divergence between this line of inquiry, focusing on the commonality and shareability of human experience, indeed on the unity and continuity of being, and Charles Fried's plea for a greater tolerance of diversity is perhaps a matter of emphasis. I wonder, however, whether the centrality of recognizing the identity of persons as a background assumption for the morality of free, rational choosing beings does not itself presuppose a primordial awareness that despite the distinctness of persons, equality of respect is possible. After all, Kant "who sees in freedom the heart of moral value" (C. Fried, this volume) feels it is fitting to define moral *choice* as a duty, a categorical imperative. A fiduciary commitment (in Michael Polanyi's sense (11)) to the value of the human, I believe, is a basis for the "principle of the autonomy of morals."

REFERENCES

(1) Chan, W. T., trans. 1962. Instructions for Practical Living and other Neo-Confucian Writings by Wang Yang-ming. New York: Columbia University Press.

(2) ———. 1973. A Source Book of Chinese Philosophy. Princeton: Princeton University Press.

(3) Fingarette, H. 1972. Confucius—The Secular as Sacred. New York: Harper and Row.

(4) Geertz, C. 1973. The Interpretation of Cultures. New York: Basic Books.

(5) Kaltenmark, M. 1969. Lao Tzu and Taoism. Trans. R. Creaves. Stanford: Stanford University Press.

(6) Kant, I. 1969. Foundations of the Metaphysics of Morals. Trans. L. W. Beck, Indianapolis: Bobbs-Merrill.

(7) Lau, D. C., trans. 1976. Mencius. New York: Penguin Books.

(8) Mote, F. W. 1971. Intellectual Foundations of China. New York: Alfred A. Knopf.

(9) Munro, D. J. 1969. The Concept of Man in Early China. Stanford: Stanford University Press.

(10) Needham, J., and Wang, L. 1954–1976. Science and Civilization in China. Vol. 2. Cambridge: Cambridge University Press.

(11) Polanyi, M. 1964. Personal Knowledge, Towards a Post-Critical Philosophy. New York: Harper and Row.

(12) Tu, W. 1976a. Centrality and Commonality: An Essay on Chung-yung. Honolulu: University Press of Hawaii.

(13) ———. 1976b. Neo-Confucian Thought in Action—Wang Yang-ming's Youth (1472–1509). Berkeley, Los Angeles, London: University of California Press.

BIOLOGY AND ETHICS: NORMATIVE IMPLICATIONS

C. Fried

THE AUTONOMY OF ETHICS

The task of identifying nontrivial normative implications of an empirical science—which is what biology is and sociobiology purports to be—is a daunting one, at least if one is convinced that ethics is (in Thomas Nagel's phrase, see this volume) an autonomous subject. I shall start by giving the sense in which I believe ethics to be autonomous. It is straightforward. If it puts me in the camp of those who hold that one cannot derive an "ought" from an "is," so that naturalism is indeed a fallacy, then I must comfort myself with the otherwise conflicting company of both Hume and Kant.

The persistence of this view that naturalism is fallacious is in large part due to the fact that the attempts to show that one can derive an "ought" from an "is" rely on some very fishy, fancy, and suspiciously "ought"-like "is"es from which to launch the derivation.

I assume the version of autonomy which holds simply enough that ethics relates to choice, and normative ethics (which is to say first-order ethics) is concerned with guiding choice—by prescription, exhortation, analysis, or clarification. There is, to be sure, a body of more or less general theoretical-descriptive propositions about what kind of choices persons *do* make, but this body of propositions is surely not normative: from its empirical propositions only empirical propositions follow. I take it to be clear that when it is a matter of recommending a choice, no description of past or present states of the world can of itself determine that recommendation. Though the recommendation, or normative argument, may *mention* nothing other than possible or actual states of the world, there are always hidden premises that these states of the world are relevant to certain goals, and that these goals are to be affirmed. Ethical discourse at the deepest level is not content to leave these goals unanalyzed and to offer only technical or hypothetical advice about their attainment. Ethics is about goals. Indeed it is not just about goals, but about some subset of goals, which has variously been identified as our more important goals, or as those that govern our relations with other people, or as those that relate to how we live our lives. However the domain of goals is further specified, (normative) ethics disappears as a subject if it treats goals as given, if it assumes directive (i.e., normative) force only over the means of attaining our goals. But this deepening of the subject as one that directs us in the choice of ends, establishes the autonomy of ethics, establishes that no system of statements about the way the world is or has been can of itself compel conclusions in an ethical argument. And of course the propositions of biology (including sociobiology) do not—in any reputable scientific circles of which I am aware—purport to be anything other than propositions about the way the world is and about the laws which describe the world at some level of abstraction or generality.

It might seem that this description of the proper domain of ethics requires us to take sides in the free will/determinism debate. Together with many philosophers I suspect that the terms of the debate have not been clearly drawn; but even if they have and even if the deterministic principle is correct, I do not believe that the account I have given of the autonomy of ethics would be undermined. Though it is true that if the deterministic principle is correct choices could in theory be accurately predicted, this does not mean that one cannot continue to reflect meaningfully on what our choices should be and what our proper goals are. That the outcomes of both those reflections and of the situations of choice on which those reflections are brought to bear are in principle predictable invalidate neither the reflection nor the offering of its conclusions as reasons for action. I would suppose that determinism includes not only ethical deliberation but also theoretical deliberation within its arguments. Nevertheless, no one is pressing us to conclude that because of the allegedly deterministic nature of theoretical deliberation we should cease to engage in mathematical speculation, or cease to seek to govern our mathematical choices by the outcome of such speculation. Whatever may or may not be true about the neurophysiology of thought, logic is still a field of inquiry independent of the science of neurophysiology. It is autonomous and gives us reasons for making choices about logic. So also is ethics an autonomous subject and gives us reasons for making choices about our goals.

The choice of goals may be determined in the sense that any future event is determined by its causal antecedents. But if the choice is in fact a choice, then the person choosing acts upon reasons, and the principle of the autonomy of morals simply holds that a description of the present or past state of the world can never supply a sufficient reason for action even though in a causal sense these prior states of the world may determine what the outcome of the choice will be. What we have, then, are two relations between states of the world and choice: (a) the relation as it appears to the choosing individual and those who engage in ethical discourse with him, whereby the choosing individual must act upon reasons and the states of the world never supply a sufficient reason for action; (b) the point of view of an observer of states of the world including the choices of the choosing individual. For the observer the future conduct of the choosing individual may be wholly a function of prior states of the world.

These two perspectives—the perspective of the chooser and the perspective of the observer—account for the tensions and difficulties that scientific theories such as sociobiology (or psychology, or sociology, or neurobiology) seem to create for morals. Sociobiology claims that behavior, just as the physical structures of organisms, may be accounted for by evolutionary theories, and that therefore behavior is a function of the two interacting vectors relevant to evolutionary theory: genetics and environment—that is, past and present states of the world. Theories regarding the evolution of altruistic behavior are simply the most recent, striking examples of this familiar trend. The problem, therefore, is not whether we can make choices at all, given the theories of such disciplines as sociobiology or psychoanalysis, but rather what choices we *should* make given these theories. The question is not whether biology has superseded morals, but rather whether biological theories have any relevance, and if so, have what relevance to our moral choices.

There are a number of important but theoretically boring answers to this question. Obviously the facts of biology, like many other facts about the world, can be of enormous instrumental value in attaining our goals, and thus are highly relevant to our choices. If we wish for a world with a particular level of material welfare, then the facts of biology are crucial to our purposes. What is far more interesting, because it forces a confrontation between the two levels of concern—the level of observational theory and the level of choice or moral theory—is the question dealing with the manipulation of the very fulcrums of choice or desire. I insist that no amount of information about how we reached our present status (icluding information about how we developed our present behavioral tendencies) can provide sufficient reasons for our present choices, even though from an observational point of view our choices may actually be determined by just those factors. But what are we to say when presented, as we may be to an increasing degree, with the possibility of determining ever more closely the fulcrums of choice—not just the external circumstances of choice but the internal circumstances, our perceptions, habits, and desires? What this possibility does is to force us to make decisions (at the level of choice or morality) that have as their object the future behavior of human agents viewed at the level of observation. This is the interesting normative dilemma that arises when ethics is seen as autonomous.

INCORPORATION AND PERSONAL IDENTITY

The most general, distinctive biological, indeed genetic, fact about persons that bears on normative questions is that persons, the moral entities with which we are concerned, are physical, biological entities. It is not just that persons have bodies but that they *are* bodies. Moreover, bodies are different from one another. One need not vouch in Leibniz's identity of indiscernibles to make the point that even if we were a race of identical twins our bodies would be different, if only by virtue of the fact that at any one time no two bodies can be in the same place. Now the fact of individuality is *not* a trivial matter in ethics. Indeed some of the most discerning recent works in moral philosophy—that of John Rawls and Bernard Williams—have pointed to the importance of identifying the kinds of entities that are primary in moral theory. Rawls has pointed out that in utilitarian theory the primacy of happiness or utility makes persons secondary entities, their significance in moral theory being derived solely from the fact that they are among the possible receptacles of happiness, utility, value. That it is the sum or average of happiness that counts, and not how satisfactions are distributed over persons (except as such distribution affects the total or average quantum), is the sign of the basic utilitarian indifference to the individuality of persons. If just distribution, however, has an importance independent of its tendency to increase happiness overall, then to that extent the status of the distributees is given an independent moral significance—they do not merge into the mass. In other words persons have rights—that is, they have claims which must be met without regard to (some) utilitarian considerations. The point is, then, that the status of persons makes a difference for moral theory. If persons are the primary entities, then the experiences that persons will have are important, to be sure, but only insofar as they are the experiences of *persons*. Next, we may note that these entities, persons, are physical entities, incorporated entities. Furthermore, ethics may not be indifferent to bodies, or may not treat bodies as simply adventitious receptacles of moral values— to be changed, manipulated, or cast aside as our more urgent concerns dictate—because some bodies are persons, and it is persons about whom we are concerned.

But there is a further point still which is of importance in discerning whether biology has any normative implications at the most general level. Bernard Williams has noted that just as utilitarianism ignores the *separateness* of persons, by treating the whole mass of humanity as if it were one unit within which the value of pleasure or utility is to be maximized, so Kantian or other excessively impartialistic theories abstract from the *identity* of persons. Williams is objecting to arguments found in Rawls (and even in some of my own writings) claiming that as long as no person is sacrificed to the common good, as long as all persons are treated equally, then morality has been satisfied. Williams objects to these arguments, because they deny the right, or even the duty, to make distinctions between persons on other than impartial grounds, and thus denies the right, or even the duty, to recognize the identity of individuals. For Williams the identity of individuals consists not only in their separateness from other individuals but also in their distinctness from other individuals. Now I suppose that Williams's point might hold even if we were indeed a race of genetic clones; in so far as we would be distinct from each other, we would have individuality at least in the Leibnizian sense. We would still be able to recognize our own identity and, perhaps using tempero-spatial coordinates, the identities of certain particular persons in whom we were interested. But one would have to say that a world of genetic clones, in which identities depended only on tempero-spatial coordinates, would be one in which the point about identity would be very thin indeed. I might be able to have special concern for my own identity in such a world (though I doubt it), but I would not be able to have any concern for a friend or a child in such a world, because I could never be quite sure who this friend was. Perhaps I could be sure because my friend is the person who is the bodily continuity of some person in a particular spatial location whom I selected to be my friend—perhaps he was closest at the time. But obviously this is a fragile notion indeed. If our normative structures depend not only on the separateness but also the identity of persons, then differences between people are indispensable. A morality of respect for persons would, using William's argument, be virtually inconceivable among a race of clones.

Identity is necessary to anything recognizable as our system of morals, and difference or distinctness is necessary to identity. Now it is true that even a race of clones might develop significant differences as they went through life and were affected by their varying environments. But this would be an insecure sort of differentiation. First, we would all start out the same, and second, we could control the degree of difference. And so I would suggest distinctness in dress, hairstyle, or even life history might *not* be enough to accomplish the necessary sense of identity. Dress and hairstyle may be changed, and the psychological deposits of life history may be altered. It is only when our distinctness is *also* a distinctness of body that the distinctness of persons (who, as I have said, are bodies) is on a secure foundation, and with that distinctness identity is on a secure foundation.

Now one might ask whether I have not, after all, begged the question. At most I have shown that *a* conception of morality, perhaps that conception which is ours, depends on the concept of identity, and thus on the distinctness—including the bodily distinctness—of persons. But who is to say that a morality which did not recognize the importance of identity, or even the separateness of persons would not be a better morality? Or at least as good a morality? All I have shown is that perhaps it would be a more unfamiliar morality than many might think. Now I cannot make the argument here, I am not sure I can make it in a conclusive way at all, but I would want to assert that a morality of persons, a morality which respects the identity of persons, is not only one morality among others, but is indeed the only thing which in the end can be considered a morality. Other moralities are confused approximations of it. I have argued that morality is tied to choice, to the sense of responsibility for what one does. In this I follow Kant who sees in freedom the core of moral value. The argument I would suggest is that if we were a race of clones, if we had no sense of identity, if distinctiveness, and thus if our conceptions were conceptions which made no room for the identity of persons, we would not have a morality at all. And if we did not have a morality at all, we would indeed not be the rational choosing beings which we are. In short, in order to be free, choosing beings, we must have a morality. And in order to have a morality we must recognize the identity of persons. If I may be permitted a further, even wilder conjecture, I would suggest that our very success (as well as failure) as a species depends upon the freedom of choice, the ability to reflect about possibilities which is inextricably related to conceiving ourselves as moral, that is, choosing entities, and thus as discrete individuals.

NORMATIVE IMPLICATIONS

Subjects such as sociobiology, or the relation between biology and ethics tend to invite speculation on a cosmic scale—such as speculations on the future of mankind. On that scale these reflections do have implications, although one feels rather embarrassed about some of the most farfetched. Farthest out is a prospect like that offered in Frank Herbert's science fiction novel, *The Eyes of Heisenberg* (3), a world in which persons are literally made to order by genetic tailors (Herbert calls them engineers). Herbert sketches quite convincingly the dehumanizing effect of a world in which all randomness is suppressed. The positive implication of this is that the randomness of human difference is based on the randomness of genetic difference. Thus if we felt we had been manufactured rather than conceived in the ordinary way, then our sense that we belong to ourselves would be radically undermined, and as we did not feel we belonged to ourselves, so also our sense of freedom, responsibility and therefore human creativity would also be undermined. Of course this does not mean that negative eugenics—interventions to prevent the expression of seriously deleterious genotypes—poses such threats. It also does not mean that genetic engineering to overcome diabetes or other enzyme deficiencies is such a threat, nor yet even that the occasional artificial insemination poses such threats. The point really is one of balance and degree, of what the prevailing background understandings are. Against a background in which persons were secure in their own identities, the occasional product of artificial insemination need be no more prejudiced than the occasional adopted child. An adopted child is treated *as if* it were the parents' own child. So long as the "as if" continues to have a strong hold it can serve as a model for literal departures from it.

A more down-to-earth set of implications relates to the institution of the family. Social theorists have always been troubled by the tendency of the family to interfere with their projects for the ideal society, whether it be a community of perfection, as in Plato's Republic, or of equality, as in the Marxist state. Thus Rawls is troubled by the tendency of the family to make more difficult the establishment of a regime of distributive justice. My suggestion is that the family is the cradle of individuality. To separate reproduction from the affection and nurture which naturally follows upon it is, I suggest, to separate body from person, the physical and contingent from the domain of choice and value. But that is a separation which is lethal to the secure possession of a sense of self, to our success as persons and thus to our success as a species. If we are reared by the state, then we belong to it almost as much as if the state had determined one's genes. Here again I should not be understood as arguing against day-care centers, orphanages, nor public education but only for the maintenance of a certain set of background assumptions.

Finally, I would enter a general plea for a greater toleration of diversity, even where that diversity threatens the tidiness of our most well-meaning schemes of social justice. I urge that we be willing to pay a fair price in inequality and foregone opportunities for social betterment in order to avoid a pernicious *Gleichschaltung* of the human condition. It is equality of respect, not of circumstances for which we should aim.

REFERENCES

(1) Fried, Charles. Right and Wrong. Chap. 5. Cambridge, Mass.: Harvard University Press. In press.

(2) ———. 1973. Ethical issues in existing and emerging techniques for improving human fertility. *In* Law and Ethics of AID and Embryo Transfer, Ciba Foundation Symposium 17 n. 5. The Hague: Mouton.

(3) Herbert, Frank. 1973. The Eyes of Heisenberg. New York: Berkeley Publishing Co.

(4) Rawls, John. 1971. A Theory of Justice. Cambridge, Mass.: Harvard University Press.

(5) Williams, Bernard. 1976. Persons, character and morality. *In* The Identities of Persons, ed. A. O. Rorty. Berkeley, Los Angeles, London: University of California Press.

(6) ———. 1973. The idea of equality. *In* Problems of the Self. Cambridge: Cambridge University Press.

ETHICS AS AN AUTONOMOUS THEORETICAL SUBJECT

T. Nagel

The usefulness of a biological approach to ethics depends on what ethics is. If it is just a certain type of behavioral pattern or habit, accompanied by some emotional responses, then biological theories can be expected to teach us a great deal about it. But, if it is a theoretical inquiry that can be approached by rational methods, and that has internal standards of justification and criticism, the attempt to understand it from outside by means of biology will be much less valuable. This is true for the same reason that the search for a biological explanation of mathematical or physical theories, or biological theories for that matter, would be relatively futile. First, we have no general biological understanding of human thought. Second, it is not a fixed set of behavioral and intellectual habits but a process of development that advances by constant reexamination of the total body of results to date. A being who is engaged in such an open-ended process of discovery cannot at the same time understand it fully from outside: otherwise he would have a decision procedure rather than a critical method. In most interesting subjects we do not want a decision procedure because we want to pursue a deeper level of understanding than that represented by our current questions and the methods we have for answering them.

No one, to my knowledge, has suggested a biological theory of mathematics; yet the biological approach to ethics has aroused a great deal of interest. There is a reason for this. Ethics exists on both the behavioral and the theoretical level. Its appearance in some form in every culture and subculture as a pattern of conduct and judgments about conduct is more conspicuous than its theoretical treatment by philosophers, political and legal theorists, utopian anarchists, and evangelical reformers. Not only is ethical theory and the attempt at ethical discovery less socially conspicuous than common behavioral morality but the amount of disagreement about ethics at both levels produces doubt that it is a field for rational discovery at all. Perhaps there is nothing to be discovered about it by such methods, and perhaps it can be understood *only* as a social and psychological peculiarity of human life. In that case biology will provide a good foundation, though psychology and sociology will be important as well.

In this paper I want to explain the reality of ethics as a theoretical subject. The progress of that subject is slow and uncertain, but it is important, both in itself and in relation to the nontheoretical forms that ethics take, because the two levels influence each other. The ethical commonplaces of any period include ideas that may have been radical discoveries in a previous age. This is true of modern conceptions of liberty, equality, and democracy, and we are in the midst of ethical debates that will probably result in a disseminated moral sensibility two hundred years hence which people of our time would find very unfamiliar. Although the rate of progress is much slower, the form of these developments is somewhat analogous to the gradual assimilation of revolutionary scientific discoveries into the common world view.

As in science, also, by the time one advance has been widely assimilated, it is being superseded by the next, and further developments use accepted current understanding as the basis for extension and revision. In ethics the two levels interact in both directions, and the division between them is not sharp. Acute questions of social policy produce widespread attempts to theorize about the basic principles of ethics.

A common idea of progress is found in all these fields, although it is not very well understood in any of them. It is assumed that we begin, as a species, with certain primitive intuitions and responses that may have biological sources. But in addition we have a critical capacity that has allowed us, starting a long time ago, to assess, systematize, extend, and in some cases reject these prereflective responses. Instead of estimating size and weight by touch and vision, we develop devices of measurement. Instead of guessing about numerical quantities, we develop mathematical reasoning. Instead of adhering to an idea of the physical world that comes directly from our senses, we have progressively asked questions and developed methods of answering them that yield a picture of physical reality farther and farther removed from appearance. We could not have done any of these things if we had not, as a species, had some prereflective, intuitive beliefs about numbers and the world. Progress beyond this has required both the efforts of creative individuals and the communal activities of criticism justification, acceptance, and rejection. The motivating idea has been that there is always more to be discovered, that our current intuitions or understanding, even if commendable for their time, are only a stage in an indefinite developmental process.

In applying this idea to ethics we must allow for the big difference that ethics is meant to govern action, not just belief. In trying to solve ethical problems we are trying to find out how to live and how to arrange our social institutions—we are not just trying to develop a more accurate picture of the world and the people in it. Therefore, ethics is connected with motivation. It begins not with prereflective ideas about what the world is like, but with prereflective ideas about what to do, how to live, and how to treat other people. It progresses by the subjection of these impulses to examination, codification, questioning, criticism, and so on. As in other areas, this is partly an individual process and partly a social one. And the progress of earlier ages is included as part of the socialization of members of later ones, some of whom may make advances in turn.

The development in this case is not just intellectual but

motivational, and it cannot be pursued exclusively by small groups of experts, as some scientific or technical subjects can. Because the questions are about how men should live and how societies should be arranged, the answers must be accepted and internalized by many people to be effective, even if only as steps in a continuing process. Though they need not be internalized equally by everyone, this requirement makes ethics a more democratic subject than any science, and severely limits its rate of progress. The community of debate does not comprise a set of experts, except in special institutional cases like the judicial system.

Still, the premise of this view of ethics as a subject for rational development is that motives, like beliefs, can be criticized, justified, and improved—in other words that there is such a thing as practical reason. This means that we can reason not only, as Hume thought, about the most effective methods of achieving what we want but also about what we should want, both for ourselves and for others.

It is of the utmost importance that such an investigation, such reasoning, is internal to the subject. It does not proceed by the application to this subject of methods developed in relation to other subjects, or of a general method of problem-solving and question-answering. While there are some extremely general conditions of rationality, they will not get one very far in any specific area of inquiry. Whether it is molecular biology, algebra, or distributive justice, one has to develop questions, concepts, arguments, and principles by thinking about that field and allowing reason and intuition to respond to its specific character. It happens again and again that the methods of one subject are taken as a model of intellectual respectability or objective rationality, and are then applied to a quite different subject for which they were not developed and for which they are unsuited. The results are shallow questions, nonexplanatory theories, and the anathematization of important questions as meaningless. Fields that lack a well-developed method of their own, such as the social sciences, psychology, and ethics, are particularly vulnerable to such intellectual displacement.

What then is the right way to think about ethics, and what kind of validity or objectivity is to be found within the subject as opposed to standards taken from without? Naturally opinions differ about this. If we set aside religious, Platonic, and natural law theories of moral knowledge on the ground that they no longer have sophisticated adherents, the methodological positions that are currently influential are of two types—these may be called deductive and inductive.

The deductive type tries to arrive at self-evident first principles about what is good and what is right—axioms knowable a priori by direct moral insight—and then works out a substantive ethical system by applying these principles to the complex circumstances and choices of human life. The results for the correct standards of conduct and the correct design of social institutions may be very complex. The two most prominent historical examples of the deductive method are utilitarianism and Kantianism. Apart from this similarity they are very different from each other and in fundamental ways morally opposed. The basic principle of utilitarianism, on the one hand, is that something is good if it satisfies the desires of persons or other sentient beings and that given a choice of actions or policies, the right one is that which will result in the maximum utility, or expected balance of satisfaction minus dissatisfaction taking together all the beings affected. The basic axiom of Kantianism, on the other hand, is the categorical imperative, which states that an act is wrong if the agent could not consistently will that the principle on which he is acting should be a universal law. This was thought by Kant to yield some very strict prohibitions, but all acts not ruled out by the categorical imperative are supposedly permissible, even if they do not maximize utility. (Recently, however, R. M. Hare (1) has argued that the correct application of a neo-Kantian requirement of universalizability implies utilitarianism as a moral consequence.)

The inductive method, by contrast, does not start with self-evident axioms, for it regards nothing as self-evident. Instead it regards moral intuitions at various levels of generality and specificity as data for ethical theory. Principles are adopted and revised on grounds both of intrinsic plausibility and of their ability to explain more specific judgments of which we feel confident. But no judgments or principles are beyond the possibility of revision, because none are axioms. Moreover the decision what to revise and what to reject when principles and judgments collide is itself a process of ethical judgment, and not the mechanical application of a consistency procedure. It is especially important that the body of data is not closed: it is continually being expanded by new practical problems and moral reactions to them. Some are actual and some are devised by the moral imagination specifically to test principles and to aid in their development.

Rawls (4) is the most important modern defender of the inductive method. He calls it the method of reflective equilibrium. While he says that it can be regarded provisionally as an investigation of our moral capacity, this quasi-psychological interpretation is not essential. The process of developing our considered judgments and bringing them under coherent principles can have as its aim not only internal consistency but greater objectivity. Each new development of the moral sense yields new judgments which create pressures for further changes in principles, criticisms, and justifications. Each stage of moral theory must collide with the world anew, and each stage will be complex enough to generate pressures for revision in its application to the world. I do not mean to imply that all such changes are progressive. That is not true in any area of human development. But the possibility of progress exists, and it is accepted by deductive as well as by inductive theorists.

Having said something about the general character of moral reasoning, let me turn briefly to the state of substantive opinion about ethics. The divisions among theorists have some relation to ordinary differences of moral opinion. I have mentioned utilitarianism and Kantianism. Both have been developed in fairly sophisticated ways. One example is rule-utilitarianism, the application of utilitarian reasoning to social institutions, with the result that certain institutions or policies that prohibit individual decisions based on utility have greater utility than the policy of making a utilitarian decision about every case. Thus a rule-utilitarian justification can be given for institutions like property and contract, even though they often require individual acts contrary to utility.

One of the unsettled questions about utilitarianism is how radical its implications are. Some utilitarians, like Mill, have thought that utilitarianism can justify the familiar individual rights and special obligations and does not require that we devote our lives to the service of the unfortunate. Among modern utilitarians, Peter Singer (5) has argued not only that we should give much more individual help than we are accustomed to giving to starving people in distant countries but that we should also become vegetarians and stop using animals as experimental subjects, except in rare cases.

Such assertions have been rejected by various opponents of utilitarianism who claim that it requires us to abdicate our individuality by subordinating our choices to the claims of the general welfare (6). The question whether ethics demands the protection of all individuals against certain internally or externally imposed sacrifices, or whether those sacrifices can be justified by enough advantage to others, is among the most controversial in contemporary moral philosophy. It emerges in the discussion of rights. One extreme view, libertarianism, has it that there are inviolable rights that may not be overridden for any purpose, that ethics begins and ends with these, and that utility and the general welfare create no moral claims at all (3). This gives each person a kind of moral veto on what may legitimately be done to him, but does not insure that anything must be done for him.

More moderate positions, that of Rawls for example, require each person's rights and interests to be respected in a more complex way. Not only are basic liberties to be protected but misfortunes resulting from arbitrary social and natural contingencies are to be rectified if possible by a redistributive social system. This is intended to express a version of the social contract, according to which a system, to be fair, should be freely acceptable to each of its members. Difficult problems have arisen about the interpretation of this requirement and about the grounds of acceptability that should be admitted in applying it. Some philosophers argue that only an actual social agreement, implicit or explicit, can give rise to moral requirements (2). But the moral conception is obviously very different from that which determines right and wrong on the basis of the general welfare rather than on each individual's point of view.

Underlying these disputes is a deep problem about the meaning of moral equality. Most modern ethical positions would subscribe to the principle that the moral claims or rights of all persons are equal. The requirements of morality are supposed to take into account everyone's point of view. The problem is that this principle by itself is not well defined. It does not say what the claims are which should be accorded equally to all persons. A libertarian would say they require only freedom from certain kinds of deliberate interference, assault, or violation. A utilitarian would say moral equality has been achieved if each person's satisfaction and dissatisfaction have been given the same importance as everyone else's in the calculation of general utility which in turn determines what is to be done. A contractarian would say it requires that everyone be guaranteed certain freedoms from interference but also that some forms of social control be used to rectify unfair substantive inequalities of welfare produced by social and natural contingencies that are outside of individual control. At present each of these positions has some plausibility, and theoretical methods do not exist that are powerful enough to rule out any of them decisively. Further explication of the idea of moral equality would also have to deal with the question of how membership in the moral community should be determined—whether the conditions are general enough to warrant the inclusion of animals other than humans as moral claimants, or conversely, whether they are special enough to limit the reach even of human claims within the boundaries of actual social or political communities.

My point is that ethics is a subject. It is pursued by methods that are continually being developed in response to the problems that arise within it. Obviously the creatures who engage in this activity are organisms about whom we can learn a great deal from biology. Moreover their capacity to perform the reflective and critical tasks involved is presumably somehow a function of their organic structure. But it would be as foolish to seek a biological evolutionary explanation of ethics as it would be to seek such an explanation of the development of physics. The development of physics is an intellectual process. Presumably the human intellectual capacity that has permitted this extremely rapid process to occur was in some way an effect, perhaps only a side-effect, of a process of biological evolution that took a very long time. But the latter can provide no explanation of physical theories that is not trivial. What human beings have discovered in themselves is a capacity to subject their pre-reflective or innate responses to criticism and revision, and to create new forms of understanding. It is the exercise of that rational capacity that explains the theories.

Ethics, though more primitive, is similar. It is the result of a human capacity to subject innate or conditioned prereflec-tive motivational and behavioral patterns to criticism and revision, and to create new forms of conduct. The capacity to do this presumably has some biological foundation, even if it is only a side-effect of other developments. But the his-tory of the exercise of this capacity and its continual reap-plication in criticism and revision of its own products is not part of biology. Biology may tell us about perceptual and motivational starting points, but in its present state it has lit-tle bearing on the thinking process by which these starting points are transcended.

There may be biological obstacles to the achievement of certain kinds of moral progress. Without question there are psychological causes. That does not make them insurmoun-table. They must be recognized and dealt with by any moral theory that is not utopian. But this recognition does not amount to acceptance of a biological foundation for ethics. It is no more than an acknowledgment that morality, like any other process of cultural development, must reckon with its starting points and with the nature of the materials it is attempting to transform.

REFERENCES

(1) Hare, R. M. 1976. Ethical theory and utilitarianism. *In* Contem-porary British Philosophy, 4th Series, ed. H. D. Lewis. London: George Allen and Unwin.

(2) Harman, G. H. 1975. Moral relativism defended. Philosoph. Rev. *84*: 3–22.

(3) Nozick, R. 1974. Anarchy, State, and Utopia. New York: Basic Books.

(4) Rawls, J. 1971. A Theory of Justice (sec. 9). Cambridge, Mass.: Harvard University Press.

(5) Singer, P. 1972. Famine, affluence, and morality. Philosophy & Public Affairs. *1*: 229–243.

(6) Williams, B. 1973. A critique of utilitarianism. *In* Utilitarianism For and Against, by Smart and Williams. Cambridge: Cambridge University Press.

PART
3

REPORTS
ON THREE GROUP
DISCUSSIONS

GROUP ONE:

H. S. Markl, Rapporteur
E. Butenandt,
D. T. Campbell,
F. J. G. Ebling,
L. H. Eckensberger,
C. Fried, H. Kummer

INTRODUCTION

Our working group addressed itself to the general problem of how the results of biological research, particularly of evolutionary biology, can contribute to an understanding of the nature and the evolution of morality, and to the question of where the limits to these contributions can be seen. We further discussed whether phenomena that are comparable to human morality can be found in animals. There was unanimous agreement that a purely nonnaturalistic approach to morality that ignores the results of biological research would lack important information for a full comprehension of moral phenomena.

The group took as its focus sociobiological views of morality, if "sociobiology" is taken to designate the field of scientific inquiry into the forms, mechanisms, functions, and evolution of social behavior in animals and man—as far as man can be regarded as an object of such inquiry by biological methods. However, we took pains not to be guided or limited by any particular set of sociobiological theories on the evolution of man's social system, especially not as they may be found in the often oversimplified and even distorted popular accounts of sociobiological arguments.

We proceeded by first explicating the essential attributes of morality, then inquired whether and how the presence of these attributes can be ascertained in animals; how and at which levels morality can affect fitness; what the biological prerequisites for the development of morality are; and whether there are universal biological dispositions that affect human morality.

THE ESSENTIAL ATTRIBUTES OF MORALITY

Neither specific features of overt behavior nor their consequences can be regarded as defining attributes of moral behavior. In particular, the often referred to altruistic self-sacrifice of one life for the benefit of another cannot be regarded as the touchstone of the presence of morality. On the one hand, entirely "nonmoralistic" explanations of such alleged nonselfish behavior are possible ((16–18) kin-selective explanation of worker caste "altruism" in insects) and, on the other hand, moral systems can readily be conceived that do not prescribe altruistic behavior as a moral goal.*

Any explication of morality that uses the word in its normal sense as applied to human morals has to refer to the decision-making processes preceding the occurrence of overt behavior. Thus, most of us found the following set of criteria necessary and sufficient for the concept of morality

*The joint use of the term altruism for both truly moral voluntary nonselfishness in the human sense as well as for the outcome of a particular behavioral interaction between organisms—where the "altruist" increases the beneficiary's fitness at the expense of his own (3, 16–18, 28–30, 52, 54–56) may seem deplorable, especially since the sociobiological theories were so successful in finding purely mechanistic, neo-Darwinian genetical explanations for the evolution of such behavior in animals and by this, as it were, explained the altruism out of animal "altruism." It seems futile, however, to try to completely avoid the usage of the term "altruism" in the sociobiological context. (J. Maynard Smith made a strong plea at the conference not to be too puristic in the application of language to phenomena of different natures for the purpose of creative thinking.) In order to avoid confusion in this report, altruism will be used only in its ordinary sense as applied to conscious human behavior, whereas the more technical and differently definded use of the term in sociobiology will always be enclosed in quotation marks, i.e., "altruism."

in that sense. (An alternative minority opinion on this matter can be found in the paper by D. T. Campbell, this volume.)

1. At the level of behavior there must be a situation of choice that entails as a consequence the possibility of conflict.

2. At the cognitive level there must be at least the potential for reflection about the action. This is tantamount to the postulate of self-consciousness.

3. At the level of rational thought, this reflection has to be of a purposive nature; reasons, not just causes, must potentially be given. This seems inseparable from the capacity for language either because language is the very medium of rational argumentation, which otherwise would not be possible, or because language seems to be the only way to communicate this rational reasoning.

4. But, not all rational reasoning can be considered as moral reasoning. Reasons have to be evaluative rather than purely instrumental, and there must be at least an attempt to universalize reasons to norms, that is, an attempt at objectivity that is reached by rational argumentation. Therefore, moral norms are typically referred to in order to justify one's actions to others.

5. Finally, this reasoning must somehow be related to purposes affecting individuals, for example, to their welfare, or to their survival (in contrast, for instance, to the purpose of solving a mathematical equation). Therefore, altruistic reasons would be one type, for most moral systems maybe even a very important type, of moral reason; but it is by no means the only or the decisively defining one. Hence, altruism seems neither a necessary nor a sufficient criterion for defining morality on the formal level.

CAN THESE CRITERIA OF MORALITY BE APPLIED TO ANIMALS?

Do animals make choices involving conscious purposes and intentions? While there is as yet probably no evidence specific to moral purposes and choices, it may be helpful to review the type of evidence employed in inferring the existence of purposeful choice in animals.

This problem is part of the more general philosophical problem of "other minds," that is, the problem of how I can know that another person has conscious experience. This knowledge cannot be established with certainty, just as solipsism cannot be decisively refuted. Our general conviction that other persons are conscious during most of their waking hours is based on an extension to others of our own private experience, by use of what philosophers refer to as the "argument from analogy," and, in addition, on the availability of a language containing terms for intentions, reasons, and conscious experience, which one can use to question others about their experiences. Whereas the availability of language does not "solve" the problems of "other minds," it does add great pragmatic conviction and subtlety to our judgment. Unfortunately, language is clearly *not* immediately available for determining the existence of animal purpose. The "argument from analogy" remains available, but the closeness of the analogy is greatly reduced.

Tolman's *Purposive Behavior* (51) summarizes substantial experimental literature bearing on this problem (partially updated by Campbell (2)). In this literature animals are reported to show consistency and persistence of goals and learned subgoals, rather than merely consistency of means, when tested by transposition experiments, in which instinct or learning is tested in a novel setting. For instance, Lashley (25) tested trained rats after a cerebellular operation that caused them to run in circles. These rats still navigated a maze they had previously learned and found the food box without entering any blind alley by use of a set of motor acts entirely different from that employed in training. What the rats had learned may be regarded as a series of subgoals, mediational purposes, in the service of a general food-seeking purpose. Such results turned Lashley away from Watson's behaviorism at a time when he was Watson's major student (see (35)).

Tolman also generated and summarized a literature on choice behavior, which focused particularly on hesitation accompanied by looking back and forth from one alternative route to another. Such "vicarious trial and error" increases in frequency during the early stages of training, later decreasing as training becomes complete and choice routinized. From careful inspection of their behavior, almost all ethologists and other observers of the behavior of mammals, birds, and even lower animals conclude that a genuine capacity for choice exists. Tolman (50), Mowrer (36), and others have used this as an observational clue for conscious experience in animals, and it is one of the "analogies" used by Lorenz (6).

Admittedly, an agnostic viewpoint on the question of animal awareness is certainly the safest ground for statements of irrefutable fact and certain knowledge. But what is called for from an evolutionary perspective are much bolder working hypotheses in order to find ways to explore and probe into the stages of mental development. This is particularly true for consciousness in animals, especially in primates, since fossil evidence for the mental correlates of the transition from ape to man is either entirely lacking or highly speculative and debatable. Very detailed analysis of an animal's behavior in solving problems, as previously stated, is to be regarded as one way of giving strength to the "argument from analogy." Another most exciting and promising approach can be seen in the efforts to teach "language" to chimpanzees or other apes (8, 9, 11–13, 43–46). As has recently been argued by Griffin (14), this approach may allow the formulation of tasks for apes to be carried out by using this learned "language" or the direct asking of questions to be answered by the animal. This might enable us to deepen our understanding of the mental processes involved and to explore the limits of animal "reasoning."

Although many students of animal behavior might prefer a parsimonious explanation in purely mechanistic terms of seemingly intentional, purposive, conscious behavior in animals, caution in interpreting phenomena should not fetter imaginative thought about animal awareness, whenever the results of the study of an animal's behavior call for an explanation at a higher level of integration. Here we may recall the widely held views of psychophysical parallelism, that is, the notion that human mental activity also requires constantly complementary explanations, both at the level of physiological mechanisms *and* at the level of a psychological "inner reality." In view of this prevalent dualistic approach to the human mind, the hypothesis of a conscious mind, at least in higher mammals, is by no means nonparsimonious. On the contrary, it is almost unavoidable in the search for the evolutionary transformation of this "inner reality" from an animal state to that of man.

If we therefore apply the criteria of morality listed above to animals, there is no disagreement about finding criterion number 1, or the capacity for behavioral choice, fulfilled. As to criterion number 2, it remains to be more fully explored whether in any animal cognitive development has approached the necessary level of reflectiveness and self-consciousness. "Mirror-image-experiments" (10) do, however, suggest for apes a considerable level of development in this respect. With regard to criterion 3, or purposive rational reasoning, the question of whether it is within the scope of apes remains to be further pursued. Although the capacity for language, in the full human sense, is clearly not present in apes, two lines of evidence caution us not to be too ready to reject the possibility of the presence of rational thought in animals purely on that ground:

1. As the studies on split-brain patients (47) have revealed, the "nonlanguage half" of the brain has considerable capacities for evaluation of information and reasoning of some kind. Sperry has come to the conclusion that after hemisphere disconnection, each hemisphere has a separate, autonomous consciousness and selfhood. This is diagnosed with great difficulty in the case of the nondominant hemisphere, because of its inability to generate speech and because, except under unusual test conditions, the same environment is represented visually and auditorially to both hemispheres.

2. The analysis of the development of "moral behavior" in the "prelanguage" child provides a singularly important source of information on the transformation of morality from a stage without fully developed language to a stage with access to it. This ontogenetic transformation could be a model for a process which must have occurred in evolution in the phylogenetic transition from animal to man. As the paper by Rheingold and Hay (this volume) demonstrates, empirical work on the development of prosocial behavior of the one- to two-year-old child, which is of crucial importance in answering these questions, is still in its very beginnings.

With regard to criteria 4 and 5, no indication so far exists that the level of universalization to norms and the relation of reasoning to purposes affecting individuals is reached in animals. In any case, 5 is almost subsumed by 3, since it seems difficult to conceive of reasoning in animals without at the same time assuming the capacity to apply that faculty to purposes affecting conspecific individuals.

We may therefore conclude that at present evidence is lacking that animals are capable of morally guided behavior—as the concept is ordinarily understood. Nevertheless, further inquiry along the lines indicated seems clearly not futile, since it may provide a better understanding of the stages of the evolutionary development of morality. The group concluded that usage of the term "moral-analogous behavior" should be avoided. This term is misleading, since it refers to comparisons at the level of the function of overt behavior from which, as set forth, the presence of morality cannot be inferred.

HOW AND ON WHICH LEVEL CAN MORALITY AFFECT FITNESS?

There is a rather crude and oversimplified way of applying biologistic reasoning to human morals (already clearly anticipated by F. Nietzsche). This leads to the suggestion that morality may just be a clever way to make us do what our genes want us to do anyway, namely, to reproduce them most efficiently, even though we may not be aware of serving these and only these goals. This notion could include the hypothesis that we are genetically guided, if not determined, to select our morals and to implement moral norms only to increase our genetic fitness—as survival machines with noble delusions about the real ends of our moral efforts and about our freedom of moral decision.

A much more cautious and sensible sociobiological interpretation would, of course, be to suppose that morals can (along with having other effects) also increase evolutionary fitness but that they do not do so inevitably by force of genetical determination. It is entirely within the frame of biological evolutionary reasoning to assume that there is no genetic disposition toward specific moral norms and that man is free to select moral goals, while granting that only those moral systems that give their adherents higher fitness than the followers of competing moral systems could and will prevail. In this way moral systems would be subject to selection in the process of cultural evolution according to their ability to confer greater fitness, that is, survival capacity on their adherents. This view, however, leads to the truisms that in the past the moral norms we hold cannot have lowered man's fitness too much (otherwise we would not be here to obey them), and that no universal morality that drastically lowers fitness is possible in the long run, since it would run out of adherents. Therefore, the real questions pertaining to the consequences of morality for fitness are:

1. What are the possible positive effects of morality on fitness and,

2. Can there be moral norms that lower fitness, thus proving that moral norms are not just the laws of Darwinian evolution in disguise?

Three levels in the evolutionary development of the contribution of behavior to fitness may be distinguished:

1. At the most primitive level there is the predominantly genetically determined neural circuitry of Stimulus-Response (S-R) programs (e.g., the stinging and sucking response of a mosquito to specific chemical stimuli). This state provides well for fitness as long as the environment is sufficiently invariant and changes only so slowly that adaptive genetic change can cope with changes in the environmental conditions.

2. At an intermediate and more flexible level, it is not the neuronal circuitry of an S-R-program that is genetically wired into the organism, but a set of "drives." Their satisfaction serves survival, while the different ways to satisfy them in a variety of environments are individually learned, for example, by conditioning.

3. At the highest level, insight into the long-range goals of behavior, that is, most importantly into the ultimate goals of survival and procreation, allows not only the satisfaction of innate "drives" but the attainment of these goals by use of rational reasoning and deliberate decision. The fitness value of moral reasoning at that level is given by its provision of insight into the long range goals and by the voluntary selection of motivations and of ways to meet them.

This last level of development implies that knowledge about the unknown future has to be approximated by inference from past experience which is codified in the form of moral norms. At the same time the acquisition of time-representation which is necessary for recognizing and considering the long-range purposes of behavior entails, as clearly set forth in Bischof's paper (this volume), that anxiety about the merely unreliably predictable future becomes a price to be paid for this insight. The freedom to select behavior on the basis of subjective reasoning makes the behavior of the social partner menacingly unpredictable (see also Kummer's paper, this volume). Therefore moral norms take on the additional function of reducing this anxiety by assuring that there is wisdom from the past available to help master an uncertain future, and at the same time, to make the behavior of social partners more predictable by "normation." Moral norms—as rules that govern the behavior of their adherents—can have an additional fitness-increasing effect, especially in their form of culture-dependent conventions (as to the development of the concepts of conventions and norms, see Turiel, this volume): by their adherence to a specific set of behavior-regulating rules, members of a social group or culture define themselves as distinctly different from members of other groups holding different moral convictions. It is well known from modern evolutionary theory that group-exclusiveness and intergroup discrimination are prerequisites for kin-selection and its beneficial effects on the evolution of cooperative sociality at the animal level (30, 31). Thus, insofar as the development of social cooperativeness increases the fitness of the members of a social group, the group-membership designative effect of holding common moral convictions and of obeying common behavioral rules can be a powerful mechanism for increasing the evolutionary fitness of individuals and groups.

An inborn propensity to strive for survival and reproduction has obviously caused man in the past not to disregard the effect of moral norms on fitness. Sociobiological hypotheses about the fitness value of morality are therefore certainly relevant to an understanding of existing moral systems. However, equally clearly, morality transcends "the morality of the genes" by being not inexorably bound to survival as the ultimate value to which any valid moral norm must conform. Morality can even renounce survival as a norm, although at the risk of extinguishing its adherents. However, as a moral norm for a subgroup of a population, this need not even endanger a population, if the remainder of the population continues to procreate efficiently and as long as the population as a whole gains from this polymorphism of morality. (It should be noted that this explanation resorts to the possibility of group selection, the occurrence of which some sociobiologists vigorously deny.) Thus morality can, and as a universal system of norms undoubtedly has, served to increase fitness. It can also serve other ends that may enhance, reduce, or fail to affect fitness. Therefore the answer to the question of whether moral norms are possible that lower fitness is clearly yes, not only on theoretical but also on empirical grounds.

As to the levels of selection at which morality can affect fitness, all levels—of the gene, of the individual, of kinship, of the group, and even of the species (as we have learned to be afraid of)—can be clearly involved, if one follows common biological practice to invoke higher level selection whenever selection at the lower level fails to explain results. Thus, if a genotype lowers the fitness of its carrier, but is nevertheless positively selected, selection has to be effective at a higher level, for instance of the kin-group—compensation for the lack of fitness in one individual by a sufficient increase of fitness in others. Since there is not the slightest evidence for assuming that there are genes for encoding specific moral capacities, discussion of effects of morality on the gene level seems of little relevance. However, one can profitably ask whether adoption of a "conduct by moral" strategy may lead a group adopting it to a fitness exceeding that of a population relying on an "evolutionary stable strategy" (ESS) in a "prisoner's dilemma" or "tragedy of the commons" type of situation as inferred by game-theoretical analysis at the level of individual selection (see Maynard Smith on ESS, this volume). By "agreeing" to act cooperatively, to adhere to the moral norms set for all and not to "cheat" (i.e., to receive social benefits without reciprocating, see Trivers (52)), it indeed seems possible to reach a higher level of fitness both on the individual and on the group level. To be workable such a system would have to include efficient ways to detect and sanction a cheater ("mobbing"), a sufficiently high level of cooperativeness by the social organization to make the benefit of "moral cooperation" felt, and a sufficiently high level of cognitive development to have behavior conducted by moral reasoning. It seems possible that these conditions were fulfilled at early stages of human evolution:

1. Kin selection in fairly exclusive groups coud have allowed cooperativeness to evolve, making an individual dependent on the benefits of communal support and making it difficult for one to switch groups (e.g., when detected at "cheating").

2. This enabled these societies to inflict without costly means severe punishment on the "cheater" who deviated from the group's moral norms, by withdrawing the social support and expelling him.

By this the stage is set for selection between groups according to their ability to develop, apply, and enforce moral norms that increase the fitness of individual group members by saving them the costs incurred by a game-theoretical solution for aggressive competition between group-members.

This line of reasoning suggests that morality might have arisen as a mechanism increasing the fitness of a group in competition with other groups, but only on a level of freedom of rational reasoning which at the same time opened a way to transcend the striving for fitness as an ultimate goal.

WHAT ARE THE PREREQUISITES FOR MORALITY?

The group dealt only cursorily with prerequisites for developing morality, that is, biological and psychological conditions, referring to the papers by Bischof, Rheingold and Hay, Turiel, and Kowalski et al. (this volume). Beyond the purely instrumental level of the capacities of the nervous system, for example, for cognition, the following abilities were considered particularly relevant: (1) the ability to differentiate between "self" and "other" (pointing, as analyzed by Rheingold and Hay, could be seen as one of the earliest indications of this capacity in the developing child); (2) the ability to infer feelings in others; (3) the ability to recognize goals and intentions (purposes) in others. (2) and (3) might be subsumed under the capacity to feel sympathy and to comprehend the role of the other, which is clearly the prerequisite for any generalization of norms and which entails the development of concepts of fairness and of resentment, taking offense, and sanctioning a deviant individual (e.g., Hoffman's (21) concept of "sympathetic distress" that occurs early in child development), and finally (4) the ability to be aware of the consequences of one's behavior and from there to develop the concept of responsibility for one's actions. This may have its roots in the "effectence motive" (53) or in "tertiary circular reactions" (42) of the very young child who has a "Funktionslust" (1).

ARE THERE GENETIC DISPOSITIONS THAT INFLUENCE HUMAN MORALITY?

By genetic dispositions we understand the inherited range of capacities of the organism to respond to influences from the environment, that is, the developmental potential defining the "reaction norm" both by the limits of modifiability and by the environmental conditions that allow optimal development of the organism.

Biological methods of investigating the involvement of genetic information in the development of behavioral traits are (a) "strong" methods—experimental selection of mutants and cross-breeding of different phenotypes in order to pinpoint the involvement of Mendelian genes and (b) "weaker" methods—ontogenetic development under conditions of stimulus deprivation or stimulus substitution, in order to ascertain whether and at which stage specific environmental input is necessary for the expression of a behavioral trait.

The "strong," genetical methods are not applicable to man for ethical reasons; the "weaker" ones (twin research; behavioral development of congenitally deaf-mute and blind children) yield important evidence. However, this evidence usually shows little more than a highly polygenic hereditary influence on human behavioral development—an influence that is far from rigidly deterministic in its effect (with the possible exception of very simple motor patterns).

The available evidence forces one to conclude that behavioral capacities of even a moderate degree of complexity are only very rarely dependent on single Mendelian genes (although that occurs also). Usually they are only very indirectly and highly polygenically influenced by genetic factors rather than specifically determined by a small number of genes. Therefore the development of most behavioral traits is strongly dependent on environmental conditions. Consequently, to ask about genetic influences on behavior in higher vertebrates, and especially in man, means usually to inquire about the influence of genetic programs on the ontogeny of behavior, stressing once more the developmental approach to an understanding of the moral nature of man.

Two additional lines of argument caution against assuming deterministic genetic programming of a particular behavior in animals and therefore even more so in man, just because that behavior is universally exhibited by all the members of a species:

1. The analysis of the ontogeny of bird song (19, 24, 32–34, 37–40, 48, 49) has shown that a given type of behavior (a complex courtship song) serving similar functions in different species arises in some species without any specific information ("model") from the environment during the development, whereas in other species it arises, as it were, as a "phenocopy" of this process by pure imitation of an external song model. It must be noted, however, that even in the latter case not *any* song model, but only a species-specific restricted class of models, can be imitated (see "constraints on learning," below.) There exist yet other bird species in which a basic, albeit imperfect species-specific song will develop autonomously, but for whose perfection the environment has to provide the information.

2. The artificial selection experiments of Ewing (7) with Drosophila show that a given gene pool has many ways of responding to the same selection pressure. Batches of flies were released in the first of a series of glass chambers connected by narrow funnels that prevented flies from returning to the previous chamber. Ewing successfully selected for "fast" and "slow" flies. Interestingly, closer inspection as to *how* fast or slow flies managed to be revealed various unexpected behavioral means. In some experiments, flies were "fast," not because they were inclined to walk more; rather, their gene pool had yielded to the selection pressure by making the flies socially less tolerant: they were "fast" because they ran away from the crowd in the start cham-

ber. In another experiment, slow flies were not found to walk less, but to be claustrophobic: they hesitated to pass through the narrow funnels and therefore were judged to be "slow." The lesson is: A trait may not have been selected for as an end, but as one of several possible mechanisms to reach an end. There is a certain accidentiality or freedom in genetic and epigenetic means by which an organism responds to a given selection pressure.

Genetic dispositions

The influence of a specific genotype on the expression of animal behavior is known to take several forms (6) (and all of these forms can also be expected to be present in man to a more or less pronounced degree; therefore they could conceivably enter in the formation of man's "moral nature"):

1. There exist genetic *constraints on learning* (see (20)) that determine what can be learned easily, what only with difficulty, and what not at all. Some things can be learned, or easily only, during one or more "critical" periods. The most effective learning paradigms are different at different developmental stages. And there can be differences in the permanence of an engram for different tasks, reinforcements, contexts, ontogenetical stages, learning processes, and sexes.

2. There is a genetic influence on the development of motivations, that is, of *propensities for specific activities*, as quantified by parameters of releasability ("drives"—ranging from easily modifiable tendencies to irrepressible compulsory action).

3. *Motor performance* can be genetically programmed to varying degrees (see bird song development, above). In some cases this hereditary program is only used in early stages of development, to be later refined or even replaced by learned motor programs (e.g., development of locomotory movements in human babies).

4. There is ample evidence for genetic programming in the *sensory domain* in animals and man ("releasing mechanisms" or "feature detectors," see (33)).

The discussions of the influence of genetic dispositions on morality usually focus on moral norms (since it is indisputable that there must be genetic prerequisites for the capacity to develop the cognitive attributes of morality, as set forth

above). *We may define norms as general rules for ordering
conduct derived from reflective moral reasoning.* The question of genetic influence on moral norms can be considered
in at least three ways.

1. *Is there a genetic disposition in man to develop norms
(of whatever contents)?*—Norms clearly seem to be a universal characteristic of man. Formation of habits, conforming to
habits, may be a stage of development that leads to the control of conduct by norms, although obviously a moral norm
that "degenerates" into a mere habit will lose the very essence of its moral quality. An inclination to accept the outcome of social conflict (e.g., to accept rank or property relations, see Kummer, this volume), a behavioral characteristic
that already clearly exists on the animal level, may be seen
as one of the preadaptations that facilitate the acceptance of
control of behavior by moral norms in evolving man. From
there it seems but a small step to the development of norms
that regulate social relations.

Pertinent material to the development of norms is presented in the papers by Nagel and Turiel (this volume). In
the child, development of norm orientation (4, 23, 41) proceeds from a stage at which primarily the consequences of
actions are taken into account (e.g., punishment, reward),
to one in which the intent of various concrete actors is
focused upon (instrumental hedonism); later both intentions
and consequences are simultaneously considered (15, 22),
first relating to peers and the family, then expanding to
groups and/or systems (5), and ultimately to general principles. These processes can be regarded as being driven by
the desire of the child to reduce uncertainty (unpredictabil-
ity) and insecurity (anxiety) by bringing order into actions
relating to environmental events, that is, to find and follow
rules of conduct.

2. *Are there inherited dispositions for specific contents of
norms?*—To find some universality in the content of moral
norms would not be surprising if one considers them from a
functional viewpoint. After all, there are many universal aspects of social life that have to be regulated by consistent
rules in order to make the actions of the social partners
more predictable, in spite of their behavioral freedom. As
seen at the most basic ecological level, this saves "costs"

(time, energy, etc.) by reducing competition and inefficient cooperation.

Among the domains to be regulated by norms, the following stand out most prominently and are regularly dealt with by moral systems, although not necessarily in the same fashion:

—aggression within and between groups
—sexual relations
—group allegiance and reliability of partnership
—reciprocity and sharing of essential resources and information as a basis for barter
—ownership and property (in primates we already see respect for the right of possession of the first-comer).

Behavioral regulation of all these aspects of social life are of course also necessary in animal societies. Many authors have therefore seen functional analogies between the adaptative function of social behavior in animals and of moral systems in man.

There are also universal conditions for valid, generalizable, stable norms, for example, the concepts of justice, equality, solidarity.

Is there, in addition to these very general "boundary conditions" for the contents of norms, evidence of genetic dispositions for specific rules? The group discussed this question only briefly in respect to incest prohibitions (see Kowalski et al., this volume), antihomicide norms, and sex-specific norms (topics to be further explored, but going beyond the scientific competence represented in the working group).

3. *Are there inherited dispositions influencing the ability or the willingness to behave according to norms or to violate them?*—This question may point to the most promising line of investigation into the influence of natural selection on man's genetic constitution relevant to the expression of morality. For instance, selection may have given rise to a heritable tendency to accept universal norms, but to implement some of them only under certain conditions, for example, when of advantage to one's own fitness or to that of one's kin ("nepotism"). In that case, the selection of a human genotype that develops guilt as a mechanism of self-sanctioning could then be viewed as the "simplest" way of en-

forcing universal application of norms, or to extend the norms beyond the biological kin-group to larger social units ("tribes"), and finally to all members of the species or even beyond that boundary.

It seems worth pursuing through further anthropological, ethnological, sociological, and psychological research the validity of an important sociobiological line of argument. This argument maintains that some norms can be much more easily implemented than others because they conform to the goal of increasing an individual's inclusive fitness. By contrast, norms that potentially lower inclusive fitness are more difficult to follow, or—on statistical average—are not actually followed at all, although they may be held in high esteem in a society. To put it differently: transgressions of norms would be more probable in directions that lead to an increased individual or inclusive fitness than in directions that lead to reduced fitness. Hence it would follow that systems of norms that exact behavior that runs counter to the dominant propensity to increase fitness are much more difficult to be implemented, are liable to engender more cheating and transgression, are inherently less stable, and inflict considerable stress on a society adhering to them. Such norms should therefore be counter-selected in the context of competing groups with different value systems. This argument does not demand that genes determine moral norms to conform to gene-survival goals; morality may transcend these goals, although it is likely that this can be done only against resistance. The same arguments could be applied also to alleged dispositional differences between the sexes and to norms regulating sex-specific roles of conduct. This clearly needs further exploration.

Whereas "cheating" can be regarded as a way of trying to take advantage of universal norms by letting others conform to them while making an exception for oneself at the other's expense, refusal to obey norms ("disobedience") under specific circumstances can of course also be the result of moral reasoning and of finding fault with existing norms. As set forth previously, norms embody traditional wisdom about the past which is used to extrapolate into the future in order to produce optimal behavior. Norms therefore tend to "fossilize" and resist changes, and hence are liable to becoming obsolete in a changing social and natural environment. Thus continuously new derivation and refoundation of norms by rational reasoning by every individual has to probe in each generation the continuing validity of traditional knowledge crystallized in norms. Or, according to J. W. von Goethe's epigram: "Was du ererbt von deinen Vätern hast, erwirb es, um es zu besitzen."

CONCLUDING REMARKS

It seems appropriate to sum up this group report by considering the levels at which a biological approach to morality could affect our understanding of that phenomenon.

1. At the instrumental, mechanistic level, biological functions (e.g., of the brain) set important boundary conditions for the possibility of moral conduct, as exemplified by hereditary or acquired neurological disorders.

2. Closely connected to that, the possibility of voluntary manipulation of these biological functions involves most important moral considerations: neurosurgery, drug administration, eugenics, or behavioral control techniques are examples of such manipulation.

3. Biological evolution determined the development of some of the fundamental capacities necessary for making moral decisions: cognition, self-consciousness, language, capacity for sympathetic generalization, and so forth. The identification of the sources of these capacities in the evolution of animal behavior, and the "reconstruction" of the evolutionary mechanisms that brought about the transition from animal to man, are genuine fields of biological research, highly pertinent to an understanding of man's moral nature.

4. Finally, at the rational level, one important source for the selection of reasons, not as ultimate goals, but as reasons among other possible reasons, is given by the biological concern for survival and increase of fitness of one's genes. Biology cannot prescribe survival or fitness as ultimately legitimate goals or "oughts." But if we decide, upon rational reflection, to accept survival as an important aim of our behavior, as almost every person seems inclined to do, biological knowledge indicates important conditions for the implementation of this goal. True morality may have to transcend the "multiplication morality" of the genes, so as to

make it possible to bring about consent among humans for a deliberate limitation of population size. Such consent may reduce the Darwinian fitness of some individuals, but it would increase the chance of survival of mankind as a humane species.

REFERENCES

(1) Bühler, K. 1919. Abriss der geistigen Entwicklung. Leipzig.

(2) Campbell, D. T. 1954. Operational delineation of "what is learned" via the transposition experiment. Psychol. Rev. *61*: 167–174.

(3) Dawkins, R. 1976. The Selfish Gene. Oxford: Oxford University Press.

(4) Eckensberger, L. H., and Reinshagen, H. 1977. Eine alternative Interpretation von Kohlbergs Stufentheorie der Entwicklung des Moralischen Urteils. Beitrag für das Internat. Seminar für Entwicklungspsychologie (ISEP). Trier.

(5) Edwards, C. N. 1974. The effect of experience on moral development: results from Kenya. Ph.D. dissertation, Harvard University.

(6) Ehrmann, L., and Parsons, P. A. 1976. The Genetics of Behavior. Sunderland: Sinauer.

(7) Ewing, A. W. 1963. Attempts to select for spontaneous activity in *Drosophila melanogaster*. Anim. Behav. *11*: 369–378.

(8) Fouts, R. S. 1975. Communication with chimpanzees. *In* Hominisation und Verhalten. Ed. I. Eibl-Eibesfeldt and G. Kurth. Stuttgart: Fischer.

(9) Fouts, R. S., and Rigby, R. L. 1977. Man-chimpanzee communication. *In* How Animals Communicate. Ed. T. A. Sebeok. Bloomington: Indiana University Press.

(10) Gallup, G. G. 1970. Chimpanzees: Self-recognition. Science *167*: 86–87.

(11) Gardner, B. T., and Gardner, R. A. 1969. Teaching sign language to a chimpanzee. Science *165*: 664–672.

(12) ———. 1971. Two-way communication with an infant chimpanzee. *In* Behavior of Non-Human Primates. Ed. A. M. Schrier and F. Stollnitz. Vol. IV. New York: Academic Press.

(13) ———. 1975. Evidence for sentence constituents in the early utterance of child and chimpanzee. J. Exp. Psychol. *104*: 244–267.

(14) Griffin, D. R. 1976. The Question of Animal Awareness. Evolutionary Continuity of Mental Experience. New York: Rockefeller University Press.

(15) Gutkin, D. G. 1973. An analysis of the concept of moral intentionality. Human Dev. *16*: 371–381.

(16) Hamilton, W. D. 1964. The genetical theory of social behavior. I, II. J. Theoret. Biol. 6: 371–371,

(17) ———. 1971. Selection of selfish and altruistic behavior in some extreme models. In: Man and Beast: Comparative Social Behavior, eds. J. F. Eisenberg and W. S. Dillon. Washington: Smithsonian Press.

(18) ———. 1972. Altruism and related phenomena, mainly in the social insects. Ann. Rev. Ecol. Sys. *3*: 193–232.

(19) Hinde, R. A., ed. 1969. Bird Vocalization. Cambridge: Cambridge University Press.

(20) Hinde, R. A., and Stevenson-Hinde, J. 1973. Constraints on Learning. Limitations and Predispositions. London: Academic Press.

(21) Hoffman, M. L. 1975. Developmental synthesis of affect and cognition and its implications for altruistic motivation. Dev. Psychol. *11*: 607–622.

(22) Holstein, C. B. 1976. Irreversible, stepwise sequence in the development of moral judgement: a longitudinal study of males and females. Child Dev. *47*: 51–61.

(23) Kohlberg, L. 1969. Stage and Sequence: A cognitive-developmental approach to socialization. *In* Handbook of Socialization. Theory and Research. Ed. D. A. Goslin. Chicago: Rand McNally.

(24) Konishi, M. 1963. Effects of deafening on song development in two species of juncos. Condor 66: 85–102.

(25) Lashley, K. S., and McCarthy, D. A. 1926. The survival of the maze habit after cerebellar injuries. J. Comp. Physiol. Psychol. 6: 423–432.

(26) Lorenz, K. 1963. Haben Tiere ein subjektives Erleben? (Do animals undergo subjective experience?) *In* Studies in Animal and Human Behavior. Vol. II. Cambridge, Mass: Harvard University Press.

(27) ———. 1965. Das sogenannte Böse. Wien: Borotha Schöller.

(28) Markl, H. S. 1971. Vom Eigennutz des Uneigennützigen. Naturwiss. Rundschau 24: 281–289.

(29) ———. 1974. Die Evolution des Soziallebens der Tiere. In Verhaltensforschung. München: Kindler.

(30) ———. 1976. Aggression and Altruismus. Konstanz: Universitätsverlag.

(31) ———. 1977. Biology of Discrimination. VI. Int. Forum Psychoanal. Berlin.

(32) Marler, P. 1970. A comparative approach to vocal learning: song development in the white-crowned sparrow. J. Comp. Physiol. Psychol. 71: 1–25.

(33) ———. 1977. Development and learning of recognition systems. In Recognition of Complex Acoustic Signals. Ed. T. H. Bullock. Berlin: Bahlem Konferenzen.

(34) Marler, P., and Peters, S. 1977. Selective vocal learning in a sparrow. Science 198: 519–521.

(35) Merleau-Ponty, M. 1963. The Structure of Behavior. Boston: Beacon Press.

(36) Mowrer, O. H. 1954. Ego psychology, cybernetics, and learning theory. In Learning Theory, Personality Theory, and Clinical Research. New York: Wiley.

(37) Nottebohm, F. 1968. Auditory experience and song development in the chaffinch, Fringilla coelebs. Ibis 110: 549–568.

(38) ———. 1969. The critical period for song learning. Ibis 111: 386–387.

(39) ———. 1970. Ontogeny of bird song. Science 167: 950–956.

(40) ———. F. 1972. Neural lateralization of vocal control in a passerine bird. II. Subsong, calls, and a theory of vocal learning. J. Exp. Zool. 179: 35–50.

(41) Piaget, J. 1948. The Moral Judgement of the Child. Glencoe, Ill.: Free Press.

(42) ———. 1952. The Origins of Intelligence in Children. New York: Int. University Press.

(43) Premack, D. 1971a. Language in Chimpanzees? Science 172: 808–822.

(44) ———. 1971b. On the assessment of language competence and the chimpanzee. In Behavior of Non-Human Primates.

Ed. A. M. Schrier and F. Stollnitz. Vol. IV. New York: Academic Press.

(45) ———. 1976. Intelligence in Ape and Man. Hilsdale: Lawrence Erlbaum Ass.

(46) Rumbaugh, D. M., ed. 1977. Language Learning by a Chimpanzee. The Lana Project. New York: Academic Press.

(47) Sperry, R. W. 1968. Hemisphere deconnection and unity in conscious awareness. Amer. Psychologist. *23*: 723–733.

(48) Thorpe, W. H. 1958. The learning of song patterns by birds with special reference to the song of the chaffinch, *Fringilla coelebs*. Ibis *100*: 535–570.

(49) ———. 1961. Bird Song. Cambridge: Cambridge University Press.

(50) Tolman, E. C. 1927. A behaviorist's definition of consciousness. Psychol. Rev. *34*: 433–439.

(51) ———. 1932. Purposive Behavior in Animals and Men. New York: Century.

(52) Trivers, R. L. 1971. The evolution of reciprocal altruism. Q. Rev. Biol. *46*: 35–57.

(53) White, R. W. 1960. Competence and the psychosexual stages of development. *In* Nebraska Symposium on Motivation. Ed. M. R. Jones. Lincoln, Nebraska.

(54) Wickler, W. 1967. Vergleichende Verhaltensforschung und Phylogenetik. *In* Die Evolution der Organismen. Ed. G. Herberer. Vol. I. Stuttgart: G. Fucher Verlag.

(55) Wickler, W., and Seibt, U. 1977. Prinzip Eigennutz. Hamburg: Hoffmann und Campe Verlag.

(56) Wilson, E. O. 1975. Sociobiology: The New Synthesis. Cambridge, Mass: Harvard University Press.

GROUP TWO:

G. W. Kowalski, Rapporteur
N. Bischof, J. R. Searle,
J. Maynard Smith,
H. L. Rheingold, E. Turiel,
B. Williams, P. H. Wolff

INTRODUCTION

In dealing with the problem of the limits of the naturalistic approach to morality, the discussion was directed toward (a) clarifying the basic theoretical presupposition of its members; (b) confronting both the members and their presuppositions with empirical data on incest prohibition, differentiation of sex roles, and ontogeny of morality in the child; and (c) considering the possibilities for, and limits to, further research along sociobiological lines on human morality.

THEORETICAL PRESUPPOSITIONS
A Characterization of Morality

B. Williams proposed the following characterization of morality as a phenomenological grid to enable us to look at what morality (a Western concept) might look like from the perspective of another culture. Morality is a system of assessing actions as being good or bad, for which the following conditions hold:

Morality is opposed at some level to egoism, and necessarily involves some degree of altruism, taken in the minimum sense of a disposition to take others' interests into account. (In this minimum sense altruism does not necessarily imply a particular kind of affect, e.g., benevolent emotion.) But the presence of this disposition seems importantly related to the cognitive capacity for empathy. (The selection of altruism as the basic condition of morality is influenced by a hypothesis about the function and hence perhaps about the origins of morality.) Moreover, moral behavior must have a representation at the intentional, conscious level. As far as the concept of intentionality is concerned J. R. Searle (17) pointed out that intentions belong to the class of mental state that is directed at objects and/or states of affairs in the world. Other members of that class are beliefs, fears, and desires: if I have a belief, it is a belief that such and such is the case; if I have a fear, it is a fear that such and such will happen; and if I have a desire, it is a desire for such and such to occur. This class is to be contrasted with another class of mental states that are not necessarily about anything or directed at the world, such as pain, tickling, and itching. The representative contents of intentions are the conditions of satisfaction under a given state of the world that is to be brought about.

The intentional representation of moral behavior may involve a variety of concepts. For instance, it does not necessarily involve the (Kantian) conception of *duty*, which is a particular, historically contingent, and not very satisfactory moral concept. Moral concepts relate, in particular, to the following items: (a) rules and prohibitions; (b) consequences of acts, particularly with regard to welfare and happiness; (c) human qualities and dispositions that are to be admired, emulated, or deplored.

A feature of *our* (Western) morality is that actions are typically assessed in the dimension of subjective voluntarism— the "mens rea" conditions. These conditions are the product of historical development; they have not been, perhaps could not be, perfectly carried out in our thought. The relation of these conditions to a supposed absolute and unfettered free will is still a matter of dispute.

In the complex, differentiated societies moral rules are to be distinguished from at least two other sorts of rules: laws (typically marked by formal sanctions applied to a public agency) and etiquette, or social conventions (typically marked by explicit relativism, "when in Rome . . ."). (Turiel observed [this volume] that three- to four-year-old children can distinguish between moral rules and social conventions.)

The moral system has a constituency. It is to be noted, though, that the class of its beneficiaries is not necessarily identical with the class of agents who are held (fully) responsible under it. (For instance, small children, the insane, and even animals are beneficiaries but not responsibles.) The Kantian ideal envisages a universal constituency, but the concept of a nonuniversal constitutency of a "tribal morality" is not self-contradictory.

The "Naturalistic" Approach

The term "naturalistic" has a very broad meaning. If "naturalistic" is taken to be the equivalent of "empirical," then the limits of the naturalistic approach to morality would refer to the limits of empiricism, a subject much too broad to treat in this discussion. We therefore arbitrarily restricted the use of the term "naturalistic" to that of the sociobiological system of explanation of morality. In that approach the strategy of optimal gene transmission is the basic functional explanation of social behavior and of its regulatory mechanisms. But, although social behavior necessarily pertains to groups, these gene transmission strategies are not necessarily group selection strategies. More frequently, they are kin selection strategies (see Maynard Smith, this volume).

Problems in Applying Sociobiological Explanation to Morality

Morality presupposes a real possibility of *alternative action*. Thus social behavior for which there is no inclination (e.g., eating someone else's excrements) is outside the province of morality. How then does one establish conceptually from the sociobiological perspective whether the nonoccurrence of a particular behavior is or is not attributable to a morally relevant gene transmission strategy? Morality is characterized by *intentional states*. How can such states be explained by the sociobiological approach? Morality is subject to a tremendous cultural elaboration of prohibitions and rules. How does one determine which components of morality have resulted from cultural adaptations and which from strategies of gene transmission?

Tentative Answers

N. Bischof attempted to clarify why the claims of the Naturalistic Fallacy do not follow from evolutionary considerations. An evolutionist version of the Naturalistic Fallacy is contained in two statements:

1. Instinctive inclinations ("what comes naturally") exist because they have been favored by selection; hence they are adaptive.

2. What is adaptive is good and should therefore be accepted as the natural basis of morality.

It is easy to see that the second statement is not valid. "Good" in the sense of "favored by selection" and in the sense of "morally desirable" are different concepts misleadingly referred to by the same word. The first concept is descriptive, the second normative, and there is no way of deducing an "ought" from an "is." It follows neither from the earlier group-selectionist definition of adaptation ("good for the species") that altruism ought to be morally more highly esteemed than egoism nor from modern gene selectionist considerations ("the selfish gene") that the opposite ought to be the case. The contribution of biology, or of any other empirical science, to the scientific treatment of morality is confined to two levels:

1. Biology may help answer the question of the *origin* of moral universals (e.g., of the incest taboo). This does not imply that it could justify why those universals *ought to be* universals.

2. Once a society has agreed as to what morality its members ought to follow, a better knowledge of human nature, as provided by biology and other behavioral sciences, could help to indicate what measures (e.g., strategies of education and socialization) would be taken in order to insure that these norms are optimally obeyed and that undesired side-effects are avoided. Again, biology cannot justify the claim that moral laws *ought to* conform to human nature.

Returning to the first of the two statements of the Naturalistic Fallacy, Bischof questioned whether a sociobiological explanation of a phenomenon is bound to assign an adaptive function to that phenomenon. In order to clarify this question, he developed the following schema:

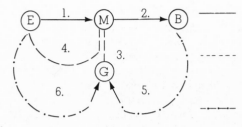

actual causation of processes:
1. stimulation,
2. release,

ontogenetic shaping of structure:
3. genetic programming,
4. environmental modification and nurturance,

phylogenetic selection according to degree of adaptation of
5. behavior to
6. environmental factors relevant to survival

Due to particular brain mechanisms (M) (including those underlying intentional mental activity), a human organism will respond with a particular behavioral program (B) to a particular environment (E). This behavioral program may or may not be adaptive in a given environment. If it is not, selection will act on the genome (G) of the organism and of its descendents. Thus G will change until, in the presence of modifying influences from E, it is able to shape the brain mechanisms M in such a way that a better adapted B is likely to be produced. If E is sufficiently stable, the whole feedback system will reach an equilibrium, in which case we call the behavior B "optimally adapted" to E.

Any marked environmental change from E to E' is likely to disturb this equilibrium: E' may, together with the unaltered G, cause brain mechanisms M' to develop that respond to particular stimuli from E' with a new behavior tendency B', where B' is no longer adaptive under E'. Admittedly, selection will at once start to readapt B' to E' by way of process number 6 of the schema; but this may take thousands of generations, and if the environment keeps shifting quickly enough, then no equilibrium can ever be reached. Hence, certain behavioral tendencies, albeit "coming naturally," may nevertheless be maladaptive.

To give an example: Suppose that humans have a natural tendency to protect children, which was probably adaptive (i.e., furthering selection of the genome via inclusive fitness) under paleolithic conditions (E). In the environment created by modern industrial society (E'), the same tendency is about to abolish infant mortality, that is, to disable the hitherto most efficient tool of natural selection. This counterselective effect is liable to lead to a depression of vitality of future human generations and therefore it is maladaptive. If a modern industrial society determined that the health of future generations be of paramount value, it might set moral norms which partially curb the natural tendency to protect children. If, however, another society deemed the emotionally dehumanizing effect of such a breeder's attitude applied against fellow humans to be more deleterious than possible eugenic drawbacks, it will arrive at quite different moral prescriptions. Both moral systems, albeit mutually contradictory, are based upon, but cannot be deduced from, a biological assessment of human nature.

E. Turiel criticized Bischof's schema as far as its relevance for sociobiological explanations of morality is concerned. He asked the following questions:

What is the exact nature of the mechanisms M? Are they specific brain functions or general brain structures? Inasmuch as the capacity for empathy and compassion is central to the development of morality, how can one envisage this capacity as a particular brain mechanism?

What is the relationship between the brain mechanisms M and the behavioral tendency B? Is this relationship a causal, direct one, as implied by the arrows in Bischof's diagram, or is it indirect, mediated by intentionality? Is not the mediation of intentionality and its relationship to culture necessarily interposed between M and B, if B is morally relevant behavior? Does the relationship between M and B in this diagram not develop through experience, being subject to change throughout life? Hence, because of the interposition of intentionality, the relation between M and B is not fixed, and B can change to B' without M changing to M'.

Thus, Turiel proposed the following modification of Bischof's schema:

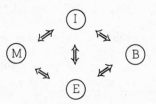

Here I represents intentionality, and the G element representing the genome is absent. Therefore, Turiel's modified schema would deprive the sociobiological approach of its relevance for explaining any relation between environment and intentional, morally relevant behavior.

Another perspective on the relationship between sociobiology and morals, not necessarily in conflict with that put forward by Bischof, opens up when biology is taken as a metaphor. One can envisage two such perspectives: (1) As outlined by Dawkins (2), the development of cultures can be viewed as being analogous to the development of biological organisms, whereby "memes" (e.g., ideologies) are to institutions what genes are to morphology; (2) as pointed out by G. Kowalski, biology can be considered not as the reality of organisms but as a scientific model that explains observational data about the living world. Accordingly, as a scientific model, biology is subject to cultural pressures. As recognized by students of the sociology of biology, one of these pressures is the demand that only such evidence is acceptable which supports biological models that conform with the central interests of a given society or group. For example, in a society attempting to legitimize population control and in which science is the major source of legitimation, biologists would look for data supporting a theory of a genetic strategy that controls reproduction to ensure survival of the species. Thus from this second perspective, the relationship between sociobiology and morals is reciprocal and mutually reinforcing. However, once the social interest component of scientific concepts has been exposed by critical review of their actual basis, the facile use of biological theories to implement ideological goals loses credibility. The recent history of sociobiology seems to confirm this finding. This aspect is more fully disclosed in the report of Solomon et al. (this volume).

CONFRONTING THEORETICAL PRESUPPOSITIONS WITH EMPIRICAL DATA
Incest

The incest taboo appears at first sight as a quasi-universal feature of the most diverse cultures. The interpretations given to this taboo can vary; but it remains by dint of its universality a very good test case for comparing sociobiological with other explanations. It should be noted, however, that in the Solomon et al. report (this volume) this claim is contested. The social anthropologist members of that group

seem to regard the incest taboo as an abstract generalization from an extremely heterogeneous collection of
phenomena. Instead of focusing on the universality of the
phenomenon, the social anthropologists appear to find explanations in terms of specific functions in the structure of a
particular society more promising, enabling them to understand the concrete form of the taboo. Nonetheless, the abstract concept of the incest taboo does not seem to be devoid
of all utility, since one can try to find out more about the
common ground in the complex cross-cultural evidence by
describing the taboo in quantitative terms and discussing it
as a sociobiological phenomenon. The group discussed the
presentation of the biological basis of the incest taboo by N.
Bischof and an alternative psychological interpretation derived from psychoanalytic theory.

According to Bischof (1) the function E relating the intensity a of approval/disapproval of sexual relations to the distance d of a possible sex partner presents an inverse U-
shaped curve. The distance d refers to proximity in kinship,
or culture, or geography, or physiognomy, defined in quantitative terms through an appropriate scaling device, or
metric. The relation $a = F(d)$ presented in graphical form
below is thus the statement of an extant moral norm.

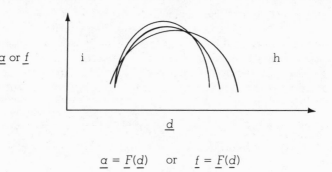

$$\underline{a} = \underline{F}(\underline{d}) \quad \text{or} \quad \underline{f} = \underline{F}(\underline{d})$$

We obtain an analogous function F if a is replaced by the
statistical frequency of sexual relationships f. (There are of
course differences in the scales of the graph, depending on
different cultures.) The relation $f = F(d)$, however, is the
statement of a sociobiological finding.

For animal species an analogous relation $f = F(d)$ can be obtained. The i limb of the curve corresponds to the avoidance of sexual relationships with close kin; the h limb represents the avoidance of hybridization. In almost all known cases there is a complete absence of sexual relationships within the core family (small values of d), and there is no example of obligatory inbreeding—except in some parasites.

The following functional explanation of the i branch of the $a = F(d)$ function can be provided. The selective advantage of preventing inbreeding is identical with that of biparental reproduction: the multiplication of genetic diversity that increases the rate of evolutionary change. Hence the progeny of individuals reproducing biparentally and avoiding inbreeding adapt more quickly to a changing environment than do their uniparental or inbreeding competitors.* The mechanism that insures the exclusion of close-kin sexual relationships seems to be based on (a) family dissolution at a certain stage of offspring development and (b) instinctive avoidance of sexual relations with individuals with whom one is highly familiar. In accord with Bischof's schema, the incest-related brain mechanisms M determined by the genome G would result in an emotional reluctance to engage in sexual relationships with close kin—individuals familiar since early childhood. This reluctance in turn would then be interpreted by various cultural prohibitions, to insure behavior B, or observance of the incest taboo.

The major countertheory to the sociological explanation of the avoidance of incest comes from psychoanalysis. According to this theory there is an innate tendency to engage in incest, with the taboo arising from the strong social element of competition with the father and ensuing fear of castration—the father's reaction to the challenge to his possession of mother and children. One can refine this simplistic scheme by taking into account that incest can provoke intrafamilial warfare, with the incest taboo evolving in Lamarckian terms.

Another psychological explanation would see incest prohibition as a social generalization of the reluctance on the

---

*J. Maynard Smith does not support this argument and points to negative pressure (e.g., avoidance of genetic disease) as the cause of outbreeding.

part of parents to introduce children to sexuality at too young an age. There exist also sociological versions of these arguments (cf. Durkheim (3, 4), Levi-Strauss (9, 10), Parsons (15)), and a general survey of the theories on incest has been provided by Bischof (1).

In discussing the relative merits of these approaches it was conceded that Bischof's account of the incest taboo has the virtue of establishing a bridge between the sociobiological finding $f = F(d)$ and the extant moral norm that $a = F(d)$. That function F has a similar shape in both cases suggests an underlying common cause. Nevertheless, the similarity of the F functions describing the approval of sexual relationships on the one hand and their frequency on the other hand does not mean that the two phenomena are identical. It merely suggests their common evolutionary origin. But so far we can only describe this parallelism, without giving it a causal explanation.

The difficulties with the psychoanalytic explanation of the incest taboo are related to the whole set of general criticisms of Freud's theory that have been made from the empiricist perspective.

In this connection the group made an observation which constitutes a kind of paradox. In animals, the incest-avoiding behavior (a) is given the functional explanation of avoidance of breeding with genetically closely related partners, but (b) it must be based on an attribute other than proximity of genetic relation, such as proximity in upbringing, since an animal cannot read another animal's birth certificate. However, in the rules against incest which humans consciously follow, it is of course kin, and therefore genetic proximity, that figures in most moral representations. Although it may be the case that proximity in upbringing does, in fact, inhibit sexual relations (as suggested by evidence from kibbutzim), this inhibition is represented in consciousness not as a prohibition, but merely as a disinclination or lack of interest. Thus there would exist a direct correspondence between the ultimate functional purpose envisaged by the sociobiological explanation and the intentional content of the moral prohibition. Is this kind of "cunning of nature," by which covert, ancient strategies found a way to reflect themselves in human intentional states? To elaborate some of the questions arising from this paradox we resorted to the following schema:

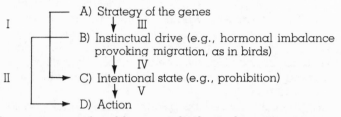

If we assume a hard-line sociobiological position we envisage relations III and II. In this case, cultural intentionalities would be merely an epiphenomenon of the genetically coded instinctual drives of relation III that provoke action directly via relation II. The direct correspondence found in the human incest taboo between the intentional content of the prohibition and the covert strategy of the genes imply the existence of relation I. One can then see intentional states as foam on the wave of genetic strategies. There would arise a problem for the sociobiological explanation if relation IV were absent and if there were autonomous reasons on level C explaining behavior D. In that case, an explanation for the "cunning of nature" would have to run something like this: In human evolution, relation IV has disappeared, or never arose in the first place. Hence intentional states no longer are, or never were, dependent on instinctual drives. The inner structure of intentional states is directly governed by the genome and is the relevant causal explanation of action. Relations I, II, and V are, of course, maintained, and relation III would then account for observations such as the reluctance to have sexual relations with people familiar from childhood (according to the kibbutzim experience).

Another interesting problem falling within the domain of psychophysiology would be the role played by a reversal of relation IV, that is, by the modification of instinctual drives by intentional states, and hence by moral prohibitions.

Sex Role Differentiation

At present there rages an ideological controversy regarding various issues raised by human sexual dimorphism. One of these issues is whether biological factors determine sex differences in behavior, from which society draws conclusions as to how men and women are to be treated (legitimation of privilege versus moral prescription of equity). Another such issue is whether biological factors determine sex differences in morality (due either to general cognitive capacities or to specific moral dispositions). These ideological issues surface clearly whenever social norms or policies are based on the data of sociobiology, that is, when "ought" is derived from "is."

As already argued by Bischof, evolutionary considerations cannot be used to support the kind of reasoning generally rejected as the Naturalistic Fallacy. Yet one must ask whether an ought derived from a description of a social role is not immune from the usual criticism of the Naturalistic Fallacy. A description of one's social role is a description of what in a given social context one *ought* to do. The question is still more cogent when the roles are not simply based on social conventions, but seem to have some biological substratum, such as sex. Because of this ideological situation it would seem important to examine sociobiological position on sex role differentiation and the psychological evidence. The sociobiological position on sex role differentiation was discussed by J. Maynard Smith. The problem to be explained is that there is in all, or almost all, societies both an economic role differentiation between the sexes, and a difference between the characteristics held to be desirable or virtuous in either sex. The question of whether, and to what extent, there are cross-cultural similarities in the nature of these differences is an empirical one, to be answered by anthropologists rather than by biologists.

Explanations are needed at two levels, functional (i.e., what selective pressures were responsible for the human tendency to adopt a role differentiation between the sexes?) and causal (i.e., what psychological/developmental processes are responsible for their appearance?). Causal explanations vary from the extreme environmentalist one, that people behave differently because they are treated differently (if so, the functional explanation is simply the functional explanation of our cognitive capacity which acts alike in men and women), to the one extreme genetic determinism that men and women develop differently by genetic processes, and that society merely reflects this underlying genetic reality.

Animal studies suggest that in species without parental care it is usual for the female to be selective in her choice of a mate and for the male to mate as often as he can; a male can increase the fitness of his genome most easily by mating as often as possible. In species that have evolved parental care, however, it may pay a male to expend energy in parental care rather than in mating with more females. In primates selection has produced three main patterns of behavior: harem groups with one male, several adult females and their offspring; monogamous pairs; and multi-male groups in which the males are polygamous or promiscuous. In monogamous pair situations males care for the young. There is no mammalian group which is both multi-male and monogamous, although this does occur in birds.

It is hard to guess what the social system in man has been for the past million years. In present human societies, one generally observes that one male lives with one female, at least temporarily, within a larger group. It is a question for anthropology whether the exceptions to this general finding are so numerous as to cast doubt on the idea that this social system is ancient in evolutionary terms. Man has been killing large game for at least one million years, which probably implies the existence for that length of time of a group bigger than the monogamous pair. The present sex dimorphism in the size of men and women is suggestive of the existence of ancient hunting groups composed of males, since in other primates size dimorphism is absent in monogamous species.

How ancient is economic role differentiation of the sexes? It is hard to see how we can gain direct evidence on this point. If it is in fact ancient, and if the nature of the differentiation has had constant features, there would be strong prima facie reasons for expecting some differences in genetic predispositions for economic role differentiation. For, if the sexes played different roles, the selection pressures on them would be different. However, in the absence of reliable information either on social structure or role differentiation in our remote ancestors, we are driven to psychological investigations to answer the causal question. P. Wolff noted in this connection that females mature earlier than males, which results in a different balance between right and left brain hemispheres in the two sexes. This can be related to difference in cognitive modes, and therefore to differences in the assignment of roles.

H. Rheingold, however, questioned the relevance of sex-role differentiation to the question of the naturalistic limits of ethical behavior. Admittedly, an individual's sex role is probably the most salient of his or her many social roles. "No other social role directs more of his overt behavior, emotional reactions, cognitive functioning, covert attitudes, and general psychological and social adjustment" (14). And all cultures assign men and women different activities, tasks, characteristics, and attitudes. But, not only do the assignments differ among cultures but so too does the extent of differentiation (e.g., (12)).

According to Rheingold, the most general statement attributes sex-role differentiation to the interaction of genetic and environmental influences. Because environmental influences, in the form of differential rearing for boys and girls, begin at birth, the separate effects of genetic predisposition and culture cannot easily be assessed. "In the theory of psychosexual differentiation, it is now outmoded to juxtapose nature versus nurture, the genetic versus the environmental, the innate versus the acquired, the biological versus the psychological, or the instinctive versus the learned. . . . The basic proposition should not be a dichotomization of genetics and environment, but their interaction" (13).

Physical, or biologic, differences are present at birth. Male infants weigh more at birth, have fewer fat cells, and by three weeks of age have more and larger muscle cells than females. Yet, on the day of birth the skeletal maturation of the female infant, a measure of biological age, is one month ahead of that of the male infant's. The female, therefore, comes into life a biologically older, more highly developed organism. The more advanced maturation of the female infant, enabling her to attract more attention and nurture, has been attributed to the greater selective pressure on her through a tendency to neglect girls differentially in early childhood (5).

Beyond such behavioral differences as may result from the earlier maturation of females, the greater physical strength of males, and the later differences in sexual function, the evidence for other psychological differences between boys and girls may be questioned, at least in Western culture. Some evidence suggests that girls have greater verbal ability than boys, that boys excel in visual-spatial and mathematical ability, and that boys are more aggressive. No such evidence, however, exists for the belief that girls are more social or suggestible than boys, have lower self-esteem, or lack achievement motivation (11). Of paramount importance is the very considerable overlap between the sexes in the distribution of any psychological attribute.

In contrast to the absence of convincing evidence of sex differences in psychological attributes is the presence of convincing evidence for differences in the rearing of boys and girls. Anthropological studies abundantly reveal many differences not only in how the two sexes are treated as children but also in expectations of how they will behave as adults. Both treatments and expectations become sex-role stereotypes; that is, they provide oversimplified and standard views that are held in common by the group. Just such stereotypes may well be responsible for the very early differences in rearing believed to start with the answer to the first question asked about a newborn, namely, "Is it a boy or a girl?" Recent studies of maternal behavior in the United States have not shown clear sex effects in *amounts* of care, except when the sex of the second child (especially a boy after a girl) differs from that of the first (7). Some evidence suggests that mothers talk more often in response to their daughters' vocalizations, but a recent review of many studies did not reveal any consistent differences in parental behavior; overall uniformity of socialization was more impressive than differences (11). The absence of differences in the studies, however, does not mean that differences do not exist; the samples of subjects were small, represent only middle-class persons, the measures may not have been appropriate, and the behaviors of mothers were studied more often than those of fathers, and so forth.

Quite a different conclusion was reached in one of Rheingold's own studies that showed marked differences in the toys and furnishings in the rooms of boys and girls under six years of age in a university town (16). Boys not only had more toys than girls but also were provided more vehicles, education-art materials, sports equipment, toy animals, depots, machines, fauna, and military toys. Girls, in contrast, were provided more dolls, dollhouses, and domestic toys. These differences in what parents provide for their children may well document differences in other classes of their behavior toward their sons and daughters. Without question, boys and girls are treated differently in school, and even today their vocational training and expectations for success in different occupations differ. But once again, the differences may not be as great as measures of overlap and uniformity. Various processes have been proposed to account for what differences do obtain. They include psychoanalytic propositions that implicate the mechanism of identification; social-learning theory that emphasizes direct tuition, observational learning, and reward and punishment; and a cognitive-developmental explanation that specifies the effect of knowing one's sex (the label, boy or girl) on acquiring the behaviors appropriate to that sex.

In most cultures men are more aggressive and dominating than women. Generally men are assigned the more physically strenuous, dangerous tasks, and those requiring absences from home. Women, on the other hand, play a more subordinate role; they care for the children and the other members of the family. A closer examination of the female role in any culture suggests that subordination may be more imagined than real. Women as rearers of children possess tremendous power, power that customarily goes unremarked, even by the women themselves. In this role they can transmit or transmute the culture. To women also has been ascribed the origin of complicated linguistic practices. "Women gossiping may have provided linguistic richness that both sexes then could use. . . . This feminine verbal preoccupation may be very important in human evolution" (6). Then, in many cultures women not only prepare food but by their own efforts produce the larger part of it. Furthermore, at least since the Industrial Revolution, large numbers of women have worked outside the home and thus shared with men in the production of income. Yet the development of tradition-fixed roles, produced by the biological differences of men and women, makes for a degree of efficiency and thus possesses greater survival value.

As Rheingold points out, in our time we have witnessed some alterations in the roles of men and women. It would be a mistake to attribute the alterations only to the discovery of simple birth control measures; the alterations began decades ago, grew firm with the civil rights movement, and became only more general with the easier control of births. After all, the reduction in family size antedated the "pill." It is true that totalitarian states need women in the work force and therefore routinely provide child care. In the democratic states, however, the movement of women into the work force has been accelerated by the women's liberation movement, by the technological inventions that reduce home and family care operations, and by the family's need for extra income to purchase these very inventions. A by-product of these cultural changes in the woman's role has been the increased caretaking of children by men. It remains for future history to determine the benefits to culture of human beings who within themselves integrate what hitherto have been considered to be masculine or feminine roles, a state of affairs imagined by the science-fiction writer U. K. Le Guin in the *The Left Hand of Darkness* (8). Women should consider carefully the extent to which the power that stems from their primary responsibility for rearing the young may be lessened when shared with men. In the last analysis, however, the chief concern of all responsible men and women should be what most benefits children.

In the discussion of the sex role differentiation, three different and perhaps contradictory arguments were advanced. First, the sociobiological data presented are open to multiple interpretations. This situation can be contrasted with the relatively simple identification of the function of sexual preference versus distance adduced by Bischof. Second, there is no definite cross-cultural and cross-species universality as evidence for a biologically based sex role differentiation, whereas such evidence does exist for the incest taboo. Third, it would appear that the strong environmentalist position—that all social behavior is the product of society—can have just as strong a political implication as

the genetic determinist position. If the kind of general sociobiological explanation proposed by Bischof is accepted, the
women's liberation movement would have to take into account a possible anxiety produced by what would amount
to going against an innate sex role.

Development of Morality in Children

The data on development of morality in children were interesting to the group particularly in those areas where they
seemed to offer a lever on the question: Is there a specific
brain mechanism that controls the acquisition of morality?
The question has some analogy with the language acquisition problem. There is a hypothesis, which not all developmental psychologists accept, that language is acquired by
a species-specific mechanism; that is to say, the child can
learn natural human languages such as French, German,
and Chinese only because all these languages, however diverse may appear their surface structures, are all based on
certain linguistic universals, or deep structures, and because there emerges an innate capacity to grasp these linguistic universals in the child's developing nervous system.

The question may then be asked whether or not there is
any evidence for a mechanism that predisposes to certain
forms of morality that have some common "grammatical"
deep structure, if we can carry over these metaphorical
terms from language to morals.

There was a general consensus among the developmental psychologists of the group that regardless of whether
language is acquired thanks to an innate development of
the capacity to grasp linguistic universals, or putative deep
structures, there is no evidence, or at least insufficient evidence to support the hypothesis that morality is acquired by
an analogous process. More generally their argument was
that developmental studies are consistent with a weaker
position: that is, that sociobiological trends provide cognitive capacities enabling humans to engage in moral behavior. The argument was developed along the following lines:

1. The developmental contribution to morality seems to be
that:

   a) Pro-moral (pro-social) behaviors appear as early
   as the first years of life, albeit in rudimentary form
   (Rheingold).

   b) Ability to verbalize moral reasons appears by three

years of age, as well as the ability to distinguish between moral behavior and social conventions (Turiel).
c) Moral behavior and moral reasoning increase steadily
with the maturation of cognitive abilities.
This development is not limited to a critical period or restricted to early infancy. Rather, a continuous process of
change (and under some theories, a continuous transformation) of what was earlier acquired turns later into more refined versions of a moral disposition.
2. These changes in moral action and moral judgment,
however they may be defined, are very real in a substantive sense. Once one considers the differences between infants, children, and adults in their moral dispositions, one
has to look seriously into the basis for such changes. Both
moral behavior and moral reasoning are acquired by experience; that is by interaction with people (i.e., with their responses to the subject's behavior):
—by being a recipient of the moral behavior of caretakers
and
—by observation, imitation, reward, and punishment.
In that sense biology does not substantively explain moral
action (and one can assume that moral action here includes
moral judgment). No special learning mechanisms need to
be invoked; the primary mechanism is the capacity to learn.
3. Research is needed to bridge the gap between moral
action and moral reasoning. The distinction between moral
action and moral judgment seems important in certain theories of the ontogenesis of morality. Action and judgment
probably represent different lines of development that cannot be studied as one unit, but the feedback one on the
other. However, theories differ on the nature of this feedback. There would generally be a departure from the exclusive consideration of moral judgment, as is the case for certain followers of Piaget.
4. The question whether the "cognitive disposition" for
morality is cognition in the most general sense or is a system
of acquisition of a subset of rules or notions (such as notions
of mathematics or biology), that go through somewhat similar developmental sequences could not be settled.
These reflections leave many unanswered questions. The
developmental psychologists suggested that a solution may
come from further study of the developmental transition

from the behaviors of very young children to those of older children who can report on their judgments and reasoning for moral behavior.

STRATEGIES FOR FURTHER RESEARCH

We do not think that the problem at issue is the "proof" or "disproof" of the sociobiological approach to morality, although we recognize the general limitations that may be imposed on that approach by the central role of intentionality. The general discussion showed that there exists no "crucial experiment" to be looked for in sociobiology, no more than it exists anywhere else in science. We would rather approach the question in terms of what results would indicate progress or lack of progress in a research program of applying sociobiological concepts to morality. We take it that progress in such a program would be shown by the production of convincing explanations of the following kinds.

1. The demonstration of the existence of a *universal* moral behavior, universal among human cultures, or still better, universal across species (such as the incest taboo) for which the research program can produce sociobiological explanations that take into account the environment of early hominids. This behavior, of course, might now be either functional or dysfunctional with respect to man's present environments; *functional* here, as throughout this discussion, is taken to mean, in accordance with the more stringent kind of sociobiology program, conducive to leaving more copies of one's genome.

2. The provision of functional explanations for *variable* moral behaviors among human cultures in terms of available environment. The idea underlying this kind of sociobiological explanation would be that what evolved in the original hominid environment was a flexible behavioral disposition, which is activated in different forms by different contemporary environments. Some members of this group (Bischof, Searle) are skeptical that explanations of this form could ever contribute to the validation of a sociobiology research program. They reason that where such variable behavior exists, there would always necessarily be an alternative, nonsociobiological explanation in terms of a general learning capacity, man having learned what moral behaviors are valuable in such environment. However, if the con-

nection between the postulated variable disposition and the present behavior were very tight, and the postulated variable disposition were of a very specific kind, some credit for the sociobiology program might be gained from explanations of this kind.

3. The finding of explanations for *variable* moral behaviors which in some cases are actually *dysfunctional* with respect to the present environment. A sociobiological explanation would be effective in such a situation if it could explain the disposition to such behavior as having been functional in relation to an environment plausibly supposed to have been that of early hominids.

It is of course not disputed that sociobiological explanations of some kind could be invented to meet these various cases. However, there is a real question about how many behaviors fall into the class of universal moral phenomena in any case. A question also arises when sociobiological explanation is advanced for a dysfunctional behavior in respect to present environment: is the corresponding moral rule still sociobiologically founded? (cf. population control issues versus sociobiological trends of kin selection).

The question is how convincing, how simple, or how epicyclic such explanations might turn out to be. This is a question not different in principle from the evaluation of other complex research programs. In this sense, subject to the important limitations discussed elsewhere in this report, we do regard the question of the limits of the sociobiological approach to the explanation of human morality as open to future research.

REFERENCES

(1) Bischof, N. 1972. The biological foundations of the incest taboo. Soc. Science Info. *11*: 7–36.

(2) Dawkins, R. B. 1977. The Selfish Gene. Oxford.

(3) Durkheim, E. 1898. La prohibition de l'inceste. *In* L'année Sociologique. Vol. 1. Paris.

(4) ———. 1925. Les formes elementaires de la vie religieuse. 2d ed. Paris.

(5) Hutchinson, G. E. 1965. The Ecological Theater and the Evolutionary Play. New Haven: Yale University Press.

(6) ———. 1976. Man talking or thinking. Amer. Scientist 64: 22–27.

(7) Jacobs, B. S., and Moss, H. A. 1976. Birth order and sex of sibling as determinants of mother-infant interaction. Child Devel. 47: 315–322.

(8) Le Guin, U. K. 1969. The Left Hand of Darkness. New York: Walker.

(9) Levi-Strauss, C. 1958. Anthropologie structurale. Paris.

(10) ———. 1967. Les structures elementaires de la parenté. 2d ed. Paris-La Haye.

(11) Maccoby, E. E., and Jacklin, C. N. 1974. The Psychology of Sex Differences. Stanford: Stanford University Press.

(12) Mead, M. 1935. Sex and Temperament in Three Primitive Societies. New York: Morrow.

(13) Money, J., and Ehrhardt, A. A. 1972. Man and Woman, Boy and Girl. Baltimore: Johns Hopkins University Press.

(14) Mussen, P. H. 1969. Early sex-role development. In Handbook of Socialization Theory and Research. Ed. D. A. Goslin, pp. 707–731. Chicago: Rand McNally.

(15) Parsons, T. 1954. The incest taboo in relation to social structure. In Br. J. Sociology 5.

(16) Rheingold, H. L., and Cook, K. V. 1975. The contents of boys' and girls' rooms as an index of parents' behavior. Child Devel. 46: 459–463.

(17) Searle, J. R. 1977. What is an intentional state? (to be published).

GROUP THREE:

R. C. Solomon, Rapporteur
C. Geertz, E. A. Gellner,
J. Goody, F. A. Jenner,
T. Nagel, G. S. Stent,
W. Tu, G. W. Wolters

INTRODUCTION

Sociobiology is the recently promulgated name of a currently controversial discipline which seeks to account for the social organization of animals, including humans, in Darwinian and, ultimately, in genetic terms (Wilson, 1975). The special concern of our group was to examine this attempt to explain human society and "human nature," in particular the phenomenon usually designated by the term "morality." We wanted to see if, and in what sense, human morality could be "illuminated" or "explained" by genetic biology and if, as some proponents of sociobiology have contended (usually in the final chapters of their books), the Darwinian analysis of social behavior can or does in fact yield substantial moral conclusions.

Our group consisted of anthropologists, philosophers, one biologist, a scholar of Chinese philosophy, and a psychiatrist. Accordingly, our bias was markedly toward cultural rather than biological accounts of human society, toward an appreciation of human differences rather than universal similarities, and we were more concerned with the values implicit in, claimed on the basis of, or suggested by sociobiology than we were with the validity or fruitfulness of the enterprise itself. Our conclusions, therefore, might best be summarized by a recommendation of "caution," both where bold moral claims are made from sociobiological science and, even more so, where they are not explicitly made but implied or suggested all the same.

The validity of evolutionary explanatory schemes and the nature of biological explanation in general are outside the domain of our discussion. We discussed such problems only briefly, reminding ourselves to be suspicious of trivial and ad hoc accounts, dubiously extended to humans. So too, the seemingly undeniable points of contact between biology and ethics, for example, problems of population control, pollution, and medical ethics, were not discussed. There, of course, biological findings influence or, in some cases, dictate (together with certain normative principles) substantial moral conclusions. Our concern was limited to sociobiology as defined by Wilson, Trivers, and others (see Suggested Readings) and its claims to substantial moral implications. Wilson (1975) for example, states quite explicitly that questions about justice should be taken out of the hands of the philosophers and handled by the biologists. He also implies that sociobiological research shows that ideals of justice may not, in fact, be justified: "While few will disagree that justice as fairness is an ideal state for disembodied spirits, the conception is in no way explanatory or predictive with reference to human beings" (Wilson, 1975, p. 562).

We wanted to find out if such studies have or could have such moral implications; or whether sociobiology itself has certain moral presuppositions, which may appear as conclusions, or may not be stated at all, but in fact are assumed from the start as part of the nature of the enterprise. And, we remained fully aware of those moral implications which were suggested by some of these studies, even in cases where (as in Dawkins, 1976) these implications are explicitly denied. Whereas a scientist may not be responsible for the abuse of his theories or its gross misinterpretations (e.g., some of the absurd accusations leveled against Wilson), he or she is responsible for what C. Geertz called "the atmosphere" created by a theory. Terminology, notably, is important here. We therefore asked whether sociobiology accurately presents its own explanandum and its terms, for example "morality" and "altruism"; and whether there is, in fact, anything for sociobiology to explain, namely, moral universals which obtain in every human society and are at least *candidates* for biological explanation.

Accordingly, we divided our group discussion, and therefore this report, into three questions and sections:

1. Does sociobiology have moral presuppositions? If so, what are they?

2. What are the meta-ethical presuppositions and concepts of sociobiology?

3. Are there social universals, such that a sociobiological attempt to explain them is appropriate?

I. THE MORAL PRESUPPOSITIONS OF SOCIOBIOLOGY

Wilson (1975) has pointed to the evolution of the hypothalamus and limbic systems evolved by natural selection with the comment "that simple biological structure must be pursued to explain ethics and ethical philosophers, if not epistemology and epistemologists, at all depths. . . ." It is the phrase "at all depths" that signals a radical claim, far more than the tepid and uncontroversial claim that, if such structures had not evolved, then people would not have anything like the conceptual and behavioral capacities that they do have, and so could not have anything like what we normally call "morality." Wilson's aim and the aims of some other sociobiologists (e.g., Lorenz, 1966), concern specific and substantial moral claims as well, including prohibitions against certain sexual activities and the principles of human welfare, justice, and fairness.

It is therefore important to itemize these various levels ("depths") of both biological explanation and specificity of moral claims, since Wilson claims to be operating on "all" of them. Biological explanations may focus on the genetic level (that is, the level of the individual genotype), on the level of the individual organism, the group, population, or species. On the genetic level, questions of human morality as such would seem to be excluded entirely but, with the aid of some significant terminological slippage (see section II), moral institutions have been discussed in terms of their "selfish" advantages for the individual genotype (Dawkins,

1976). On the individual level, questions of morality are obviously pertinent, but the role of the individual in the scope of the evolutionary process is negligible, and individuals do not evolve genetically. At the group and population levels, morality is relevant and an evolutionary theory of social organization is plausible, but conditions needed for group selection rarely exist in nature (Maynard Smith, this volume). At the species level, both morality and theories of evolution are relevant and plausible, so it is at this level that most sociobiologists presume to operate. "Humanity," it can be pointed out, is a central concept, and "universality" the aim of a great many moralities and moral theories, from ancient Chinese thought to the European Enlightenment, in Kant and utilitarianism. Also, the species is (virtually by definition) the maximum range of cross-breeding possibilities and so the most convenient and common unit of evolutionary explanation, that is, in terms of the genotype(s) of the species, which in turn explain its defining features. Thus Wilson, for example, undertakes the explanation of human universals, with the understanding that these may have a genetic base. He does not deny that a great many differences within the human species are products of culture and environment rather than of genetics and biological evolution, but he insists that at least some essential human traits can be so explained. On each of these levels, however, it is the survival of the genotype that is the key to sociobiological theory.

Regarding the various levels ("depths") of morality, it is important to distinguish at least (1) the human *capacity* for moral reasoning and behavior, (2) the *fact* that humans reason and behave morally and, (3) *specific* moral principles and/or practices, which may or may not be universal, for example, taboos against incest and intermarriage, (qualified) injunctions against killing, or treating others (whether of the same tribe, nation, or species) with regard to their interests. Furthermore, it is important to distinguish moral *behavior* and its consequences from the motives and intentions that motivate such behavior. Level (1) can, of course, be handed over to the sociobiologists, without objection, as having a (partially) specifiable biological and genetic base. However, very little if anything is now known about it, and any nontrivial biological explanation seems very far off. Level (2) raises the obvious problem, to be treated in section

II, of defining or at least circumscribing those features which deserve to be called *moral*. Level (3) leaves open the question whether any of these specific principles are in fact universal and thus appropriate candidates for sociobiological explanation. It is important to note that level (2) also leaves this question open, pending some adequate definition/circumscription of what is to count as moral. On some accounts, moral behavior itself (for example, action according to certain categorical principles) may be demonstrably not universal. Sociobiology claims to explain all three levels, both behavior and motivation. Our question was whether it can, or whether it instead has presupposed what it presumes to explain.

We have already pointed out the importance of the difference between moral presuppositions and moral conclusions: the first are assumed at the outset of an inquiry, the second are, presumably, drived from the findings of the inquiry. It is also important to point out the difference between those presuppositions *inherent in the very project* of the sociobiologists on the one hand, and those which are simply "tacked on," whether by an individual researcher or by sociobiologists as a group. In our discussion, we found out that it was often difficult to make this distinction in practice. On the one hand, we all agreed that there was a "pure" conception of sociobiology, which simply made the limited claim that it would provide an evolutionary account of the advantages of a certain existing trait in a given surviving species. It would in no way be presumed that the survival of that species or its basic genotypes was a "good" in any but the trivial sense of "having made the survival of the species possible." But when the species in question is homo sapiens, the survival of the species or of its basic genotypes suddenly appeared as just such a "good," in fact, an ultimate good, and the trait in question accordingly appeared as a virtue.

We were unable to agree on exactly where this "impurity" entered into the investigation—as part of the very conception of sociobiology *applied to humans* or as part of the psychodynamics of certain sociobiologists. But insofar as this concept of the good of the survival of the human species or genotypes entered into sociobiological investigations, it seemed to enter as a moral presupposition, rather than as a conclusion. It was not clear to us whether a sociobiological study of human social organization could be purged of such a presupposition.

Insofar as sociobiology (applied to humans) has moral presuppositions, there seemed to be a number of argument forms emerging, though rarely, if ever, so explicitly as we present them here. Where the presupposition in question is a substantial moral assumption, such as the above ("survival is good"), the argument looks something like:

(a) moral assumption (e.g., survival is good),
(b) sociobiological findings (e.g., aggression aids survival in n-n$_z$ species studies),
(c) ergo: a principle of conduct (e.g., people ought to be aggressive).

In subsequent discussion, it became obvious that, in addition to the question of the propriety of the initial assumption in (a) and the obvious problem with the inductive leap hidden in the seemingly deductive inference from (b) to (c), the same pseudo-practical syllogism could be used in exactly the opposite way, to support a principle of conduct directed at combatting a dubious "natural" tendency.

Or consider:

(a) Survival of one's own genotype is good, that is, for each of us (moral assumption).
(b) "Altruistic" behavior of certain kinds increases fitness and thus increases the likelihood of the survival of one's own genotype (sociobiological finding).
(c) "Altruistic" behavior (of certain kinds) is good.

It is this sort of argument that marks the enormous difference between some of the new sociobiological implications and traditional social Darwinism. Some authors, however, continue to argue the older Darwinian "selfishness" line, but without the moral consequences of that tradition. Dawkins, for example, argues that, "If there is a moral to be drawn, it is that we must teach our children altruism, for we cannot expect it to be part of their biological nature" (Dawkins, 1976). Both arguments, however, share the controversial form:

(Sub-human) animals are P. (altruistic/selfish)
ergo: People are also "naturally" P.

The problems with any such argument should be obvious.

An argument that is almost explicit in Wilson's last chapter is that:

(a) It is unreasonable to expect people to act contrary to their nature.

(b) People "naturally" act preferentially toward their own kind.

(c) *ergo*: Principles that instruct us to treat everyone equally are unreasonable.

Such arguments use sociobiological findings to set limits to human moral goals. The crux of the matter, however, is whether sociobiology can establish the second premise and move to the conclusion, since it can be argued that: (1) where social and moral institutions are involved, no number of findings, among animals or men, can show that something is "natural" and necessary rather than contingent and potentially variable; (2) that no such findings, however conclusive, can undercut the rationality of moral ideals—at most, they can show us how difficult it may be to obey them; and (3), it is also true, not only according to sociobiologists but anthropologists and developmental psychologists too, that human behavior is enormously "plastic," so that culture makes humans adaptable with minimal biological restraints. (Consider the difference between "Isn't it terrible the way lions treat antelopes" and "Isn't it terrible the way people only consider their own interests and those of their friends and family.")

Given the leap from inductive evidence regarding some species to what is "natural" for humans, and given the leap from an empirical generalization about what is natural to what *ought* to be done, we seriously doubted that any such arguments could be sound. Furthermore, the nature of such logical leaps made us doubt whether any such arguments could be made formally valid, and, if not, just what kind of logical force they could possibly have. For example, it is one thing to argue that biology *determines* certain behavior or inclinations to behave, something else to say that biology imposes certain *constraints* on human behavior and proposed moral principles, and something else again to say that biology offers us certain considerations and suggestions concerning our moral principles and behavior.

Not all morally-implicative assumptions are moral assumptions as such. Some of the most important arguments implicit in some sociobiological writings instead involve a meta-ethical premise, that is, an assumption about the concept of morality and related concepts, or assumptions about proper source or justifications of moral principles. Most evident among these, as one would expect, is the assumption that morality *should* have a naturalistic (that is, in this context, biological) source. (Sociobiologists are resoundingly quiet on the question of justification, but source and justification are often intimately related.) This argument scheme would look something like this:

(a) meta-ethical assumption (e.g., ethics should be natural),

(b) sociobiological findings (e.g., living things have a natural tendency to act toward survival of their genotype),

(b₁) humans are living things),

(c) ergo: principles of conduct (e.g., humans ought to act to preserve their genotype).

Or:

(a) Altruistic behavior is behavior that benefits another organism's genotype at the expense of one's own genotype (meta-ethical stipulation).

(b) There is no altruistic behavior (sociobiological finding).

(b₁) There is no point encouraging something that doesn't exist anyway) (covert premise).

(c) ergo: There is no point in encouraging altruistic behavior.

This argument, whose conclusion is sometimes denied as soon as it appears (e.g., by Dawkins, 1976) nevertheless permeates the atmosphere in which sociobiology is discussed. It is therefore important that it be made explicit, if only to be rejected, and that its crucial use of moral terminology in the stipulation of a technical biological concern be critically scrutinized (see section II).

Of course, these arguments become more provocative, as well as more dubious, as the premises and conclusions become increasingly specific. But it is worth mentioning another form of argument that is controversial just because of its grand abstraction. This is the argument, clearly indicated by Wilson, that begins with certain philosophical assumptions and proceeds to a rejection of morality as such, at least in some of the forms in which we think of it. For example:

(a) philosophical assumption (e.g., morality presupposes free choice),

(b) sociobiology can/will provide deterministic explanations (in terms of natural selection of our moral "choices"),

(b_1 deterministic explanations show that there is no free choice),

(c) *ergo*: morality has no objective validity.

Premise (b_1) has long been a matter of controversy among philosophers, since whether determinism undermines the objective validity or morality depends on how one understands "determinism." We scrupulously avoided delving into the formidable so-called free will problem, and so left the issue unresolved, with about half the group believing that deterministic explanations by biologists, if true, would entail the rejection of morality as such and some of the group arguing that deterministic explanations, if sound, would only complement moral arguments, not undermine them. Consequent to this discussion, a further argument emerged:

(a) One can critically assess only what one can "step away from," and consider rejecting only what is not determined.

(b) Biological evolution determines our values, so that we can neither "step away" from them nor consider rejecting them.

(c) *ergo*: Our values cannot be critically assessed nor can we even consider rejecting them.

One objection to this argument was that, even if biological determinism is accepted, what is determined is our critical capacities just as well as certain values. In fact, one can argue (following both Kant and Aristotle) that our critical capacity is itself determined as our most important value. Another set of objections, though not pursued, were directed, again, at the notion of biological determinism itself. The danger of these deterministic arguments, in particular, is that they can be used to silence disagreement with all the earlier arguments. Our conclusion, therefore, was that whatever one believes about biological determinism, reflective criticism must be absolutely essential to any discussion of morals.

We have already mentioned the most evident moral presupposition of sociobiology—the value of the survival of one's own genotype, that is, at least when it is human evolution being discussed. One way of stating this argument is this: the sociobiologist can say, for each member of each species, its own good is the survival of its genotype. But when the species in question is the human species, the sociobiologist is included, and the "its own good" becomes "my/our own good." Thus, what in the other cases could be described simply as a norm in accordance with which animals (or their genes) could be discussed, now becomes for the sociobiologist the discussion of a norm which he or she accepts *for us*. One might say that, if they are right, the sociobiologists embrace knowingly the biological values which the rest of us act on in ignorance, perhaps (foolishly in their eyes) even denying their very existence.

In any case, the survival of one's own genotype emerges as an essential *moral* ingredient in any sociobiological discussion. This is not merely a *fact* about our behavior, as some cautious theoreticians insist, but it becomes a normative constraint, or perhaps a necessity, through use of one or more of the previous arguments (whether explicitly or implicitly, straightforwardly or deviously, intentionally or unintentionally). This presupposition suggests (but perhaps does not entail) others as well. Since the emphasis is on survival, and since it is the genotype and surely not the individual that survives, sociobiology includes a distinctive bias against the individual. Thus, it was pointed out, it is hard to imagine how someone who believes that sociobiology can explain ethics could even entertain conceptions such as fairness and individual rights, since these would seem to be, on any but the most ingenious ad hoc Darwinian analysis, not contributing to and probably working against the survival of the genotype. (Dawkins [1976] for example, argues explicitly that lying, cheating and other clearly immoral behavior will give one "an advantage in the gene pool.") The protection of the weak, for example, would be such an obvious incompatibility. This demotion of the individual and his or her rights is not unique in sociobiology, it should be emphasized.

Any approach to moral issues which takes a considerably larger (or smaller, e.g., individual's genes) unit than the individual will *tend* to neglect individual concerns and rights. For example, Hegel's philosophy of the State, because it takes "the State" to be the "real" entity in question tends to make individual concerns secondary or derivative of the concerns of the larger entity. Thus the bias of sociobiology away from the individual is inherent in any such approach to morality. This is *not*, emphatically, a bias that sociobiologists accept personally, but it must be made clear that it is inherent in the very nature of the enterprise. Furthermore, the emphasis on genetic survival and those human traits contributing to it produces a kind of degenerate essentialism, in which the concept of human nature is reduced to its "lowest common denominator," namely, those traits helping survival. Virtually all intellectual, cultural and critical enterprises are accordingly dismissed as "by-products" of human nature, that is, not contributing to survival. A quote from Santayana emerged at this point: "What is most valuable about humanity is most useless." Sociobiology, it would seem, has a built-in bias against much of what people have always thought best, or definitive of, human nature, for example, "reason." (Aristotle and Kant, both using functionalist explanations, argued that what made reason most valuable and essential to human nature was precisely the fact that it was biologically irrelevant.) Again, it may well be the case that many sociobiologists would deny any such biases, would fully endorse a humanistic commitment to the arts, culture, and critical thinking, and would continue to insist on the "purely scientific" and nonnormative status of their inquiry. But what emerged from our discussion was the conclusion that such moral biases and norms are difficult, if not impossible, to purge from sociobiology as applied to humans—insofar as these are presuppositions which lie at the base of the entire enterprise.

II. META-ETHICAL PRESUPPOSITIONS AND CONCEPTS

Meta-ethical principles are principles *about* morality, including the definitions or circumscription of its central concepts, including the concept of morality itself. Sociobiologists claim to explain human morality without bothering to define what they mean by morality. Thus one objection that pervaded our group discussion was that sociobiologists presupposed that morality was in fact a term denoting a single set of human practices. This presupposition was itself under severe attack, and on two separate (but related) grounds: (1) it was argued, with many examples, that a great many practices which we would call moral display significant differences between them; and (2) that various *conceptions* of morality hold that different features are definitive of morality.

The sociobiological use of morality proved to be, even in a first analysis, an extremely limited concept which omits most of what is usually referred to by that name. In fact, the sociobiological basis for talking about morality seemed to rest upon a single phenomenon, namely, the fact that animals sometimes act in such a way as to aid the survival of another animal of their species, a finding which is, in the abstract, a surprise to those who have always assumed that the basis of all animal behavior is self-interest. This self-sacrificing behavior is what sociobiologists refer to as "altruism," and it is this conception of so-called altruism which forms their most critical link with human morality. Two different sets of arguments follow from this. Some sociobiologists (e.g., Dawkins, 1976) continue to argue that such seeming altruism is in fact just selfishness on a deeper level (e.g., the level of the "selfish gene"); others (e.g., Wilson, 1975) have tried to take this apparent altruism seriously, even if, on a genetic level, such a concept would not apply. Whereas it once was believed that all animal behavior is essentially selfish (and thus human behavior too, as Hobbes argued centuries ago), some sociobiologists have now suggested that at least some animal behavior is altruistic (and thus at least some human behavior, as Hume, Shaftesbury, and Rousseau also argued several centuries ago, based on sympathy for one's fellow creatures). Two questions thus emerged which define our discussion of these topics:

(a) Is the altruism of the sociobiologists the same as, or significantly similar to, the altruism of ordinary parlance?

(b) Is altruism, even in its ordinary meaning, the same as, or an essential ingredient in, morality?

Two principles guided our discussion: first, it seemed essential that we not circumscribe these terms in such a way that we ruled out, a priori, any possibility of subhuman moral or altruistic behavior. This meant too that we had to be prepared to accept certain cautious generalizations of such terms if they proved to be heuristically valuable in discussing animal behavior. But, second, we were resolved that we would not tolerate devious stipulative definitions or ordinary terms, with verbal slippage between the technical term and the ordinary one. Needless to say, the line between generalization and slippage was often hard to find, but some of the abuses were not at all difficult to recognize.

Our first criticism of the sociobiological concept of altruism was that it is defined behavioristically, in terms of *consequences*. In other words, if an animal in fact serves the interests of another animal of its species, to its own detriment, it is behaving altruistically. This was objected to on two grounds. First, it was clear that an animal which accidentally or stupidly benefited another animal of its own species was not being altruistic on any interpretation. Altruistic behavior, even in the special sense of that term used here, must be systematic, not accidental—for example, the protective behavior of mother birds, bees, and soldier ants. Second, and more important, it was clear that an animal might regularly serve the interests of another animal of its species, but just coincidentally, or only because this is a way of serving its own interests. Accordingly, we agreed that any behavior that deserves to be called altruistic required a disposition to help other creatures (offspring, members of the same hive or tribe, or simply members of the same species) "for its own sake," not for *only* selfish reasons. The key here, however, is "only," for it may well be that some, or all, altruistic behavior is *also* motivated by selfishness. This means that a soldier ant who gives its life "for Queen and country" may also be acting in its own interests, that is, in the interest of preserving its genotype, but altruism would not apply, despite whatever appearances, if its *sole* motive were preserving its genotype. Of course, it does not seem to make much sense to talk about the motives of ants in any case, but this led us to ask whether it made sense to talk about ant altruism either. Consequently, we began to insist that whatever could be called altruism required a conscious element, an intention or motive to help the other animal "for its own sake." This addition of "internal" or mental contents may seem anathema to behavioristically inclined sociobiologists, but (1) not all sociobiology is behavioristic (e.g., Lorenz is a counterexample) and (2) anyone who is not willing to talk in terms of some such mental contents is not talking about phenomena that we can recognize as altruism, much less as moral.

What follows is that altruism, as used by many sociobiologists, and altruism in its normal English usage, are two distinct terms, one stipulated and unusual, the other familiar. In itself, this would be no objection. (Calling a function of certain subatomic particles "charm" in no way entails that the particles are charming.) But there is a dangerous tendency to slip from the artificial term to the ordinary term, thus moving from altruism, meaning simply "to another's genetic advantage at the expense of one's own," to altruism-proper, meaning "with regard to another's interests." "Regard" is obviously a mentalistic or intentional term. (It is important to add that regard requires concern, not just attention.) Thus, when Dawkins (1976) ascribes the property of altruism not only to animals but to genes, he should be committed to using only the artificial term, but he slips from one to the other, at a cost of considerable confusion. Similarly, the notion of "selfishness" means "with prominent regard to one's own interests," and must not be confused with any stipulated homonym which means, simply, "self-benefiting." The word *prominent* here can be disputed, but "sole regard" seems too strong and simply "regard" much too weak. It was argued in our group that altruistic acts do not have to be self-sacrificing, and so selfish acts do not have to be damaging to others. Since altruism and selfishness are polar (but not exhaustive) concepts, it was questioned whether it makes sense to apply one if the other could not be applied.

We spent some time discussing possible objects and agents of altruism. It was argued that, strictly speaking, altruism should be reserved to describe relationships between two (or more) conscious creatures, but it was again pointed out that it would be a mistake, and rule out the sociobiological position by *fiat*, if we thereby insisted that only humans could have such relationships. Thus the debate turned on how sophisticated the conscious contents of a creature had to be in order to describe its behavior as altruistic. Dogs and chimpanzees were obvious candidates, but it was not agreed within the group whether their behavior could be so described or not. Ants and bees seemed to be a dubious case, but not ruled out entirely. Genes, however, are clearly neither selfish nor altruistic, and it is a dangerous confusion to use such words, in any sense, regarding them. It was suggested that the *object* of altruism, as an intentional object, need in fact not be conscious at all, but altruistic behavior required the *belief* that the object had interests to be served.

The concept of "morality" provided further difficulties, not least of which was the insistence, on the part of some group members, and the suspicions, on the part of others, that there is no single set of phenomena designated by that term. We had agreed that morality, like altruism, must not be *defined* in such a way as to reject out of hand the possibility of subhuman morality. Yet some of the suggestions concerning morality clearly did exclude all subhuman animals (for example, the suggestions that morality involves choice, critical thinking, and universal principles), others did not (for example, the idea that morality involves fellow feeling).

One problem, however, was that some of these suggestions seemed to rule out some human moralities as well. The most important example was conceptions of morality which do not include the concept of *choice*, for example, Taoist morality (W. Tu) and certain ritualistic moralities in contemporary Bali and Java (C. Geertz). It was argued, and generally agreed, that for us to redescribe them in terms of our "choice" and "decision" vocabulary would be a distortion. This is *not* to say, however, that concepts like "choice" and "responsibility" cannot be applied to these people (by us), or that they do not *have* choices (as if they were automatons rather than human beings). It is rather the case that their *concepts* of right and wrong are not applied to decisions but rather to something else. Transgressions, accordingly, are considered not sins or immoral so much as mistakes or signs of faulty development. Similarly, critical reflection, which seems so important to us in some of our conceptions of morality, is of little importance in other societies, in some of which such an activity is itself considered wrong. And even fellow feeling or compassion, which some members of the group argued to be the most essential single ingredient of morality, seemed to be lacking in some, particularly in those moralities whose essential features seemed to be rules or rituals, rather than personal relations in our sense.

We agreed that altruism alone did not suffice and was not necessary to characterize morality. For example, it was suggested that Buddhist morality, with its stress on the earning of "merit," rendered all other-serving behavior self-interested and thus not altruistic. That is, in leading the moral life, one would still be striving for self-perfection, not for the disinterested goal of satisfying other's interests. The same might be said of certain versions of Christianity, in which the ultimate goal of all good (altruistic) acts is personal salvation. Such cases have been controversial in philosophy for centuries, but their moral status will usually be conceded even if their altruism is in question. Moreover, moralities that are defined in terms of law or principles (e.g., the Ten Commandments) need not include altruism as an ingredient but only commitment to the Law. (It is another question whether such laws serve, or once served, human interests.) Moralities defined in terms of ritual (e.g., certain forms of Buddhism) need not include altruism either, but only norms of "correctness." Yet these seem to be moralities, literally speaking. (Notice that by this point in our discussion, we talked almost always of moralities and rarely of morality [Morality].)

It was pointed out that moralities might differ not only in different societies but at different levels of the same society. For instance, the moral concerns of the family seem very different from those of political institutions. The concerns of the latter have very little to do with altruism, for example, and much more to do with general principles of anonymous fairness. Family morality, however, stresses altruism and compassion, principles of rare political relevance or utility in a large society.

Even granting that altruism is an ingredient in most, if not all moralities, it was agreed that they necessarily consisted of something more. The question then became, what more?

We could not settle this issue, not only because of disagreement about what other ingredients might be required but more critically, because we had by this time agreed that no one set of ingredients uniquely deserved the honorific title "morality." We also agreed that any attempt to define morality would be arbitrary and unavoidably rule out or gloss over some of the most important phenomena which go under that name. However, we also agreed that, in what we loosely referred to as "our morality" (which was not to say that our morals were loose) certain conceptions going far beyond altruism and anything that could plausibly be identified in animal behavior were involved. In particular, the notions of "rights," "obligations," "justice," "equality," and "duties" have an essential place in our moral thinking (although their relative importance has been often debated) together with our concepts of social roles and responsibilities and the value we place on individual self-realization. It is here that "our" conception of morality moves furthest from the sociobiological concepts, for no matter how persuasive their evidence concerning sharing and other- as opposed to self-benefiting behavior, nothing approaching these concepts seems even plausible with regard to nonhuman animals. The concept of individual *rights*, we agreed, would be the (or at least a) primary concern of any analysis or explanation of our morality, and nothing in the concept of "survival of the genotype" seemed even relevant to any such analysis or explanation. In addition, the following suggestions for moral ingredients were debated, without conclusion: (1) compassion; (2) choice; (3) critical reflection; (4) concern for interests of others; (5) a concern for social welfare; (6) any set of norms or principles; (7) any set of constraints or proscriptions; (8) a dominant set of norms or principles; (9) certain kinds of principles (e.g., categorical commands); (10) principles about certain matters (e.g., social relations, religion, social welfare); (11) a certain set of principles (e.g., the Ten Commandments); and (12) universal principles (applying to everyone everywhere). But whether or not morality can be circumscribed by some single formula, the sociobiologist still can claim to explain specific moral principles. So it is to such principles that we then turned our attention.

III. THE SEARCH FOR SOCIAL UNIVERSALS

Since our group had the advantage of a number of anthropologists, we felt it part of our group's contribution to examine the availability of those social or moral universals which the sociobiologists claim ultimately to be able to explain. The question, of course, is whether there are any such universals, for if there are not, then species-level explanations will not have anything to explain. It was important to remind ourselves, however, that human universals as such are not necessary for there to be biological explanations. Other subspecies variations, for example, fat distribution, skin color and texture, and eye color, are biological in origin and can be explained by an evolutionist. However, it has been agreed that human differences, in general, have come about and changed much more rapidly than evolutionary mechanisms could explain and that cultural accounts, rather than biological accounts, are usually the most plausible and informative.

The anthropological arguments against the idea of human universals took three forms. The first, that whatever universals could be found would tend to be "vacuous" and "uninteresting," seemed plausible but not of great consequence to the sociobiologist, who only needs some human social organizational structure to explain, regardless of its "interest" to others. This objection, in other words, seemed more of a difference between fields than a refutation of one by the other. The charge of "vacuousness," however, led to other criticisms far more damaging. The second charge was that, given their vagueness and forced all-inclusiveness, the universals "discovered" by sociobiologists were in fact invented rather than found. It was objected that the very idea of sociobiology has pushed its practitioners into inventions of specious generalizations that were either false or irrefutable. For example, the supposedly universal incest taboo that has been the subject of some very far reaching sociobiological arguments was argued to be such a fabrication. The third objection was that social universals—even when they were substantial, stood up to scrutiny and were not vacuous—were only deviously explained by sociobiological principles when sociocultural principles seemed to do the job specifically and convincingly.

Underlying all three objections was the idea, basic to philosophers, anthropologists, and psychiatrists but usually not of central importance in biology, that understanding is an interpretative (hermeneutic) process, and, regarding human practices and cultures, appreciating them "from the inside" and understanding the *particular* role that this or that institution or practice plays in the organization of the society. Sociobiology, on the other hand, derives its principles from a superficial gloss (even if the principles themselves are supposed to be a "deep structure") over societies in general, thus capturing, in the words of one of our anthropologists, "an overly general and uninformative description of an impoverished institution." The argument is not so much that such descriptions cannot be *true*: it is rather that they tend to say very little, aggregate very different phenomena (considering the various roles they play in different societies) under the same heading, and then explain them in an often ad hoc and speculative way when cultural explanations (still perhaps functional and evolutionary, but not biological, that is, genetic) are readily available.

As a test case, we looked at the so-called incest taboo, which has been widely claimed to be just such a social universal and explainable through evolutionary accounting. What was made clear to our group, however, was that this taboo was a conglomerate of a great many different practices, with different roles to play in different societies. There is a tendency to lump together sexual relations, marriage, morals, and religious beliefs. Lack of sexual preference is sometimes confused with sexual avoidance, and sexual avoidance conflated with taboos and prohibitions. Preferring to have sex with *b* rather than *a* is very different from avoiding sex with *a*, and avoiding sex with *a* is very different from doing so because one *ought* or *must* (that is, morally ought or must) not have sex with *a*. It was argued that brother-sister sex was common in some societies in which sibling marriage was forbidden. F. A. Jenner pointed out that father-daughter sex is not uncommon in psychiatric practice, for example, in England. Sibling sex is often treated very differently from parent-child sex, and so to treat them together as a single prohibition is a serious oversimplification. Marriages are indeed surrounded by taboos of various kinds, but these are often of a legal nature and more conducive to socioeconomic rather than biological explanations. In fact, in a great many societies, marriage arrangements are almost wholly unrelated to sexual preferences. There are a number of societies where marriages between brothers and sisters are encouraged or arranged, not just among the Pharaohs of ancient Egypt but throughout the levels of ancient Egyptian society, in early Bali and Hawaii as well. Any claim for the universality of the incest taboo, accordingly, will have to be formulated much more carefully than general statements to the effect that intrafamily marriage and sex is universally forbidden.

One of the arguments we used in our group was that discussions of incest frequently confused kinship with proximity, in the much discussed example of the fact that Israeli children raised together in a kibbutz did not marry, despite the fact that they are not brother and sister nor, often, even of the same national origins. This seemed to us to be a confusion, and it had already been argued that the empirical evidence on kinship relations and marriages alone did not support the idea that incest, in this sense, is a universal taboo. This argument, however, was quashed by J. Searle, who argued, and we agreed, that one could connect the evolutionary function (that is, avoidance of inbreeding) with the hypothesis that children raised together at a certain crucial age (2–4) did not later have sex or get married, by arguing that the latter provided the evolutionary *mechanism* for the former. This nullified the argument that the two had been confused; however, the evidence on the proximity claims was no better than the evidence on the kinship claim. It too confused having sex, which, it turns out, is not entirely uncommon between children growing up together, and marriage, and it too confuses a lack of interest in getting married with a taboo against getting married. Moreover, if the proximity hypothesis were correct, and such an inhibition did in fact serve the evolutionary function, then sex and marriage between cousins raised together should be significantly different from sex and marriage between cousins raised separately. No such luck. Marriage between cousins is common and even encouraged in many instances of *both* situations.

It was pointed out, by G. Stent, that some recent claims had been made that inbreeding might have certain evolutionary *advantages*. If so, we wondered how long it would take for sociobiologists to destroy their own incestual Freud-wagen. But, in any case, we concluded that the incest taboo has not been shown to be universal in any sufficiently well-defined sense such that biological accounts are appropriate and, where such various prohibitions and inhibitions exist, cultural explanations on a local scale seem far more persuasive.

CONCLUSION

We in no way concluded that biology, or even sociobiology, had no proper place in studies of human society and morality. What we did find was that such accounts and claims that now receive such excessive attention are often specious as explanations, dangerous as potential ideological tools, and antiheuristic regarding the cooperation of the biological and distinctively human sciences and moral philosophy. The sociobiological ambitions to, "in the end," explain all human morality, are presently irrefutable, useless and dangerous. An explanation is not useful, or anything else until it exists, and all we seem to have at present is a number of provocative threats and promises. (If the history of science serves us at all, it at least demonstrates to us that there is no "in the end" for science.) None of our views were intended to rebuke the advances of the sociobiologists; on the contrary, we wanted to say that we believe that there are indeed interesting and important points of contact between biology, culture and morality which should be probed, but that recent sociobiological claims to "undermine" and "take over" moral investigations from its supposed competitors in anthropology and philosophy have only resulted in an antagonism that makes interdisciplinary cooperation impossible.

SUGGESTED READINGS

I. The Moral Presuppositions of Sociobiology

Dawkins, R. 1976. The Selfish Gene. London: Oxford University Press.

Hamilton, W. D. 1964. The genetical theory of social behavior. J. Theor. Biol. 7: 1.

Lorenz, K. S. 1966. On Aggression. London: Methuen.

Trivers, R. L. 1971. The evolution of reciprocal altruism. Q. Rev. Bio. 46: 35.

Wilson, E. O. 1975. Sociobiology. Cambridge: Harvard University Press.

II. Meta-Ethical Presuppositions and Concepts

Frankena, W. 1973. Ethics. 2d ed. Englewood Cliffs, N.J.: Prentice-Hall.

Fürer-Heimendorf, C. 1967. Morals and Merit. A Study of Values and Social Controls in South Asian Societies. Chicago: University of Chicago Press.

Harman, G. 1977. The Nature of Morality. New York: Oxford University Press.

Nagel, T. 1970. The Possibility of Altruism. Oxford: Oxford University Press.

Williams, B. 1972. Morality. New York: Harper and Row.

III. The Search for Social Universals

Edel, A. 1961. Science and the Structure of Ethics. Chicago: University of Chicago Press.

Fingarette, H. 1967. Confucius—The Secular as Sacred. New York: Harper and Row.

Geertz, C. 1973. The Interpretation of Cultures. New York: Basic Books.

Gellner, E. 1974. Thought and Change. Chicago: University of Chicago Press.

Goldschmidt, W. 1966. Comparative Functionalism: An Essay in Anthropological Theory. Berkeley and Los Angeles: University of California Press.

Ladd, J. 1957. Structure of a Moral Code: A Philosophical Analysis of Ethical Discourse, Applied to the Ethics of the Navahoè Indians. Cambridge: Harvard University Press.

Munro, D. 1962. The Concept of Man in Early China. Stanford: Stanford University Press.

Murdock, G. P. 1965. Social Structure. New York: Free Press.

Winch, P. 1970. The Ideal of a Social Science. New York: Humanities Press.

CONCLUSION

B. A. O. Williams

I am not going to try to give a further and higher level summary of the group reports or of all the discussion that has taken place. I am just going to make some selective remarks about particularly interesting questions that have emerged, and obviously this is going to be a very personal interpretation.

Let me first say something about the issue of the account or definition of morality. The three groups have produced various accounts and characterizations of morality in relation to which the discussion could proceed. It seems to me that there are two requirements if any such characterization is to be useful. First, it should not excessively beg the question against a naturalistic account; and second, it should be adequately cross-cultural—that is, the concepts it uses should not be too excessively local. A particularly cogent point regarding the second requirement was brought up by Clifford Geertz in the discussion.

Needless to say, I happen to think that those requirements were best met by the account of morality given by our group (Kowalski et al., this volume). This account does contain one feature which has attracted criticism from other speakers, but I think this criticism is largely based on misunderstanding. The misunderstanding is to suppose that the term *altruism* which is built into the definition or account of morality in our group report is meant to be the name of a motive. It is meant, in fact, to be the name of a function; that is, there is supposed to be a feature of the institutions of morality which has the effect that other people's interests get observed in the behavior of agents, and this effect is no accident. It is functional in the sense that it has this consequence and its having this consequence is part of the explanation. To the extent that this is so, it contains implicitly a hypothesis about the nature of morality. Of course, it is a further condition of human moralities (all the groups agree about this) that, unlike the activities of bees, ants, fish, and so on, they have an intentional or conscious content, indeed that there are conscious motives. But the fact that all moralities contain conscious motives, and that they all display altruism, does not mean that they all contain the conscious motive of altruism; that is, that they all require agents to be motivated by the thought that what they do will be in somebody else's interest. Once one has taken that point, such things as rules, the tablets of the law, self-improvement, and so on, can be accommodated.

There still remains, however, the question of the hypothesis which is implicit in using this functional characterization of altruism. This is a hypothesis which is supposed to link the sociobiological conception with the humanist conception. And here the remarks made by more than one speaker in favor of "slippage" apply. Because, of course, slippage in the application of a term is sometimes simply called generalization; there is an explanatory idea which underlies the use of the notion of "altruism" in both of these connections. To me that seems a very good reason for not being puritanically hygienic about the use of such terms. It is not just the psychological point made by John Maynard Smith that it is difficult for most of us to think without slippage; it is that some valuable thought essentially involves slippage. It consists in generalizations of notions which have previously been used in a more restricted way.

The kind of hypothesis that underlies the use of the expression *altruism* has, I think, come out in a number of our discussions. I particularly found it in the group report by Markl et al. (this volume), in the situation set up in terms of game-theoretical models, going beyond the prisoner's dilemma. If you are going to overcome the lack of an equilibrium point in the prisoner's dilemma (a two-person conflict situation), then one of the ways in which you do this is to create an internalized norm or disposition which will increase reliability—a point that is also brought forward in Hans Kummer's paper (this volume) with the idea of increasing predictability. These ideas seem to me to be extremely fruitful for an understanding of the general nature or basis of the background of morality. Certainly in this sense, the idea that concepts drawn from sociobiology can illuminate the character of human morality seems to me to be undeniable, and we have already very interesting examples of this in some of the literature brought up in this conference.

I would like to turn now to one or two points about the conditions of applicability of sociobiological explanations. This has come up in several forms. First let me make one point about the subject of what is universal. We have heard quite a lot of discussion here about the prohibition of incest, and I do not want to add further to it. The point has been made (and interestingly it has been made both by broadly anti-sociobiological speakers, putting it very crudely, and pro-sociobiological speakers) that a distinction is to be made between prohibitions and inhibitions: between there being a normative rule against doing something, and it just being the case that people do not want to do it. This point came up in what John Searle said about marriage among the kibbutzim. Even if proximity of upbringing has led to a certain distate for marrying persons with whom you were brought up, allegedly it has not actually given rise to a normative prohibition that you must not marry them—you just are not very keen on it. The point I want to make is that to insist on this distinction is not entirely unambiguous or neutral with regard to sociobiological explanations. Of course, in one sense what sociobiological theory is bound to predict and explain are inhibitions: but that does not exclude the possibility that in species, such as man, which are capable of having prohibitions, some inhibitions should express themselves as prohibitions—that prohibitions should be cultural elaborations of some kinds of inhibitions. The notion of a "cultural elaboration" here is a mere promissory note, and we shall still be owed an explanation in terms of which inhibition and prohibition can be comprehensively related. But, on the other hand, just to insist that prohibitions are one thing and inhibitions another, and that sociobiology could in principle only explain the latter, is in danger of begging the question against sociobiological explanations of morality.

This draws our attention to an important point which John Searle made in discussing the report of Kowalski et al. (this volume). Namely, how we are to construe in the sociobiological context the relation between the intentional content of the functional explanation and the intentional content of the moral thought—whether it be a prohibition or whatever. This is an area in which it is certain that sociobiological theorists go too quickly. They find a functional explanation with a certain content; they find a prohibition with a certain content; they say "Ah! There you are." But what we need is an explanation of how the one got into the other.

I turn now briefly to cases in which we are dealing with (everyone agrees) nonuniversal moral phenomena; that is, differences in human cultural moral practice. The question here is, what are to be the contributions of different kinds of explanation—genetic, psychological, cultural—and this is an obvious area of disagreement. More than one group has tried to illuminate this area in terms of laying down some (a priori) boundaries across which the different sorts of explanation might interact. There is one point which I think all groups have either implicitly or explicitly laid aside, and, it seems to me, rightly so. This is the issue between explanations that run through conscious phenomena on the one hand and purely physicalistic explanations on the other. It is clearly possible that there exists some form of physicalistic parallelism (psychophysical parallelism) such that every explanation that runs through intentional states will, in fact, be paralleled by an account that runs through physical states. The point is, if physicalism is true, then every sort of explanation of any individual's behavior is going to have some sort of physicalistic account along with it. Therefore this does nothing to distinguish between different sorts of nonphysicalistic explanation, whether these be genetic or psychological or cultural. So the issue is not about physicalism. That of course makes it different from one of the points that Gunther Stent mentioned, as a thing he hoped we might have discussed. We haven't discussed the issue about physicalism versus mentalistic or other nonphysicalistic forms of explanation. We are concerned with the relations between explanations, none of which is in any direct sense physicalistic—namely, genetic or genetically motivational, psychological, and cultural.

We are all agreed in laying aside certain kinds of brutal reductive rhetoric which, if not offered by sociobiological thinkers, is sometimes offered by people who think they are representing what is said by sociobiological thinkers. For instance, there is the line which says, "intentionality plays no role at all." Well, that is obvious nonsense, and any form of epiphenomenalism which claims it is obviously false. "The man got out of the way because he saw the car coming" could be a true explanation, and cannot be rendered a false explanation because of a philosophical theory. What people perhaps mean when they say that that explanation is not true is that something else is true as well—for instance, a physicalistic explanation.

We are also slightly interested in the rhetorical, unfavorable, and seductive descriptions which are often produced in these connections of human motives, "people think that they are striving for patriotic motives, but all the time it is only their genes." I don't think any of us finds that a very edifying level of rhetoric, even if it is their genes; maybe what their genes do is make them act with patriotic motives. We do not have to agree with this style of eliminative reductivism, which means, in effect, that not only is everything explained by genes, but the effect of having everything explained by genes is that the world is more boring than you thought it was in the first place. But I think most of us agree that among the things that might be explained in genetic terms are actions for these kinds of motives.

Everybody agrees that individual behavior is in fact a complex function of genetic and environmental factors. The question is, is there any nontrivial way of establishing a point at which genetic styles of explanations get leverage? That is something we discussed quite a lot in our group (Kowalski et al., this volume), and others have discussed it as well. In this matter I found two very useful distinctions in the report of Markl et al. (this volume). One was the distinction in what has to be explained, namely, (a) the disposition to having norms at all; (b) the disposition to having particular norms rather than others; and (c) certain factors about the breaking and observing of norms. The other distinction was in what might be evoked, at the most general genetic level, to explain norms. This includes the following: (a) fixed behavior patterns (genetically wired-in behavior patterns—probably rare in man compared with insects); (b) a general capacity to learn; and (c) a long-range, strategic, and more elaborately time-based conception which we take to be peculiar to human beings (even allowing for squirrels' investment procedures, which I take it are not very far-sighted in any very deep sense). Nobody denies, I take it, that these capacities have evolved and are themselves the product of evolution. The question, then, seems to come to this: The more basic and general and flexible is the disposition of moral behavior, the less determinate is the biological determination of the behavior. If all I am invoking at the genetic level is a general capacity to learn, then I have not given a determinately biological explanation. It follows then that the more basic and general is the capacity invoked at the genetic level, the more work is to be done by psychological and cultural dimensions of explanation. Peter Wolff made this point in his remarks about learning morality all our lives. This is going to give us a much greater psychological component in the explanation of the moral outcome.

At the end of the report of Kowalski et al., the question was raised about what would indicate the success of a sociobiological research program with respect to these kinds of human moral phenomena. We all agree, I think, that there are no crucial experiments in this, or, as Maynard Smith rightly reminded us, in any other place in science. Geertz put it very well when he said that the question is not "is there a deciding experiment or observation?" but rather, "are these sociobiological patterns of explanation constraining at all? Do they have any constraining effects?" We do agree that the phenomenon to be explained does not itself have to be universal. We also agree that it does not have to be adaptively functional *now* in order for an explanation to apply: if we can plausibly postulate an earlier hominid environment in which there would be selection for the characteristic in question, this could provide the basis for a sociobiological type of explanation of present behavior. On the further, positive conditions that have to be satisfied in order for there to be nonvacuous sociobiological or genetic explanations of variable human moral phenomena, we do not yet have general agreement. I take it to be a philosophical question. Still less do we know what the outcome of applying the conditions would be, which I take to be a problem for research.

So far I have spoken to the issue which has concerned us all, namely, what are the general conditions for there being constraining sociobiological explanations of human moral phenomena? What can be said is that nobody has conjured out of a philosophical hat an a priori argument against there being any such well-constrained explanations at all. How many there are, we do not know.

Let us now turn to a question with which, in a way, we started: What could be the result or practical significance if we actually came up with explanations of human moral phenomena in the sorts of ways which some have suggested? This is naturalistic fallacy territory, the area of "*is* does not imply *ought.*" We all ought to remember at this point a companion to "*is* does not imply *ought,*" and which came out of the same stable, is that "*ought* does imply *can.*" Presumably one of the items that the sociobiologists might like to deliver to us is a proposition about what we cannot do, what society cannot do, on what sorts of norms it cannot run. Although that will not give us *ought,* it can give us *not ought*: if "*ought* implies *can,*" then "*cannot* implies *not ought*"; that is, you had better forget that one as a norm. The trouble is that the strongest kind of sociobiological "cannot" would mean that the question never came up at all, a point that Searle and others have mentioned. Since we cannot eat our own heads, a moral demand to do so is not valid and a moral prohibition against it not necessary. It looks as if the philosopher can produce a quick dilemma here. If the sociobiologists really deliver a "cannot," something no human being can do, then there is no need for a moral prohibition against it. As soon as he permits "can," then the philosopher says "*is* does not imply *ought*" and we have room for free choice. What the sociobiologists say here is, "Look, when we say 'can't,' we do not mean 'absolutely can't.'

What we mean is 'can't' without terrific costs that any group of human beings will count as costs." That is, there is a *Spielraum*, an area in which it is possible for human beings individually—or even for a time societally—to do things of a certain kind, but it is so against the grain that some things are just, to use the phrase used by Thomas Nagel, too much to ask. Or it might be just that it is too hard and it will not work. Someone will come along and say, "Look, of course it is possible to treat women just like men, at least almost just like men. But if you try to adopt this equality of treatment everywhere, there will be anxiety, disaster, collapse—results which everybody knows are unacceptable to human society." This is a logically respectable *form* of claim.

What form might the boundaries of this *Spielraum* take? What will these constraints be? One mentioned by several of us is constraints on learning. It might be claimed that there are certain moral standards or patterns of behavior which human beings cannot successfully internalize. That is one kind of claim. I take it that our psychologist friends' ontogenic researches would bear on that—whether there are patterns that have this characteristic, and if so, why. Second (Norbert Bischof made this point on a number of occasions), it might be that the cost of certain practices is a very high level of anxiety—that people could act against these built-in norms, but if they did, it always made them very upset, or anxious, or neurotic. Here I would make two points very quickly: Bischof thinks, as a matter of fact, that we are going to have anxiety anyway because of our time sense; that is, anxiety is a universal human condition and therefore it is only a bit of extra anxiety that we get presumably by going against certain inborn norms, rather than acting in some other way. We must also remember (and I think the psychiatrists will probably agree with us here too) that anxiety is not a 100 percent disvalue for human beings. John Stuart Mill made a memorable remark about it being "better to be Socrates and unhappy than a pig happy (or contented)." (I do not know whether it is a sound ethological observation that pigs are contented: it may be based on a misreading of their looks.) But anxiety is, in fact, quite a powerful value in human life, and presumably we must not take its avoidance as *the* norm in these connections.

Another of the problems that we discussed in our group

(Kowalski et al.) was the question of sex differentiation. This is an extremely lively issue, and what is universal with regard to sex role differentiation, is a very good question indeed. It is very unclear as to what, if anything, might be thought common to human races; and also what would follow from past common practice. Suppose it were true that up to this point in history human beings had displayed a high degree of universality in sex role differentiation in a uniform direction. It would then seem enormously important that this is *history*—the past. Radical thought says that the fact that it *is* the past is absolutely vital in this respect, because all the difference is between the past and now. Some of it is due to technological opportunities now available which we did not have in the past—this would certainly be relevant to any Marxist interpretation of this phenomenon. Another extremely important difference is that we now know something about sociobiology. Here we have an important clue to the ineliminable importance of cultural and historical studies for evaluating these things, because here it is unremovable that we are dealing with a cultural, historical phenomenon. Unless you can understand it historically and culturally, its significance—how you can even feed into a sociobiological argument—will remain totally obscure. You just will not understand, at all, what you are talking about.

As far as anxiety is concerned, let us remember our universal tendency to always suppose that there was less anxiety in the past. In past societies without all these liberated ideas, people were allegedly less anxious. This I take to be a general psychologized form of the "Golden Age" illusion, whether it be the removal from Eden, or the division of labor, or the end of the city-state, or the waning of the Middle Ages, or the Industrial Revolution—there was some time before in which it was all marvelous. This illusion, which itself needs diagnosis, is nearly universal, at least in the Western world. That is itself something which is a cultural force that can encourage the acceptance of conservative conclusions from sociobiological arguments. "Doing what comes naturally" can mean not just an idea of nature of a Rousseauite liberal kind, but "what they used to do before everything got so complex and anxiety-making as it is now."

I would summarize the situation from my point of view as

this: We are left with some unsolved, general philosophical problems about the competitiveness between sociobiological and other forms of explanation. We have no reason to think that there cannot be, in principle, effective and quite strongly constrained sociobiological explanations for these kinds of phenomena. It is not ruled out a priori, but the constraints on their being so seem to be both tight and obscure. More philosophical research is needed on that point. Second, there are many unsolved problems about the extent of those explanations, what they would actually be like if we got them, and to that we presumably do not know the answer—it is an ongoing research program. Third, we certainly will always need historical, psychological, and cultural explanations of moral phenomena; that is presumably a platitude, but not all sociobiologists seem quite able to accept it.

It is particularly important that we cultivate such understanding now, because we need cultural and historical understanding of sociobiology itself, especially sociobiology as an ideology. I do not mean the views held by Wilson and Dawkins: I am talking about what a popular ideology of this movement would be, and that is an independent point. I think there is a very interesting aspect of sociobiology as a potential ideology. That aspect relates to our present situation. One element in our present intellectual environment is scientism as an ideology. There is a very good reason for that; namely, science is one of the few paradigms of knowledge of any general kind that we have actually got. Its effectiveness, its patent and evident effectiveness, produces the notion—on the whole, it seems to me a correct notion—that this is because it actually represents a kind of concrete knowledge of the universe which had not been very widespread in human cultures before the scientific revolution. It therefore has, quite properly, a very high prestige, and that is an obvious point. The result is not that there is less superstitious belief now—obviously there is, if anything, *more* superstitious belief—but that the form of superstitious belief now is pseudoscience. The fantasies of superstition are projected into the scientific context, such as space travel, or visitors from elsewhere, rather than visitors from the underworld, which is what those same characters in paranoid fantasies used to be. On the other hand, as we all know, this is counterbalanced by an extreme degree of antitechnological and antimanipulative alarm. Now that we are aware of what can happen as a result of technological enterprises, we are above all threatened by the sense of malleability and manipulability of psychological processes. This is not just a fear of totalitarian power, but the fear of formless future progress.

Sociobiology as an ideology, and again I wish to emphasize I am not speaking of these writers (Wilson and Dawkins), but of a popular form, combines the features that it is both scientistic and conservative. It combines the notion of being in favor of science and being based on scientific explanation with a fundamentally conservative and literally conservative "keeping what is found natural" approach to various social institutions. In the present ideological climate, one can predict that that is an extraordinarily potent combination of characteristics. Most conservative outlooks are antiscientific, and therefore treated with distrust because they seem to leave aside the paradigm of modern knowledge. Many scientistic outlooks are deeply radical, such as that of B. F. Skinner: Forget everything you ever valued, all's swept away, new world, Walden II . . . we should all be listening to the gramophone all day, people having their brains cut out in the interest of social conformity. People do not like that either, for various old-fashioned reasons. When you have an outlook which can be at once scientistic and conservative, it can speak to quite a lot of our needs, and therefore, however many disclaimers Dawkins puts in, however many disclaimers Wilson puts in, however many admirable hygienic and analytic observations we have managed to achieve, I still think that, on the whole, we had better watch out.

POSTSCRIPT TO THE UNIVERSITY OF CALIFORNIA PRESS EDITION

Dahlem Konferenzen, the sponsor of the Workshop on "Morality as a Biological Phenomenon," was founded in 1974 for the promotion of interdisciplinary exchange of scientific information and ideas and the stimulation of international cooperation in research. It is supported by the *Stifterverband für die Deutsche Wissenschaft* of German industry, trade, and commerce, in cooperation with the *Deutsche Forschungsgemeinschaft*, the German National Science Foundation. The format of *Dahlem Konferenzen* workshops was designed by their founder-director Silke Bernhard to maximize the opportunity for productive and creative intellectual interchanges. No lectures are delivered, and the thirty to forty participants spend most of their time in small groups with no more than eight to ten members. In order to provide a focus for the discussions of these groups, some of the participants are commissioned to write a background paper that provides an up-to-date general overview of an assigned topic. These background papers are circulated in advance and are presumed to have been read before arrival in Berlin. After an opening statement by the chairman, the participants disperse into the small groups. After several days of intense discussion, a rapporteur prepares a report of the conclusions of each group regarding the overall theme. The workshop ends with a general discussion of the group reports in plenary session and a grand synthesis of the whole meeting in a conclusion. Finally, the proceedings of the workshop, consisting of the chairman's Introduction, the Position Papers, the Group Reports, and the Conclusion are published by *Dahlem Konferenzen* as one of its *Science Reports*. Because of the rather general interest in the topic of this particular workshop, *Dahlem Konferenzen* has authorized publication of this slightly revised edition by the University of California Press, so as to make these proceedings available to a broad audience.

LIST OF PARTICIPANTS

BISCHOF, N.
Abteilung für Biologische-
  Mathematische Psychologie
Attenhoferstrasse 9
8044 Zürich, Switzerland
Field of research: Experimental
  psychology

BUTENANDT, E.
Lehrstuhl Für Nachrichtentechnik
Technische Universität
Arcisstrasse 21
8000 München 2, F.R. Germany
Field of research: Neuro-
  physiology, cybernetics

CAMPBELL, D. T.
Department of Psychology
Northwestern University
Evanston, IL 60201, USA
Field of research: Social sci-
  ence (psychology)

EBLING, F. J. G.
Department of Zoology
University of Sheffield
Sheffield S10 2TN, Great
  Britain
Field of research: Endocrinol-
  ogy and mammalian skin

ECKENSBERGER, L. H.
Fachrichtung Psychologie
Universität des Saarlandes
6600 Saarbrücken, F.R.
  Germany
Field of research: Moral
  development

FRIED, C.
Harvard Law School
Cambridge, MA 02138, USA
Field of research: Philosophy
  and Law

GEERTZ, C.
Institute for Advanced Study
Princeton NJ 08540, USA
Field of research: Cultural anthropology

GELLNER, E. A.
The London School of Economics and Political Science
Houghton Street
London WC2A 2AE, Great Britain
Field of research: Sociology, social anthropology

GOODY, J.
Department of Social Anthropology
University of Cambridge
Downing Street
Cambridge CB2 3DZ, Great Britain
Field of research: Literary and oral cultures

JENNER, F. A.
M.R.C. Unit
Middlewood Hospital
P.O. Box 134
Sheffield S6 ITP, Great Britain
Field of research: Metabolic studies in psychiatry

KOWALSKI, G. W.
61 Rue Madame
75006 Paris, France
Field of research: Science and theology; behavior and systems

KUMMER, H.
Ethologie und Wildforschung
Universität Zürich
Birchstrasse 95
8050 Zürich, Switzerland
Field of research: Primate social behavior

MARKL, H.S.
Fachbereich Biologie der Universität Konstanz
Postfach 7733
7750 Konstanz, F.R. Germany
Field of research: Animal behavior

MAYNARD SMITH, J.
School of Biological Sciences
University of Sussex
Brighton, Sussex BN1 9QG
Great Britain
Field of research: Evolution theory

NAGEL, T.
Department of Philosophy
Princeton University
Princeton, NJ 08540, USA
Field of research: Philosophy

RHEINGOLD, H. L.
Department of Psychology
University of North Carolina
Davie Hall O13A
Chapel Hill, NC 27514, USA
Field of research: Developmental psychology

SEARLE, J. R.
Department of Philosophy
University of California
Berkeley, CA 94720, USA
Field of research: Philosophy

SOLOMON, R. C.
Department of Philosophy
University of Texas
Waggener 316
Austin, TX 78712, USA
Field of research: Philosophy: psychology and ethics

STENT, G. S.
Department of Molecular
    Biology
University of California
Wendell M. Stanley Hall
Berkeley, CA 94720, USA
Field of research:
    Neurobiology

TU, W.
Department of History
University of California
Berkeley, CA 94720, USA
Field of research: Chinese in-
    tellectual history, philoso-
    phies of East Asia

TURIEL, E.
Department of Psychology
University of California
College V
Santa Cruz, CA 95064, USA
Field of research: Psychology

WILLIAMS, B. A. O.
Department of Philosophy
King's College
University of Cambridge
Cambridge CB2 1ST, Great
    Britain
Field of research: Philosophy

WOLFF, P. H.
Children's Hospital
Medical Center
300 Longwood Avenue
Boston, MA 02115, USA
Field of research: Develop-
    mental neuropsychology

WOLTERS, G. W.
Fachbereich Philosophie der
Universität Konstanz
Postfach 7733
6650 Konstanz, F.R. Germany
Field of research: History of
    methodology, philosophy of
    sciences

INDEX